COLLECTED
LONGER POEMS

W. H. Auden
*
Collected
Longer Poems

VINTAGE BOOKS
A Division of Random House
New York

FIRST VINTAGE BOOKS EDITION, November 1975

Library of Congress Cataloging in Publication Data

Auden, Wystan Hugh, 1907-1973.
 Collected longer poems.

 CONTENTS: Paid on both sides.—Letter to Lord Byron.
—New Year letter. [etc.]
 I. Title.
[PR6001.U4A17 1975b]   821'.9'12   75-12968
ISBN 0-394-72014-8

Manufactured in the United States of America

Contents

PAID ON BOTH SIDES   *page* 9

LETTER TO LORD BYRON   35

NEW YEAR LETTER   77

FOR THE TIME BEING   131

THE SEA AND THE MIRROR   199

THE AGE OF ANXIETY   253

A NOTE ON THE TEXT   354

Paid on Both Sides

A Charade

TO CECIL DAY-LEWIS

CHARACTERS

Lintzgarth	Nattrass
JOHN NOWER	AARON SHAW★★★★★
DICK	SETH SHAW
GEORGE★★★★	THE SPY—SETH'S BROTHER
WALTER	BERNARD
KURT	SETH'S MOTHER
CULLEY	ANNE SHAW
STEPHEN★★	

ZEPPEL—JOHN NOWER'S SERVANT
NUMBER SIX
JOAN—MOTHER OF JOHN NOWER
TRUDY

FATHER CHRISTMAS★
THE DOCTOR
BO★★★★
PO★★★★★
THE MAN-WOMAN
THE DOCTOR'S BOY★★
THE ANNOUNCER★
THE CHIEF GUEST★
THE BUTLER★

THE CHORUS

The starred parts should be doubled

[*No scenery is required. The stage should have a curtained-off recess. The distinction between the two hostile parties should be marked by different coloured arm-bands.* THE CHORUS, *which should not consist of more than three persons, wear similar and distinctive clothing.*]

[*Enter* TRUDY *and* WALTER.]

TRUDY: You've only just heard?

WALTER: Yes. A breakdown at the Mill needed attention, kept me all morning. I guessed no harm. But lately, riding at leisure, Dick met me, panted disaster. I came here at once. How did they get him?

TRUDY: In Kettledale above Colefangs road passes where high banks overhang dangerous from ambush. To Colefangs had to go, would speak with Layard, Jerry and Hunter with him only. They must have stolen news, for Red Shaw waited with ten, so Jerry said, till for last time unconscious. Hunter was killed at first shot. They fought, exhausted ammunition, a brave defence but fight no more.

WALTER: Has Joan been told yet?

TRUDY: Yes. It couldn't be helped. Shock, starting birth pangs, caused a premature delivery.

WALTER: How is she?

TRUDY: Bad, I believe. But here's the doctor.

[*Enter* DOCTOR.]

Well, Doctor, how are things going?

DOCTOR: Better, thanks. We've had a hard fight, but it's going to be all right. She'll pull through and have a fine infant as well. My God, I'm thirsty after all that. Where can I get a drink?

WALTER: Here in the next room, Doctor.

[*Exeunt. Back curtains draw.* JOAN *with child and corpse.*]

JOAN:
Not from this life, not from this life is any
To keep; sleep, day and play would not help there,
Dangerous to new ghost; new ghost learns from many,
Learns from old termers what death is, where.

12

Who's jealous of his latest company,
From one day to the next final to us,
A changed one, would use sorrow to deny
Sorrow, to replace death? Sorrow is sleeping thus.

Unforgetting is not today's forgetting
For yesterday, not bedrid scorning,
But a new begetting,
An unforgiving morning.
[*Baby squeals.*]
  O see, he is impatient
  To pass beyond this pretty lisping time:
  There'll be some crying out when he's come there.
[*Back curtains close.*]
CHORUS:
  Can speak of trouble, pressure on men
  Born all the time, brought forward into light
  For warm dark moan.
  Though heart fears all heart cries for, rebuffs with mortal beat
  Skyfall, the legs sucked under, adder's bite.
  That prize held out of reach
  Guides the unwilling tread,
  The asking breath,
  Till on attended bed
  Or in untracked dishonour comes to each
  His natural death.

We pass our days
Speak, man to men, easy, learning to point,
To jump before ladies, to show our scars:
But no,
We were mistaken, these faces are not ours.
They smile no more when we smile back:
Eyes, ears, tongue, nostrils bring

13

News of revolt, inadequate counsel to
An infirm king.

O watcher in the dark, you wake
Our dream of waking, we feel
Your finger on the flesh that has been skinned,
By your bright day
See clear what we were doing, that we were vile.
Your sudden hand
Shall humble great
Pride, break it, wear down to stumps old systems which await
The last transgression of the sea.

[*Enter* JOHN NOWER *and* DICK.]

JOHN NOWER: If you have really made up your mind, Dick, I won't try and persuade you to stop. But I shall be sorry to lose you.

DICK: I have thought it all over and I think it is the best thing to do. My cousin writes that the ranch is a thoroughly good proposition. I don't know how I shall like the Colonies but I feel I must get away from here. There is not room enough . . . but the actual moving is unpleasant.

JOHN NOWER: I understand. When are you thinking of sailing?

DICK: My cousin is sailing tomorrow. If I am going I am to join him at the Docks.

JOHN NOWER: Right. Tell one of the men to go down to the post-office and send a wire for you. If you want anything else, let me know.

DICK: Thank you.

[*Exit* DICK. *Enter* ZEPPEL.]

ZEPPEL: Number Six wishes to see you, sir.

JOHN NOWER: All right, show him in.

[*Enter* NUMBER SIX.]

Well, what is it?

NUMBER SIX: My area is Rookhope. Last night at Horse and Farrier, drank alone, one of Shaw's men. I sat down friendly next till muzzed with drink and lateness he was blabbing. Red Shaw goes to Brandon Walls today, visits a woman.

JOHN NOWER: Alone?

NUMBER SIX: No, sir. He takes a few. I got no numbers.

JOHN NOWER: This is good news. Here is a pound for you.

NUMBER SIX: Thank you very much, sir.

[*Exit* NUMBER SIX.]

JOHN NOWER: Zeppel.

ZEPPEL: Sir.

JOHN NOWER: Ask George to come here at once.

ZEPPEL: Very good, sir.

[JOHN *gets a map out. Enter* GEORGE.]

JOHN NOWER: Red Shaw is spending the day at Brandon Walls. We must get him. You know the ground well, don't you, George?

GEORGE: Pretty well. Let me see the map. There's a barn about a hundred yards from the house. Yes, here it is. If we can occupy that without attracting attention it will form a good base for operations, commands both house and road. If I remember rightly, on the other side of the stream is a steep bank. Yes, you can see from the contours. They couldn't get out that way, but lower down is marshy ground and possible. You want to post some men there to catch those who try.

JOHN NOWER: Good. Who do you suggest to lead that party?

GEORGE: Send Sturton. He knows the whole district blindfold. He and I as boys fished all those streams together.

JOHN NOWER: I shall come with you. Let's see: it's dark now about five. Fortunately there's no moon and it's cloudy. We'll start then about half-past. Pick your men and get some sandwiches made up in the kitchen. I'll see about the ammunition if you will remember to bring a compass. We meet outside at a quarter past.

[*Exeunt. Enter* KURT *and* CULLEY.]

KURT: There's time for a quick one before changing. What's yours?

CULLEY: I'll have a sidecar, thanks.

KURT: Zeppel, one sidecar and one C.P.S. I hear Chapman did the lake in eight.

CULLEY: Yes, he is developing a very pretty style. I am not sure though that Pepys won't beat him next year if he can get out of that double kick. Thanks. Prosit.

KURT: Cheerio.

[*Enter* WALTER *and* TRUDY.]

WALTER: Two half pints, Zeppel, please. (*To* KURT.) Can you let me have a match? How is the Rugger going?

KURT: All right, thank you. We have not got a bad team this season.

WALTER: Where do you play yourself?

KURT: Wing 3Q.

WALTER: Did you ever see Warner? No, he'd be before your time. You remember him don't you, Trudy?

TRUDY: He was killed in the fight at Colefangs, wasn't he?

WALTER: You are muddling him up with Hunter. He was the best three-quarter I have ever seen. His sprinting was marvellous to watch.

ZEPPEL (*producing Christmas turkey*): Not bad eh?

TRUDY (*feeling it*): Oh a fine one. For tomorrow's dinner?

ZEPPEL: Yes. Here, puss . . . gobble, gobble . . .

TRUDY (*to* WALTER): What have you got Ingo for Christmas?

WALTER: A model crane. Do you think he will like it?

TRUDY: He loves anything mechanical. He's so excited he can't sleep.

KURT: Come on, Culley, finish your drink. We must be getting along. (*To* WALTER.) You must come down to the field on Monday and see us.

WALTER: I will if I can.

[*Exit* KURT *and* CULLEY.]

TRUDY: Is there any news yet?

WALTER: Nothing has come through. If things are going right they may be back any time now.

TRUDY: I suppose they will get him?

WALTER: It's almost certain. Nower has waited long enough.

16

TRUDY:

I am sick of this feud. What do we want to go on killing each
    other for?
We are all the same. He's trash, yet if I cut my finger it bleeds
    like his.
But he's swell, keeps double shifts working all night by flares:
His mother squealed like a pig when he came crouching out.
Sometimes we read a sign, cloud in the sky,
The wet tracks of a hare, quicken the step
Promise the best day. But here no remedy
Is to be thought of, no news but the new death;
A Nower dragged out in the night, a Shaw
Ambushed behind the wall. Blood on the ground
Would welcome fighters. Last night at Hammergill
A boy was born fanged like a weasel. I am old,
Shall die before next winter, but more than once shall hear
The cry for help, the shooting round the house.

WALTER:

The best are gone.
Often the man, alone shut, shall consider
The killings in old winters, death of friends.
Sitting with stranger shall expect no good.

Spring came, urging to ships, a casting off,
But one would stay, vengeance not done; it seemed
Doubtful to them that they would meet again.

Fording in the cool of the day they rode
To meet at crossroads when the year was over:
Dead is Brody, such a man was Maul.

I will say this not falsely; I have seen
The just and the unjust die in the day,
All, willing or not, and some were willing.

Here they are.

17

[*Enter* JOHN NOWER, GEORGE, STURTON *and others. The three speak alternately.*]

Day was gone, Night covered sky,
Black over earth, When we came there,
To Brandon Walls, Where Red Shaw lay
Hateful and sleeping, Unfriendly visit.
I wished to revenge, Quit fully
Who my father at Colefangs valley,
Lying in ambush, Cruelly shot,
With life for life.

Then watchers saw They were attacked,
Shouted in fear, A night alarm
To men asleep, Doomed men awoke,
Felt for their guns, Ran to the doors,
Would wake their master Who lay with woman,
Upstairs together, Tired after love.
He saw then There would be shooting
Hard fight.

Shot answered shot, Bullets screamed,
Guns shook, Hot in the hand,
Fighters lay, Groaning on ground
Gave up life. Edward fell,
Shot through the chest, First of our lot,
By no means refused fight, Stephen was good,
His first encounter, Showed no fear,
Wounded many.

Then Shaw knew We were too strong,
Would get away Over the moor,
Return alive, But found at the ford
Sturton waiting, Greatest gun-anger,
There he died, Nor any came,
Fighters home, Nor wives shall go
Smiling to bed. They boast no more.

[STEPHEN *suddenly gets up.*]

STEPHEN: A forward forward can never be a backward backward.

GEORGE: Help me put Stephen to bed, somebody. He got tight on the way back. Hullo, they've caught a spy.

VOICES OUTSIDE: Look out. There he is. Catch him. Got you.

[*Enter* KURT *and others with prisoner.*]

KURT: We found this chap hiding in an outhouse.

JOHN NOWER: Bring him here. Who are you?

STEPHEN: I know him. I saw him once at Eickhamp. He's Seth Shaw's brother.

JOHN NOWER: He is, is he. What do you come here for? You know what we do to spies. I'll destroy the whole lot of you. Take him out.

SPY: You may look big, but we'll get you one day, Nower.

[*Exeunt all but* JOHN NOWER, STEPHEN *following.*]

STEPHEN: Don't go, darling.

[JOHN NOWER *sits. A shot outside followed by cheers.*]

[*Enter* ZEPPEL.]

ZEPPEL: Will you be wanting anything more tonight, sir?

JOHN NOWER: No, that will be all thank you.

ZEPPEL: Good night, sir.

JOHN NOWER:

 Always the following wind of history
 Of others' wisdom makes a buoyant air
 Till we come suddenly on pockets where
 Is nothing loud but us; where voices seem
 Abrupt, untrained, competing with no lie
 Our fathers shouted once. They taught us war,
 To scamper after darlings, to climb hills,
 To emigrate from weakness, find ourselves
 The easy conquerors of empty bays:
 But never told us this, left each to learn,
 Hear something of that soon-arriving day
 When to gaze longer and delighted on
 A face or idea be impossible.

Could I have been some simpleton that lived
Before disaster sent his runners here;
Younger than worms, worms have too much to bear.
Yes, mineral were best: could I but see
These woods, these fields of green, this lively world
Sterile as moon.

CHORUS:

The Spring unsettles sleeping partnerships,
Foundries improve their casting process, shops
Open a further wing on credit till
The winter. In summer boys grow tall
With running races on the froth-wet sand,
War is declared there, here a treaty signed;
Here a scrum breaks up like a bomb, there troops
Deploy like birds. But proudest into traps
Have fallen. These gears which ran in oil for week
By week, needing no look, now will not work;
Those manors mortgaged twice to pay for love
Go to another.

O how shall man live
Whose thought is born, child of one farcical night,
To find him old? The body warm but not
By choice, he dreams of folk in dancing bunches,
Of tart wine spilt on home-made benches,
Where learns, one drawn apart, a secret will
Restore the dead; but comes thence to a wall.
Outside on frozen soil lie armies killed
Who seem familiar but they are cold.
Now the most solid wish he tries to keep
His hands show through; he never will look up,
Say 'I am good'. On him misfortune falls
More than enough. Better where no one feels,
The out-of-sight, buried too deep for shafts.

[*Enter* FATHER CHRISTMAS. *He speaks to the audience.*]

FATHER CHRISTMAS: Ladies and Gentlemen: I should like to thank you all very much for coming here tonight. Now we have a little surprise for you. When you go home, I hope you will tell your friends to come and bring the kiddies, but you will remember to keep this a secret, won't you? Thank you. Now I will not keep you waiting any longer.

[*Lights. A trial.* JOHN NOWER *as the accuser. The* SPY *as accused.* JOAN *as his warder with a gigantic feeding bottle.* FATHER CHRISTMAS *as president, the rest as jury, wearing school caps.*]

FATHER CHRISTMAS: Is there any more evidence?

JOHN NOWER: Yes. I know we have and are making terrific sacrifices, but we cannot give in. We cannot betray the dead. As we pass their graves can we be deaf to the simple eloquence of their inscriptions, those who in the glory of their early manhood gave up their lives for us? No, we must fight to the finish.

FATHER CHRISTMAS: Very well. Call the witness.

[*Enter* BO.]

BO:

In these days during the migrations, days
Freshening with rain reported from the mountains,
By loss of memory we are reborn,
For memory is death; by taking leave,
Parting in anger and glad to go
Where we are still unwelcome, and if we count
What dead the tides wash in, only to make
Notches for enemies. On northern ridges
Where flags fly, seen and lost, denying rumour
We baffle proof, speakers of a strange tongue.

[*The* SPY *groans. His cries are produced by jazz instruments at the back of the stage.* JOAN *brandishes her bottle.*]

JOAN: Be quiet, or I'll give you a taste of this.

FATHER CHRISTMAS: Next, please.

[*Enter* PO.]

PO:

Past victory is honour, to accept
An island governorship, back to estates

Explored as child; coming at last to love
Lost publicly, found secretly again
In private flats, admitted to a sign.
An understanding sorrow knows no more,
Sits waiting for the lamp, far from those hills
Where rifts open unfenced, mark of a fall,
And flakes fall softly softly burying
Deeper and deeper down her loving son.

[*The* SPY *groans.* JOHN NOWER *produces a revolver.*]

JOHN NOWER: Better to get it over.

JOAN: This way for the Angel of Peace.

FATHER CHRISTMAS: Leave him alone. This fellow is very very ill.
But he will get well.

[*The* MAN-WOMAN *appears as a prisoner of war behind barbed wire,
in the snow.*]

MAN-WOMAN:

Because I'm come it does not mean to hold
An anniversary, think illness healed,
As to renew the lease, consider costs
Of derelict iron works on deserted coasts.
Love was not love for you but episodes,
Traffic in memoirs, views from different sides;
You thought oaths of comparison a bond,
And though you had your orders to disband,
Refused to listen, but remained in woods
Poorly concealed your profits under wads.
Nothing was any use; therefore I went
Hearing you call for what you did not want.
I lay with you; you made that an excuse
For playing with yourself, but homesick because
Your mother told you that's what flowers did,
And thought you lived since you were bored, not dead,
And could not stop. So I was cold to make
No difference, but you were quickly meek
Altered for safety. I tried then to demand

22

Proud habits, protestations called your mind
To show you it was extra, but instead
You overworked yourself, misunderstood,
Adored me for the chance. Lastly I tried
To teach you acting, but always you had nerves
To fear performances as some fear knives.
Now I shall go. No, you if you come,
Will not enjoy yourself, for where I am
All talking is forbidden. . . .

[*The* SPY *groans.*]

JOHN NOWER: I can't bear it.

[*Shoots him. Lights out.*]

VOICES:
Quick, fetch a doctor.
Ten pounds for a doctor.
Ten pounds to keep him away.
Coming, coming.

[*Lights.* FATHER CHRISTMAS, JOHN NOWER *and the* SPY *remain.
The* JURY *has gone, but there is a* PHOTOGRAPHER.]

FATHER CHRISTMAS: Stand back there. Here comes the doctor.

[*Enter* DOCTOR *and his* BOY.]

BOY: Tickle your arse with a feather, sir.

DOCTOR: What's that?

BOY: Particularly nasty weather, sir.

DOCTOR: Yes, it is. Tell me, is my hair tidy? One must always be
careful with a new client.

BOY: It's full of lice, sir.

DOCTOR: What's that?

BOY: It's looking nice, sir. [*For the rest of the scene the* BOY *fools
about.*]

FATHER CHRISTMAS: Are you the doctor?

DOCTOR: I am.

FATHER CHRISTMAS: What can you cure?

DOCTOR: Tennis elbow, Graves' Disease, Derbyshire neck and
Housemaid's knees.

23

FATHER CHRISTMAS: Is that all you can cure?

DOCTOR: No, I have discovered the origin of life. Fourteen months I hesitated before I concluded this diagnosis. I received the morning star for this. My head will be left at death for clever medical analysis. The laugh will be gone and the microbe in command.

FATHER CHRISTMAS: Well, let's see what you can do.

[DOCTOR *takes circular saws, bicycle pumps, etc., from his bag.*]

BOY: You need a pill, sir.

DOCTOR: What's that.

BOY: You'll need your skill, sir. O sir you're hurting.

[BOY *is kicked out.*]

[JOHN NOWER *tries to get a look.*]

DOCTOR: Go away. Your presence will be necessary at Scotland Yard when the criminals of the war are tried, but your evidence will not be needed. It is valueless. Cages will be provided for some of the more interesting specimens. [*Examines the body.*] Um, yes. Very interesting. The conscious brain appears normal except under emotion. Fancy it. The Devil couldn't do that. This advances and retreats under control and poisons everything round it. My diagnosis is: Adamant will, cool brain and laughing spirit. Hullo, what's this? [*Produces a large pair of pliers and extracts an enormous tooth from the body.*] Come along, that's better. Ladies and Gentlemen, you see I have nothing up my sleeve. This tooth was growing ninety-nine years before his great grandmother was born. If it hadn't been taken out today he would have died yesterday. You may get up now.

[*The* SPY *gets up. The* PHOTOGRAPHER *gets ready.*]

PHOTOGRAPHER: Just one minute, please. A little brighter, a little brighter. No, moisten the lips and start afresh. Hold it.

[PHOTOGRAPHER *lets off his flash. Lights out.* FATHER CHRISTMAS *blows a whistle.*]

FATHER CHRISTMAS: All change.

[*Lights.* SPY *behind a gate guarded by* FATHER CHRISTMAS. *Enter* JOHN NOWER *running.*]

24

JOHN NOWER: I'm late, I'm late. Which way is it? I must hurry.

FATHER CHRISTMAS: You can't come in here, without a pass.

[JOHN NOWER *turns back his coat lapel.*]

FATHER CHRISTMAS: O I beg your pardon, sir. This way, sir.

[*Exit* FATHER CHRISTMAS. *The* ACCUSER *and* ACCUSED *plant a tree.*]

JOHN NOWER:

Sametime sharers of the same house,

We know not the builder nor the name of his son.

Now cannot mean to them; boy's voice among dishonoured portraits

To dockside barmaid speaking,

Sorry through wires, pretended speech.

SPY:

Escaped

Armies' pursuit, rebellion and eclipse

Together in a cart,

After all journeys

We stay and are not known.

[*Lights out.*]

Sharers of the same house,

Attendants on the same machine,

Rarely a word, in silence understood.

[*Lights.* JOHN NOWER *alone in his chair. Enter* DICK.]

DICK:

Hullo. I've come to say goodbye.

Yesterday we sat at table together,

Fought side by side at enemies face-to-face meeting

Today we take our leave, time for departure.

I'm sorry.

JOHN NOWER:

Here, give me your knife and take mine. By these

We may remember each other.

There are two chances, but more of one
Parting for ever, not hearing the other
Though he need help.
Have you got everything you want?

DICK: Yes, thanks. Goodbye, John.

JOHN NOWER: Goodbye.

[*Exit* DICK.]

There is the city,
Lighted and clean once, pleasure for builders,
And I,
Letting to cheaper tenants, have made a slum,
Houses at which the passer shakes his fist,
Remembering evil.
Pride and indifference have shared with me, and I
Have kissed them in the dark, for mind has dark,
Shaded commemorations, midnight accidents
In streets where heirs may dine.

But love, sent east for peace
From tunnels under those
Bursts now to pass
On trestles over meaner quarters
A noise and flashing glass.

Feels morning steaming down,
Wind from the snows,
Nowise withdrawn by doubting flinch
Nor joined to any by belief's firm flange,
Refreshed sees all,
The tugged-at teat,
The hopper's steady feed, the frothing leat.
Zeppel.

[*Enter* ZEPPEL.]

ZEPPEL: Sir.

JOHN NOWER: Get my horse ready at once, please.
[*Exeunt.*]
CHORUS:

To throw away the key and walk away,
Not abrupt exile, the neighbours asking why,
But following a line with left and right,
An altered gradient at another rate,
Learns more than maps upon the whitewashed wall,
The hand put up to ask; and makes us well
Without confession of the ill. All pasts
Are single old past now, although some posts
Are forwarded, held looking on a new view;
The future shall fulfil a surer vow,
Not smiling at queen over the glass rim,
Nor making gunpowder in the top room,
Not swooping at the surface still like gulls
But with prolonged drowning shall develop gills.

But there are still to tempt; areas not seen
Because of blizzards or an erring sign,
Whose guessed at wonders would be worth alleging,
And lies about the cost of a night's lodging.
Travellers may sleep at inns but not attach,
They sleep one night together, not asked to touch;
Receive no normal welcome, not the pressed lip,
Children to lift, not the assuaging lap.
Crossing the pass descend the growing stream,
Too tired to hear except the pulses' strum,
Reach villages to ask for a bed in,
Rock shutting out the sky, the old life done.

[CULLEY *enters right and squats in the centre of the stage, looking left through field glasses. Several shots are heard off. Enter* GEORGE *and* KURT.]
GEORGE: Are you much hurt?
KURT: Nothing much, sir. Only a slight flesh wound. Did you get
him, sir?

27

GEORGE: On ledge above the gulley, aimed at, seen moving, fell; looked down on, sprawls in the stream.

KURT: Good. He sniped poor Billy last Easter, riding to Flash.

GEORGE: I have some lint and bandages in my haversack, and there is a spring here. I'll dress your arm.

[*Enter* SETH *finds* BERNARD, *left.*]

SETH: Did you find Tom's body?

BERNARD: Yes, sir. It's lying in the Hangs.

SETH: Which way did they go?

BERNARD: Down there, sir.

[CULLEY *observes them and runs right.*]

CULLEY: There are twenty men from Nattrass, sir, over the gap, coming at once.

GEORGE: Have they seen us?

CULLEY: Not yet.

GEORGE: We must get out. You go down to the copse and make for the Barbon road. We'll follow the old tramway. Keep low and run like hell.

[*Exeunt right.* SETH *watches through field glasses.*]

SETH: Yes. No. No. Yes, I can see them. They are making for the Barbon road. Go down and cut them off. There is good cover by the bridge. We've got them now.

[*A whistle. The back curtains draw, showing* JOHN NOWER, ANNE *and* AARON *and the* ANNOUNCER *grouped. Both sides enter left and right.*]

AARON:

There is a time for peace; too often we
Have gone on cold marches, have taken life,
Till wrongs are bred like flies; the dreamer wakes
Who beats a smooth door, behind footsteps, on the left
The pointed finger, the unendurable drum,
To hear of horses stolen or a house burned.
Now this shall end with marriage as it ought:
Love turns the wind, brings up the salt smell,
Shadow of gulls on the road to the sea.

ANNOUNCER: The engagement is announced of John Nower,

eldest son of the late Mr. and Mrs. George Nower of Lintzgarth, Rockhope, and Anne Shaw, only daughter of the late Mr. and Mrs. Joseph Shaw of Nattrass, Garrigill.

ALL: Hurrah.

[GEORGE *and* SETH *advance to the centre, shake hands and cross over the stage to their opposite sides. Back curtains close. Exeunt in different directions, talking as they go.*]

GEORGE: It was a close shave that time. We had a lucky escape. How are you feeling?

KURT: The arm is rather painful. I owe Bernard one for that.

BERNARD: It's a shame. Just when we had them fixed.

SETH: Don't you worry. You'll get your chance.

BERNARD: But what about this peace?

SETH: That remains to be seen. Only wait.

[*Exeunt. Back curtains draw.* JOHN NOWER *and* ANNE *alone.* JOHN *blows on a grass held between the thumbs and listens.*]

JOHN NOWER: On Cautley where a peregrine has nested, iced heather hurt the knuckles. Fell on the ball near time, the forward stopped. Goodbye now, he said, would open the swing doors. . . . These I remember, but not love till now. We cannot tell where we shall find it, though we all look for it till we do, and what others tell us is no use to us.

Some say that handsome raider still at large,
A terror to the Marshes, in truth is love;
And we must listen for such messengers
To tell us daily: 'Today a saint came blessing
The huts': 'Seen lately in the provinces,
Reading behind a tree and people passing.'
But love returns;
At once all heads are turned this way, and love
Calls order—silenced the angry sons—
Steps forward, greets, repeats what he has heard
And seen, feature for feature, word for word.

ANNE:
Yes, I am glad this evening that we are together.

The silence is unused, death seems
    An axe's echo.

The summer quickens all,
Scatters its promises
To you and me no less
Though neither can compel.

JOHN NOWER:

The wish to last the year,
The longest look to live,
The urgent word survive
The movement of the air.

ANNE:

But loving now let none
Think of divided days
When we shall choose from ways,
All of them evil, one.

JOHN NOWER:

Look on with stricter brows
The sacked and burning town,
The ice-sheet moving down,
The fall of an old house.

ANNE: John, I have a car waiting. There is time to join Dick before
the boat sails. We sleep in beds where men have died howling.

JOHN NOWER: You may be right, but we shall stay.

ANNE:

Tonight the many come to mind,
Sent forward in the thaw with anxious marrow,
For such might now return with a bleak face,
An image pause half-lighted in the door,
A greater but not fortunate in all;
Come home deprived of an astonishing end . . .
Morgan's who took a clean death in the north
Shouting against the wind, or Cousin Dodd's,
Passed out in her chair, the snow falling.

The too-loved clays, born over by diverse drifts,
Fallen upon the far side of all enjoyment,
Unable to move closer, shall not speak
Out of that grave stern on no capital fault;
Enough to have lightly touched the unworthy thing.

JOHN NOWER: We live still.

ANNE: But what has become of the dead? They forget.

JOHN NOWER: These. Smilers, all who stand on promontories, slinkers, whisperers, deliberate approaches, echoes, time, promises of mercy, what dreams or goes masked, embraces that fail, insufficient evidence, touches of the old wound.

But let us not think of things which we hope will be long in coming.

CHORUS:
The Spring will come,
Not hesitate for one employer who
Though a fine day and every pulley running
Would quick lie down; nor save the wanted one
That, wounded in escaping, swam the lake
Safe to the reeds, collapsed in shallow water.
You have tasted good and what is it? For you,
Sick in the green plain, healed in the tundra, shall
Turn westward back from your alone success,
Under a dwindling Alp to see your friends
Cut down the wheat.

JOHN NOWER: It's getting cold, dear, let's go in.

[*Exeunt. Back curtains close.*]

CHORUS:
For where are Basley who won the Ten,
Dickon so tarted by the House,
Thomas who kept a sparrow-hawk?
The clock strikes, it is time to go,
The tongue ashamed, deceived by a shake of the hand.

[*Enter* BRIDAL PARTY *left*, GUESTS *right*.]

GUESTS: Ssh.

31

[*The* CHIEF GUEST *comes forward and presents a bouquet to the bride.*]
CHIEF GUEST:
>With gift in hand we come
>From every neighbour farm
>To celebrate in wine
>The certain union of
>A woman and a man;
>And may their double love
>Be shown to the stranger's eye
>In a son's symmetry.
>Now hate is swallowed down,
>All anger put away;
>The spirit comes to its own,
>The beast to its play.

[ALL *clap. The* CHIEF GUEST *addresses the* AUDIENCE.]
CHIEF GUEST: Will any lady be so kind as to oblige us with a
>dance? . . . Thank you very much . . . This way miss. . . . What
>tune would you like?

[*Gramophone. A dance. As the dance ends, the back curtains draw and the*
BUTLER *enters centre.*]
BUTLER: Dinner is served.
[AARON *goes to the* DANCER.]
AARON: You'll dine with us, of course?
[*Exeunt all except* SETH *and his* MOTHER.]
GUESTS (*as they go out*): It will be a good year for them, I think.
>You don't mean that he . . . well, you know what.
>Rather off his form lately.
>The vein is showing good in the Quarry Hazel.
>One of Edward's friends.
>You must come and have a look at the Kennels some day.
>Well it does seem to show.
>>[*Etc., etc.*]
[*Back curtains close.*]
MOTHER: Seth.
SETH: Yes, Mother.

MOTHER: John Nower is here.

SETH: I know that. What do you want me to do?

MOTHER: Kill him.

SETH: I can't do that. There is peace now; besides he is a guest in our house.

MOTHER: Have you forgotten your brother's death . . . taken out and shot like a dog? It is a nice thing for me to hear people saying that I have a coward for a son. I am thankful your father is not here to see it.

SETH: I'm not afraid of anything or anybody, but I don't want to.

MOTHER: I shall have to take steps.

SETH: It shall be as you like. Though I think that much will come of this, chiefly harm.

MOTHER: I have thought of that.

[*Exit* MOTHER.]

SETH: The little funk. Sunlight on sparkling water, its shades dissolved, reforming, unreal activity where others laughed but he blubbed clinging, homesick, and undeveloped form. I'll do it. Men point in after days. He always was. But wrongly. He fought and overcame, a stern self-ruler. You didn't hear. Hearing they look ashamed too late for shaking hands. Of course I'll do it.

[*Exit* SETH.]

[*A shot. More shots. Shouting.*]

VOICES OUTSIDE: A trap. I might have known.

Take that, damn you.

Open the window.

You swine.

Jimmy, O my God.

[*Enter* SETH *and* BERNARD.]

BERNARD: The Master's killed. So is John Nower, but some of them got away, fetching help, will attack in an hour.

SETH: See that all the doors are bolted.

[*Exeunt right and left. The back curtains draw.* ANNE *with the dead.*]

ANNE:

Now we have seen the story to its end.

33

The hands that were to help will not be lifted,
And bad followed by worse leaves to us tears,
An empty bed, hope from less noble men.
I had seen joy
Received and given, upon both sides, for years.
Now not.

CHORUS:
Though he believe it, no man is strong.
He thinks to be called the fortunate,
To bring home a wife, to live long.

But he is defeated; let the son
Sell the farm lest the mountain fall;
His mother and her mother won.

His fields are used up where the moles visit,
The contours worn flat; if there show
Passage for water he will miss it:

Give up his breath, his woman, his team;
No life to touch, though later there be
Big fruit, eagles above the stream.

CURTAIN

Letter to Lord Byron

I

Excuse, my lord, the liberty I take
    In thus addressing you. I know that you
Will pay the price of authorship and make
    The allowances an author has to do.
    A poet's fan-mail will be nothing new.
And then a lord–Good Lord, you must be peppered,
Like Gary Cooper, Coughlin, or Dick Sheppard,

With notes from perfect strangers starting, 'Sir,
    I liked your lyrics, but *Childe Harold's* trash,'
'My daughter writes, should I encourage her?'
    Sometimes containing frank demands for cash,
    Sometimes sly hints at a platonic pash,
And sometimes, though I think this rather crude,
The correspondent's photo in the nude.

And as for manuscripts–by every post . . .
    I can't improve on Pope's shrill indignation,
But hope that it will please his spiteful ghost
    To learn the use in culture's propagation
    Of modern methods of communication;
New roads, new rails, new contacts, as we know
From documentaries by the G.P.O.

For since the British Isles went Protestant
  A church confession is too high for most.
But still confession is a human want,
  So Englishmen must make theirs now by post
  And authors hear them over breakfast toast.
For, failing them, there's nothing but the wall
Of public lavatories on which to scrawl.

So if ostensibly I write to you
  To chat about your poetry or mine,
There's many other reasons: though it's true
  That I have, at the age of twenty-nine
  Just read *Don Juan* and I found it fine.
I read it on the boat to Reykjavik
Except when eating or asleep or sick.

Now home is miles away, and miles away
  No matter who, and I am quite alone
And cannot understand what people say,
  But like a dog must guess it by the tone;
  At any language other than my own
I'm no great shakes, and here I've found no tutor
Nor sleeping lexicon to make me cuter.

The thought of writing came to me today
  (I like to give these facts of time and space);
The bus was in the desert on its way
  From Mothrudalur to some other place:
  The tears were streaming down my burning face;
I'd caught a heavy cold in Akureyri,
And lunch was late and life looked very dreary.

Professor Housman was I think the first
   To say in print how very stimulating
The little ills by which mankind is cursed,
   The colds, the aches, the pains are to creating;
   Indeed one hardly goes too far in stating
That many a flawless lyric may be due
Not to a lover's broken heart, but 'flu.

But still a proper explanation's lacking;
   Why write to you? I see I must begin
Right at the start when I was at my packing.
   The extra pair of socks, the airtight tin
   Of China tea, the anti-fly were in;
I asked myself what sort of books I'd read
In Iceland, if I ever felt the need.

I can't read Jefferies on the Wiltshire Downs,
   Nor browse on limericks in a smoking-room;
Who would try Trollope in cathedral towns,
   Or Marie Stopes inside his mother's womb?
   Perhaps you feel the same beyond the tomb.
Do the celestial highbrows only care
For works on Clydeside, Fascists, or Mayfair?

In certain quarters I had heard a rumour
   (For all I know the rumour's only silly)
That Icelanders have little sense of humour.
   I knew the country was extremely hilly,
   The climate unreliable and chilly;
So looking round for something light and easy
I pounced on you as warm and *civilisé*.

There is one other author in my pack:
    For some time I debated which to write to.
Which would least likely send my letter back?
    But I decided that I'd give a fright to
    Jane Austen if I wrote when I'd no right to,
And share in her contempt the dreadful fates
Of Crawford, Musgrave, and of Mr Yates.

Then she's a novelist. I don't know whether
    You will agree, but novel writing is
A higher art than poetry altogether
    In my opinion, and success implies
    Both finer character and faculties.
Perhaps that's why real novels are as rare
As winter thunder or a polar bear.

The average poet by comparison
    Is unobservant, immature, and lazy.
You must admit, when all is said and done,
    His sense of other people's very hazy,
    His moral judgements are too often crazy,
A slick and easy generalization
Appeal too well to his imagination.

I must remember, though, that you were dead
    Before the four great Russians lived, who brought
The art of novel writing to a head;
    The help of Boots had not been sought.
    But now the art for which Jane Austen fought,
Under the right persuasion bravely warms
And is the most prodigious of the forms.

She was not an unshockable blue-stocking;
    If shades remain the characters they were,
No doubt she still considers you as shocking.
But tell Jane Austen, that is, if you dare,
    How much her novels are beloved down here.
She wrote them for posterity, she said;
'Twas rash, but by posterity she's read.

You could not shock her more than she shocks me;
    Beside her Joyce seems innocent as grass.
It makes me most uncomfortable to see
    An English spinster of the middle class
    Describe the amorous effects of 'brass',
Reveal so frankly and with such sobriety
The economic basis of society.

So it is you who is to get this letter.
    The experiment may not be a success.
There're many others who could do it better,
    But I shall not enjoy myself the less.
    Shaw of the Air Force said that happiness
Comes in absorption: he was right, I know it;
Even in scribbling to a long-dead poet.

Every exciting letter has enclosures,
    And so shall this—a bunch of photographs,
Some out of focus, some with wrong exposures,
    Press cuttings, gossip, maps, statistics, graphs;
    I don't intend to do the thing by halves.
I'm going to be very up to date indeed.
It is a collage that you're going to read.

I want a form that's large enough to swim in,
    And talk on any subject that I choose,
From natural scenery to men and women,
    Myself, the arts, the European news:
    And since she's on a holiday, my Muse
Is out to please, find everything delightful
And only now and then be mildly spiteful.

Ottava Rima would, I know, be proper,
    The proper instrument on which to pay
My compliments, but I should come a cropper;
    Rhyme-royal's difficult enough to play.
    But if no classics as in Chaucer's day,
At least my modern pieces shall be cheery
Like English bishops on the Quantum Theory.

Light verse, poor girl, is under a sad weather;
    Except by Milne and persons of that kind
She's treated as *démodé* altogether.
    It's strange and very unjust to my mind
    Her brief appearances should be confined,
Apart from Belloc's *Cautionary Tales*,
To the more bourgeois periodicals.

'The fascination of what's difficult',
    The wish to do what one's not done before.
Is, I hope, proper to *Quincunque Vult*,
    The proper card to show at Heaven's door.
    Gerettet not *Gerichtet* be the Law,
Et cetera, et cetera. O curse,
That is the flattest line in English verse.

Parnassus after all is not a mountain,
    Reserved for A.1. climbers such as you;
It's got a park, it's got a public fountain.
    The most I ask is leave to share a pew
    With Bradford or with Cottam, that will do:
To pasture my few silly sheep with Dyer
And picnic on the lower slopes with Prior.

A publisher's an author's greatest friend,
    A generous uncle, or he ought to be.
(I'm sure we hope it pays him in the end.)
    I love my publishers and they love me,
    At least they paid a very handsome fee
To send me here. I've never heard a grouse
Either from Russell Square or Random House.

But now I've got uncomfortable suspicions,
    I'm going to put their patience out of joint.
Though it's in keeping with the best traditions
    For Travel Books to wander from the point
    (There is no other rhyme except anoint),
They well may charge me with–I've no defences–
Obtaining money under false pretences.

I know I've not the least chance of survival
    Beside the major travellers of the day.
I am no Lawrence who, on his arrival,
    Sat down and typed out all he had to say;
    I am not even Ernest Hemingway.
I shall not run to a two-bob edition,
So just won't enter for the competition.

And even here the steps I flounder in
  Were worn by most distinguished boots of old.
Dasent and Morris and Lord Dufferin,
  Hooker and men of that heroic mould
  Welcome me icily into the fold;
I'm not like Peter Fleming an Etonian,
But, if I'm Judas, I'm an old Oxonian.

The Haig Thomases are at Myvatn now,
  At Hvitarvatn and at Vatnajökull
Cambridge research goes on, I don't know how:
  The shades of Asquith and of Auden Skökull
  Turn in their coffins a three-quarter circle
To see their son, upon whose help they reckoned,
Being as frivolous as Charles the Second.

So this, my opening chapter, has to stop
  With humbly begging everybody's pardon.
From Faber first in case the book's a flop,
  Then from the critics lest they should be hard on
  The author when he leads them up the garden,
Last from the general public he must beg
Permission now and then to pull their leg.

II

I'm writing this in pencil on my knee,
  Using my other hand to stop me yawning,
Upon a primitive, unsheltered quay
  In the small hours of a Wednesday morning.
  I cannot add the summer day is dawning;
In Seydhisfjördur every schoolboy knows
That daylight in the summer never goes.

To get to sleep in latitudes called upper
   Is difficult at first for Englishmen.
It's like being sent to bed before your supper
   For playing darts with father's fountain-pen,
   Or like returning after orgies, when
Your breath's like luggage and you realize
You've been more confidential than was wise.

I've done my duty, taken many notes
   Upon the almost total lack of greenery,
The roads, the illegitimates, the goats:
   To use a rhyme of yours, there's handsome scenery
   But little agricultural machinery;
And with the help of Sunlight Soap the Geysir
Affords to visitors le plus grand plaisir.

The North, though, never was your cup of tea;
   'Moral' you thought it so you kept away.
And what I'm sure you're wanting now from me
   Is news about the England of the day,
   What sort of things *La Jeunesse* do and say.
Is Brighton still as proud of her pavilion,
And is it safe for girls to travel pillion?

I'll clear my throat and take a Rover's breath
   And skip a century of hope and sin—
For far too much has happened since your death.
   Crying went out and the cold bath came in,
   With drains, bananas, bicycles, and tin,
And Europe saw from Ireland to Albania
The Gothic revival and the Railway Mania.

We're entering now the Eotechnic Phase
   Thanks to the Grid and all those new alloys;
That is, at least, what Lewis Mumford says.
   A world of Aertex underwear for boys,
   Huge plate-glass windows, walls absorbing noise,
Where the smoke nuisance is utterly abated
And all the furniture is chromium-plated.

Well, you might think so if you went to Surrey
   And stayed for week-ends with the well-to-do,
Your car too fast, too personal your worry
   To look too closely at the wheeling view.
   But in the north it simply isn't true.
To those who live in Warrington or Wigan,
It's not a white lie, it's a whacking big 'un.

There on the old historic battlefield,
   The cold ferocity of human wills,
The scars of struggle are as yet unhealed;
   Slattern the tenements on sombre hills,
   And gaunt in valleys the square-windowed mills
That, since the Georgian house, in my conjecture
Remain our finest native architecture.

On economic, health, or moral grounds
   It hasn't got the least excuse to show;
No more than chamber pots or otter hounds;
   But let me say before it has to go,
It's the most lovely country that I know;
Clearer than Scafell Pike, my heart has stamped on
The view from Birmingham to Wolverhampton.

Long, long ago, when I was only four,
　　Going towards my grandmother, the line
Passed through a coal-field. From the corridor
　　I watched it pass with envy, thought 'How fine!
　　Oh how I wish that situation mine.'
Tramlines and slagheaps, pieces of machinery,
That was, and still is, my ideal scenery.

Hail to the New World! Hail to those who'll love
　　Its antiseptic objects, feel at home.
Lovers will gaze at an electric stove,
　　Another *poésie de départ* come
　　Centred round bus-stops or the aerodrome.
But give me still, to stir imagination
The chiaroscuro of the railway station.

Preserve me from the Shape of Things to Be;
　　The high-grade posters at the public meeting,
The influence of Art on Industry,
　　The cinemas with perfect taste in seating;
　　Preserve me, above all, from central heating.
It may be D. H. Lawrence hocus-pocus,
But I prefer a room that's got a focus.

But you want facts, not sighs. I'll do my best
　　To give a few; you can't expect them all.
To start with, on the whole we're better dressed;
　　For chic the difference to-day is small
　　Of barmaid from my lady at the Hall.
It's sad to spoil this democratic vision
With millions suffering from malnutrition.

Again, our age is highly educated;
    There is no lie our children cannot read,
And as MacDonald might so well have stated
    We're growing up and up and up indeed.
    Advertisements can teach us all we need;
And death is better, as the millions know,
Than dandruff, night-starvation, or B.O.

We're always had a penchant for field sports,
    But what do you think has grown up in our towns?
A passion for the open air and shorts;
    The sun is one of our emotive nouns.
    Go down by chara' to the Sussex Downs,
Watch the manœuvres of the week-end hikers
Massed on parade with Kodaks or with Leicas.

These movements signify our age-long rule
    Of insularity has lost its powers;
The cult of salads and the swimming pool
    Comes from a climate sunnier than ours,
    And lands which never heard of licensed hours.
The south of England before very long
Will look no different from the Continong.

You lived and moved among the best society
    And so could introduce your hero to it
Without the slightest tremor of anxiety;
    Because he was your hero and you knew it,
    He'd know instinctively what's done, and do it.
He'd find our day more difficult than yours
For industry has mixed the social drawers.

We've grown, you see, a lot more democratic,
   And Fortune's ladder is for all to climb;
Carnegie on this point was most emphatic.
   A humble grandfather is not a crime,
   At least, if father made enough in time!
Today, thank God, we've got no snobbish feeling
Against the more efficient modes of stealing.

The porter at the Carlton is my brother,
   He'll wish me a good evening if I pay,
For tips and men are equal to each other.
   I'm sure that *Vogue* would be the first to say
   Que le Beau Monde is socialist today;
And many a bandit, not so gently born
Kills vermin every winter with the Quorn.

Adventurers, though, must take things as they find them
   And look for pickings where the pickings are.
The drives of love and hunger are behind them,
   They can't afford to be particular:
   And those who like good cooking and a car,
A certain kind of costume or of face,
Must seek them in a certain kind of place.

Don Juan was a mixer and no doubt
   Would find this century as good as any
For getting hostesses to ask him out,
   And mistresses that need not cost a penny.
   Indeed our ways to waste time are so many,
Thanks to technology, a list of these
Would make a longer book than *Ulysses*.

Yes, in the smart set he would know his way
    By second nature with no tips from me.
Tennis and Golf have come in since your day;
    But those who are as good at games as he
    Acquire the back-hand quite instinctively,
Take to the steel-shaft and hole out in one,
Master the books of Ely Culbertson.

I see his face in every magazine.
    'Don Juan at lunch with one of Cochran's ladies.'
'Don Juan with his red setter May MacQueen.'
    'Don Juan, who's just been wintering in Cadiz,
    Caught at the wheel of his maroon Mercedes.'
'Don Juan at Croydon Aerodrome.' 'Don Juan
Snapped in the paddock with the Aga Khan.'

But if in highbrow circles he would sally
    It's just as well to warn him there's no stain on
Picasso, all-in-wrestling, or the Ballet.
    Sibelius is the man. To get a pain on
    Listening to Elgar is a sine qua non.
A second-hand acquaintance of Pareto's
Ranks higher than an intimate of Plato's.

The vogue for Black Mass and the cult of devils
    Has sunk. The Good, the Beautiful, the True
Still fluctuate about the lower levels.
    Joyces are firm and there there's nothing new.
    Eliots have hardened just a point or two.
Hopkins are brisk, thanks to some recent boosts.
There's been some further weakening in Prousts.

I'm saying this to tell you who's the rage,
  And not to loose a sneer from my interior.
Because there's snobbery in every age,
  Because some names are loved by the superior,
  It does not follow they're the least inferior:
For all I know the Beatific Vision's
On view at all Surrealist Exhibitions.

Now for the spirit of the people. Here
  I know I'm treading on more dangerous ground:
I know there're many changes in the air,
  But know my data too slight to be sound,
  I know, too, I'm inviting the renowned
Retort of all who love the Status Quo:
'You can't change human nature, don't you know!'

We've still, it's true, the same shape and appearance,
  We haven't changed the way that kissing's done;
The average man still hates all interference,
  Is just as proud still of his new-born son:
  Still, like a hen, he likes his private run,
Scratches for self-esteem, and slyly pecks
A good deal in the neighbourhood of sex.

But he's another man in many ways:
  Ask the cartoonist first, for he knows best.
Where is the John Bull of the good old days,
  The swaggering bully with the clumsy jest?
  His meaty neck has long been laid to rest,
His acres of self-confidence for sale;
He passed away at Ypres and Passchendaele.

Turn to the work of Disney or of Strube;
  There stands our hero in his threadbare seams;
The bowler hat who strap-hangs in the tube,
  And kicks the tyrant only in his dreams,
  Trading on pathos, dreading all extremes;
The little Mickey with the hidden grudge;
Which is the better, I leave you to judge.

Begot on Hire Purchase by Insurance,
  Forms at his christening worshipped and adored;
A season ticket schooled him in endurance,
  A tax collector and a waterboard
  Admonished him. In boyhood he was awed
By a matric, and complex apparatuses
Keep his heart conscious of Divine Afflatuses.

'I am like you,' he says, 'and you, and you,
  I love my life, I love the home-fires, have
To keep them burning. Heroes never do.
  Heroes are sent by ogres to the grave.
  I may not be courageous, but I save.
I am the one who somehow turns the corner,
I may perhaps be fortunate Jack Horner.

'I am the ogre's private secretary;
  I've felt his stature and his powers, learned
To give his ogreship the raspberry
  Only when his gigantic back is turned.
  One day, who knows, I'll do as I have yearned.
The short man, all his fingers on the door,
With repartee shall send him to the floor.'

One day, which day? O any other day,
   But not today. The ogre knows his man.
To kill the ogre that would take away
   The fear in which his happy dreams began,
   And with his life he'll guard dreams while he can.
Those who would really kill his dream's contentment
He hates with real implacable resentment.

He dreads the ogre, but he dreads yet more
   Those who conceivably might set him free,
Those the cartoonist has no time to draw.
   Without his bondage he'd be all at sea;
   The ogre need but shout 'Security',
To make this man, so lovable, so mild,
As madly cruel as a frightened child.

Byron, thou should'st be living at this hour!
   What would you do, I wonder, if you were?
Britannia's lost prestige and cash and power,
   Her middle classes show some wear and tear,
   We've learned to bomb each other from the air;
I can't imagine what the Duke of Wellington
Would say about the music of Duke Ellington.

Suggestions have been made that the Teutonic
   Führer-Prinzip would have appealed to you
As being the true heir to the Byronic–
   In keeping with your social status too
   (It has its English converts, fit and few),
That you would, hearing honest Oswald's call,
Be gleichgeschaltet in the Albert Hall.

'Lord Byron at the head of his storm-troopers!'
  Nothing, says science, is impossible:
The Pope may quit to join the Oxford Groupers,
  Nuffield may leave one farthing in his Will,
  There may be someone who trusts Baldwin still,
Someone may think that Empire wines are nice,
There may be people who hear Tauber twice.

You liked to be the centre of attention,
  The gay Prince Charming of the fairy story,
Who tamed the Dragon by his intervention.
  In modern warfare though it's just as gory,
  There isn't any individual glory;
The Prince must be anonymous, observant,
A kind of lab-boy, or a civil servant.

You never were an Isolationist;
  Injustice you had always hatred for,
And we can hardly blame you, if you missed
  Injustice just outside your lordship's door:
  Nearer than Greece were cotton and the poor.
Today you might have seen them, might indeed
Have walked in the United Front with Gide,

Against the ogre, dragon, what you will;
  His many shapes and names all turn us pale,
For he's immortal, and today he still
  Swinges the horror of his scaly tail.
  Sometimes he seems to sleep, but will not fail
In every age to rear up to defend
Each dying force of history to the end.

Milton beheld him on the English throne,
   And Bunyan sitting in the Papal chair;
The hermits fought him in their caves alone,
   At the first Empire he was also there,
   Dangling his Pax Romana in the air:
He comes in dreams at puberty to man,
To scare him back to childhood if he can.

Banker or landlord, booking-clerk or Pope,
   Whenever he's lost faith in choice and thought,
When a man sees the future without hope,
   Whenever he endorses Hobbes' report
   'The life of man is nasty, brutish, short,'
The dragon rises from his garden border
And promises to set up law and order.

He that in Athens murdered Socrates,
   And Plato then seduced, prepares to make
A desolation and to call it peace
   Today for dying magnates, for the sake
   Of generals who can scarcely keep awake,
And for that doughy mass in great and small
That doesn't want to stir itself at all.

Forgive me for inflicting all this on you,
   For asking you to hold the baby for us;
It's easy to forget that where you've gone, you
   May only want to chat with Set and Horus,
   Bored to extinction with our earthly chorus:
Perhaps it sounds to you like a trunk-call,
Urgent, it seems, but quite inaudible.

Yet though the choice of what is to be done
  Remains with the alive, the rigid nation
Is supple still within the breathing one;
  Its sentinels yet keep their sleepless station,
  And every man in every generation,
Tossing in his dilemma on his bed,
Cries to the shadows of the noble dead.

We're out at sea now, and I wish we weren't;
  The sea is rough, I don't care if it's blue;
I'd like to have a quick one, but I daren't.
  And I must interrupt this screed to you,
  For I've some other little jobs to do;
I must write home or mother will be vexed,
So this must be continued in our next.

III

My last remarks were sent you from a boat.
  I'm back on shore now in a warm bed-sitter,
And several friends have joined me since I wrote;
  So though the weather out of doors is bitter,
  I feel a great deal cheerier and fitter.
A party from a public school, a poet,
Have set a rapid pace, and make me go it.

We're starting soon on a big expedition
  Into the desert, which I'm sure is corking:
Many would like to be in my position.
  I only hope there won't be too much walking.
  Now let me see, where was I? We were talking
Of Social Questions when I had to stop;
I think it's time now for a little shop.

In setting up my brass plate as a critic,
   I make no claim to certain diagnosis,
I'm more intuitive than analytic,
   I offer thought in homoeopathic doses
   (But someone may get better in the process).
I don't pretend to reasoning like Pritchard's
Or the logomachy of I. A. Richards.

I like your muse because she's gay and witty,
   Because she's neither prostitute nor frump,
The daughter of a European city,
   And country houses long before the slump;
   I like her voice that does not make me jump:
And you I find sympatisch, a good townee,
Neither a preacher, ninny, bore, nor Brownie.

A poet, swimmer, peer, and man of action,
   –It beats Roy Campbell's record by a mile–
You offer every possible attraction.
   By looking into your poetic style,
   And love-life on the chance that both were vile,
Several have earned a decent livelihood,
Whose lives were uncreative but were good.

You've had your packet from the critics, though:
   They grant you warmth of heart, but at your head
Their moral and aesthetic brickbats throw.
   A 'vulgar genius' so George Eliot said,
   Which doesn't matter as George Eliot's dead,
But T. S. Eliot, I am sad to find,
Damns you with: 'an uninteresting mind'.

A statement which I must say I'm ashamed at;
  A poet must be judged by his intention,
And serious thought you never said you aimed at.
   I think a serious critic ought to mention
   That one verse style was really your invention,
A style whose meaning does not need a spanner,
You are the master of the airy manner.

By all means let us touch our humble caps to
  La poésie pure, the epic narrative;
But comedy shall get its round of claps, too.
   According to his powers, each may give;
   Only on varied diet can we live.
The pious fable and the dirty story
Share in the total literary glory.

There's every mode of singing robe in stock,
  From Shakespeare's gorgeous fur coat, Spenser's muff,
Or Dryden's lounge suit to my cotton frock,
   And Wordsworth's Harris tweed with leathern cuff.
   Firbank, I think, wore just a just-enough;
I fancy Whitman in a reach-me-down,
But you, like Sherlock, in a dressing-gown.

I'm also glad to find I've your authority
  For finding Wordsworth a most bleak old bore,
Though I'm afraid we're in a sad minority
   For every year his followers get more,
   Their number must have doubled since the war.
They come in train-loads to the Lakes, and swarms
Of pupil-teachers study him in *Storm's*.

'I hate a pupil-teacher,' Milton said,
   Who also hated bureaucratic fools;
Milton may thank his stars that he is dead,
   Although he's learnt by heart in public schools,
   Along with Wordsworth and the list of rules;
For many a don while looking down his nose
Calls Pope and Dryden classics of our prose.

And new plants flower from that old potato.
   They thrive best in a poor industrial soil,
Are hardier crossed with Rousseaus or a Plato;
   Their cultivation is an easy toil.
   William, to change the metaphor, struck oil;
His well seems inexhaustible, a gusher
That saves old England from the fate of Russia.

The mountain-snob is a Wordsworthian fruit;
   He tears his clothes and doesn't shave his chin,
He wears a very pretty little boot,
   He chooses the least comfortable inn;
   A mountain railway is a deadly sin;
His strength, of course, is as the strength of ten men,
He calls all those who live in cities wen-men.

I'm not a spoil-sport, I would never wish
   To interfere with anybody's pleasures;
By all means climb, or hunt, or even fish,
   All human hearts have ugly little treasures;
   But think it time to take repressive measures
When someone says, adopting the 'I know' line,
The Good Life is confined above the snow-line.

Besides, I'm very fond of mountains, too;
   I like to travel through them in a car;
I like a house that's got a sweeping view;
   I like to walk, but not to walk too far.
   I also like green plains where cattle are,
And trees and rivers, and shall always quarrel
With those who think that rivers are immoral.

Not that my private quarrel gives quietus to
   The interesting question that it raises;
Impartial thought will give a proper status to
   This interest in waterfalls and daisies,
   Excessive love for the non-human faces,
That lives in hearts from Golders Green to Teddington;
It's all bound up with Einstein, Jeans, and Eddington.

It is a commonplace that's hardly worth
   A poet's while to make profound or terse,
That now the sun does not go round the earth,
   That man's no centre of the universe;
   And working in an office makes it worse.
The humblest is acquiring with facility
A Universal-Complex sensibility.

For now we've learnt we mustn't be so bumptious
   We find the stars are one big family,
And send out invitations for a scrumptious
   Simple, old-fashioned, jolly romp with tea
   To any natural objects we can see.
We can't, of course, invite a Jew or Red
But birds and nebulae will do instead.

The Higher Mind's outgrowing the Barbarian,
   It's hardly thought hygienic now to kiss;
The world is surely turning vegetarian;
   And as it grows too sensitive for this,
   It won't be long before we find there is
A Society of Everybody's Aunts
For the Prevention of Cruelty to Plants.

I dread this like the dentist, rather more so:
   To me Art's subject is the human clay,
And landscape but a background to a torso;
   All Cézanne's apples I would give away
   For one small Goya or a Daumier.
I'll never grant a more than minor beauty
To pudge or pilewort, petty-chap or pooty.

Art, if it doesn't start there, at least ends,
   Whether aesthetics like the thought or not,
In an attempt to entertain our friends;
   And our first problem is to realize what
   Peculiar friends the modern artist's got;
It's possible a little dose of history
May help us in unravelling this mystery.

At the Beginning I shall *not* begin,
   Not with the scratches in the ancient caves;
Heard only knows the latest bulletin
   About the finds in the Egyptian graves;
   I'll skip the war-dance of the Indian braves;
Since, for the purposes I have in view,
The English eighteenth century will do.

We find two arts in the Augustan age:
   One quick and graceful, and by no means holy,
Relying on his lordship's patronage;
   The other pious, sober, moving slowly,
   Appealing mainly to the poor and lowly.
So Isaac Watts and Pope, each forced his entry
To lower middle class and landed gentry.

Two arts as different as Jews and Turks,
   Each serving aspects of the Reformation,
Luther's division into faith and works:
   The God of the unique imagination,
   A friend of those who have to know their station;
And the Great Architect, the Engineer
Who keeps the mighty in their higher sphere.

The important point to notice, though, is this:
   Each poet knew for whom he had to write,
Because their life was still the same as his.
   As long as art remains a parasite,
   On any class of persons it's alright;
The only thing it must be is attendant,
The only thing it mustn't, independent.

But artists, though, are human; and for man
   To be a scivvy is not nice at all:
So everyone will do the best he can
   To get a patch of ground which he can call
   His own. He doesn't really care how small,
So long as he can style himself the master:
Unluckily for art, it's a disaster.

To be a highbrow is the natural state:
   To have a special interest of one's own,
Rock gardens, marrows, pigeons, silver plate,
   Collecting butterflies or bits of stone;
   And then to have a circle where one's known
Of hobbyists and rivals to discuss
With expert knowledge what appeals to us.

But to the artist this is quite forbidden:
   On this point he must differ from the crowd,
And, like a secret agent, must keep hidden
   His passion for his shop. However proud,
   And rightly, of his trade, he's not allowed
To etch his face with his professional creases,
Or die from occupational diseases.

Until the great Industrial Revolution
   The artist had to earn his livelihood:
However much he hated the intrusion
   Of patron's taste or public's fickle mood,
   He had to please or go without his food;
He had to keep his technique to himself
Or find no joint upon his larder shelf.

But Savoury and Newcomen and Watt
   And all those names that I was told to get up
In history preparation and forgot,
   A new class of creative artist set up,
   On whom the pressure of demand was let up:
He sang and painted and drew dividends,
But lost responsibilities and friends.

Those most affected were the very best:
  Those with originality of vision,
Those whose technique was better than the rest,
  Jumped at the chance of a secure position
  With freedom from the bad old hack tradition,
Leave to be sole judges of the artist's brandy,
Be Shelley, or Childe Harold, or the Dandy.

So started what I'll call the Poet's Party:
  (Most of the guests were painters, never mind)–
The first few hours the atmosphere was hearty,
  With fireworks, fun, and games of every kind;
  All were enjoying it, no one was blind;
Brilliant the speeches improvised, the dances,
And brilliant, too, the technical advances.

How nice at first to watch the passers-by
  Out of the upper window, and to say
'How glad I am that though I have to die
  Like all those cattle, I'm less base than they!'
  How we all roared when Baudelaire went fey.
'See this cigar,' he said, 'it's Baudelaire's.
What happens to perception? Ah, who cares?'

Today, alas, that happy crowded floor
  Looks very different: many are in tears:
Some have retired to bed and locked the door;
  And some swing madly from the chandeliers;
  Some have passed out entirely in the rears;
Some have been sick in corners; the sobering few
Are trying hard to think of something new.

I've made it seem the artist's silly fault,
  'In which case why these sentimental sobs?
In fact, of course, the whole tureen was salt.
  The soup was full of little bits of snobs.
  The common clay and the uncommon nobs
Were far too busy making piles or starving
To look at pictures, poetry, or carving.

I've simplified the facts to be emphatic,
  Playing Macaulay's favourite little trick
Of lighting that's contrasted and dramatic;
  Because it's true Art feels a trifle sick,
  You mustn't think the old girl's lost her kick.
And those, besides, who feel most like a sewer
Belong to Painting not to Literature.

You know the terror that for poets lurks
  Beyond the ferry when to Minos brought.
Poets must utter their Collected Works,
  Including Juvenilia. So I thought
  That you might warn him. Yes, I think you ought,
In case, when my turn comes, he shall cry 'Atta boys,
Off with his bags, he's crazy as a hatter, boys!'

The clock is striking and it's time for lunch;
  We start at four. The weather's none too bright.
Some of the party look as pleased as Punch.
  We shall be travelling, as they call it, light:
  We shall be sleeping in a tent tonight.
You know what Baden-Powell's taught us, don't you,
Ora pro nobis, please, this evening, won't you?

A ship again; this time the *Dettifoss*.
  Grierson can buy it; all the sea I mean,
All this Atlantic that we've now to cross
  Heading for England's pleasant pastures green.
  Pro tem I've done with the Icelandic scene;
I watch the hills receding in the distance,
I hear the thudding of an engine's pistons.

I hope I'm better, wiser for the trip:
  I've had the benefit of northern breezes,
The open road and good companionship,
  I've seen some very pretty little pieces;
  And though the luck was almost all MacNeice's,
I've spent some jolly evenings playing rummy—
No one can talk at Bridge, unless it's Dummy.

I've learnt to ride, at least to ride a pony,
  Taken a lot of healthy exercise,
On barren mountains and in valleys stony,
  I've tasted a hot spring (a taste was wise),
  And foods a man remembers till he dies.
All things considered, I consider Iceland,
Apart from Reykjavik, a very nice land.

The part can stand as symbol for the whole:
  So ruminating in these last few weeks,
I see the map of all my youth unroll,
  The mental mountains and the psychic creeks,
  The towns of which the master never speaks,
The various parishes and what they voted for,
The colonies, their size, and what they're noted for.

A child may ask when our strange epoch passes,
    During a history lesson, 'Please, sir, what's
An intellectual of the middle classes?
    Is he a maker of ceramic pots
    Or does he choose his king by drawing lots?'
What follows now may set him on the rail,
A plain, perhaps a cautionary, tale.

My passport says I'm five feet and eleven,
    With hazel eyes and fair (it's tow-like) hair,
That I was born in York in 1907,
    With no distinctive markings anywhere.
    Which isn't quite correct. Conspicuous there
On my right cheek appears a large brown mole,
I think I don't dislike it on the whole.

My father's forbears were all Midland yeomen
    Till royalties from coal mines did them good;
I think they must have been phlegmatic slowmen.
    My mother's ancestors had Norman blood,
    From Somerset I've always understood;
My grandfathers on either side agree
In being clergymen and C. of E.

Father and Mother each was one of seven,
    Though one died young and one was not all there;
Their fathers both went suddenly to Heaven
    While they were still quite small and left them here
    To work on earth with little cash to spare;
A nurse, a rising medico, at Bart's
Both felt the pangs of Cupid's naughty darts.

My home then was professional and 'high'.
  No gentler father ever lived, I'll lay
All Lombard Street against a shepherd's pie.
  We imitate our loves: well, neighbours say
  I grow more like my mother every day.
I don't like business men. I know a Prot
Will never really kneel, but only squat.

In pleasures of the mind they both delighted;
  The library in the study was enough
To make a better boy than me short-sighted;
  Our old cook Ada surely knew her stuff;
  My elder brothers did not treat me rough;
We lived at Solihull, a village then;
Those at the gasworks were my favourite men.

My earliest recollection to stay put
  Is of a white stone doorstep and a spot
Of pus where father lanced the terrier's foot;
  Next, stuffing shag into the coffee pot
  Which nearly killed my mother, but did not;
Both psychoanalyst and Christian minister,
Will think these incidents extremely sinister.

With northern myths my little brain was laden,
  With deeds of Thor and Loki and such scenes;
My favourite tale was Andersen's *Ice Maiden*;
  But better far than any kings or queens
  I liked to see and know about machines:
And from my sixth until my sixteenth year
I thought myself a mining engineer.

The mine I always pictured was for lead,
 Though copper mines might, *faute de mieux*, be sound.
Today I like a weight upon my bed;
 I always travel by the Underground;
 For concentration I have always found
A small room best, the curtains drawn, the light on;
Then I can work from nine till tea-time, right on.

I must admit that I was most precocious
 (Precocious children rarely grow up good).
My aunts and uncles thought me quite atrocious
 For using words more adult than I should;
 My first remark at school did all it could
To shake a matron's monumental poise;
'I like to see the various types of boys.'

The Great War had begun: but masters' scrutiny
 And fists of big boys were the war to us;
It was as harmless as the Indian Mutiny,
 A beating from the Head was dangerous.
 But once when half the form put down *Bellus*
We were accused of that most deadly sin,
Wanting the Kaiser and the Huns to win.

The way in which we really were affected
 Was having such a varied lot to teach us.
The best were fighting, as the King expected,
 The remnant either elderly grey creatures,
 Or characters with most peculiar features.
Many were raggable, a few were waxy,
One had to leave abruptly in a taxi.

Surnames I must not write–O Reginald,
    You at least taught us that which fadeth not,
Our earliest visions of the great wide world;
    The beer and biscuits that your favourites got,
    Your tales revealing you a first-class shot,
Your riding breeks, your drama called *The Waves*,
A few of us will carry to our graves.

'Half a lunatic, half a knave.' No doubt
    A holy terror to the staff at tea;
A good headmaster must have soon found out
    Your moral character was all at sea;
    I question if you'd got a pass degree:
But little children bless your kind that knocks
Away the edifying stumbling blocks.

How can I thank you? For it only shows
    (Let me ride just this once my hobby-horse),
There're things a good headmaster never knows.
    There must be sober schoolmasters, of course,
    But what a prep school really puts across
Is knowledge of the world we'll soon be lost in:
Today it's more like Dickens than Jane Austen.

I hate the modern trick, to tell the truth,
    Of straightening out the kinks in the young mind,
Our passion for the tender plant of youth,
    Our hatred for all weeds of any kind.
    Slogans are bad: the best that I can find
Is this: 'Let each child have that's in our care
As much neurosis as the child can bear.'

In this respect, at least, my bad old Adam is
　　Pigheadedly against the general trend;
And has no use for all these new academies
　　Where readers of the better weeklies send
　　The child they probably did not intend,
To paint a lampshade, marry, or keep pigeons,
Or make a study of the world religions.

Goddess of bossy underlings, Normality!
　　What murders are committed in thy name!
Totalitarian is thy state Reality,
　　Reeking of antiseptics and the shame
　　Of faces that all look and feel the same.
Thy Muse is one unknown to classic histories,
The topping figure of the hockey mistress.

From thy dread Empire not a soul's exempted:
　　More than the nursemaids pushing prams in parks,
By thee the intellectuals are tempted,
　　O, to commit the treason of the clerks,
　　Bewitched by thee to literary sharks.
But I must leave thee to thy office stool,
I must get on now to my public school.

Men had stopped throwing stones at one another,
　　Butter and Father had come back again;
Gone were the holidays we spent with Mother
　　In furnished rooms on mountain, moor, and fen;
　　And gone those summer Sunday evenings, when
Along the seafronts fled a curious noise,
'Eternal Father', sung by three young boys.

Nation spoke Peace, or said she did, with nation;
　　The sexes tried their best to look the same;
Morals lost value during the inflation,
　　The great Victorians kindly took the blame;
　　Visions of Dada to the Post-War came,
Sitting in cafés, nostrils stuffed with bread,
Above the recent and the straight-laced dead.

I've said my say on public schools elsewhere:
　　Romantic friendship, prefects, bullying,
I shall not deal with, *c'est une autre affaire*.
　　Those who expect them, will get no such thing,
　　It is the strictly relevant I sing.
Why should they grumble? They've the Greek Anthology,
And all the spicier bits of Anthropology.

We all grow up the same way, more or less;
　　Life is not known to give away her presents;
She only swops. The unselfconsciousness
　　That children share with animals and peasants
　　Sinks in the *Sturm und drang* of adolescence.
Like other boys I lost my taste for sweets,
Discovered sunsets, passion, God, and Keats.

I shall recall a single incident
　　No more. I spoke of mining engineering
As the career on which my mind was bent,
　　But for some time my fancies had been veering;
　　Mirages of the future kept appearing;
Crazes had come and gone in short, sharp gales,
For motor-bikes, photography, and whales.

But indecision broke off with a clean cut end
    One afternoon in March at half past three
When walking in a ploughed field with a friend;
    Kicking a little stone, he turned to me
    And said, 'Tell me, do you write poetry?'
I never had, and said so, but I knew
That very moment what I wished to do.

Without a bridge passage this leads me straight
    Into the theme marked 'Oxford' on my score
From pages twenty-five to twenty-eight.
    Aesthetic trills I'd never heard before
    Rose from the strings, shrill poses from the cor;
The woodwind chattered like a pre-war Russian,
'Art' boomed the brass, and 'Life' thumped the percussion.

A raw provincial, my good taste was tardy,
    And Edward Thomas I as yet preferred;
I was still listening to Thomas Hardy
    Putting divinity about a bird;
    But Eliot spoke the still unspoken word;
For gasworks and dried tubers I forsook
The clock at Grantchester, the English rook.

All youth's intolerant certainty was mine as
    I faced life in a double-breasted suit;
I bought and praised but did not read Aquinas,
    At the Criterion's verdict I was mute,
    Though Arnold's I was ready to refute;
And through the quads dogmatic words rang clear,
'Good poetry is classic and austere.'

So much for Art. Of course Life had its passions too;
    The student's flesh like his imagination
Makes facts fit theories and has fashions too.
    We were the tail, a sort of poor relation
    To that debauched, eccentric generation
That grew up with their fathers at the War,
And made new glosses on the noun Amor.

Three years passed quickly while the Isis went
    Down to the sea for better or for worse;
Then to Berlin, not Carthage, I was sent
    With money from my parents in my purse,
    And ceased to see the world in terms of verse.
I met a chap called Layard and he fed
New doctrines into my receptive head.

Part came from Lane, and part from D. H. Lawrence;
    Gide, though I didn't know it then, gave part.
They taught me to express my deep abhorrence
    If I caught anyone preferring Art
    To Life and Love and being Pure-in-Heart.
I lived with crooks but seldom was molested;
The Pure-in-Heart can never be arrested.

He's gay; no bludgeonings of chance can spoil it,
    The Pure-in-Heart loves all men on a par,
And has no trouble with his private toilet;
    The Pure-in-Heart is never ill; catarrh
    Would be the yellow streak, the brush of tar;
Determined to be loving and forgiving,
I came back home to try and earn my living.

The only thing you never turned your hand to
  Was teaching English in a boarding school.
Today it's a profession that seems grand to
  Those whose alternative's an office stool;
  For budding authors it's become the rule.
To many an unknown genius postmen bring
Typed notices from Rabbitarse and String.

The Head's M.A., a bishop is a patron,
  The assistant staff is highly qualified;
Health is the care of an experienced matron,
  The arts are taught by ladies from outside;
  The food is wholesome and the grounds are wide;
The aim is training character and poise,
With special coaching for the backward boys.

I found the pay good and had time to spend it,
  Though others may not have the good luck I did:
For you I'd hesitate to recommend it;
  Several have told me that they can't abide it.
  Still, if one tends to get a bit one-sided,
It's pleasant as it's easy to secure
The hero worship of the immature.

More, it's a job, and jobs today are rare:
  All the ideals in the world won't feed us
Although they give our crimes a certain air.
  So barons of the press who know their readers
  Employ to write their more appalling leaders,
Instead of Satan's horned and hideous minions,
Clever young men of liberal opinions.

Which brings me up to nineteen thirty-five;
    Six months of film work is another story
I can't tell now. But, here I am, alive
    Knowing the true source of that sense of glory
    That still surrounds the England of the Tory,
Come only to the rather tame conclusion
That no man by himself has life's solution.

I know – the fact is really not unnerving –
    That what is done is done, that no past dies,
That what we see depends on who's observing,
    And what we think on our activities.
    That envy warps the virgin as she dries
But *Post coitum, homo tristis* means
The lover must go carefully with the greens.

The boat has brought me to the landing-stage,
    Up the long estuary of mud and sedges;
The line I travel has the English gauge;
    The engine's shadow vaults the little hedges;
    And summer's done. I sign the usual pledges
To be a better poet, better man;
I'll really do it this time if I can.

I hope this reaches you in your abode,
    This letter that's already far too long,
Just like the Prelude or the Great North Road;
    But here I end my conversational song.
    I hope you don't think mail from strangers wrong.
As to its length, I tell myself you'll need it,
You've all eternity in which to read it.

New Year Letter

(*January* 1, 1940)

TO ELIZABETH MAYER

PART ONE

Under the familiar weight
Of winter, conscience and the State,
In loose formations of good cheer,
Love, language, loneliness and fear,
Towards the habits of next year,
Along the streets the people flow,
Singing or sighing as they go:
Exalté, piano, or in doubt,
All our reflections turn about
A common meditative norm,
Retrenchment, Sacrifice, Reform.

Twelve months ago in Brussels, I
Heard the same wishful-thinking sigh
As round me, trembling on their beds,
Or taut with apprehensive dreads,
The sleepless guests of Europe lay
Wishing the centuries away,
And the low mutter of their vows
Went echoing through her haunted house,
As on the verge of happening
There crouched the presence of The Thing.
All formulas were tried to still
The scratching on the window-sill,
All bolts of custom made secure
Against the pressure on the door,

But up the staircase of events
Carrying his special instruments,
To every bedside all the same
The dreadful figure swiftly came.

Yet Time can moderate his tone
When talking to a man alone,
And the same sun whose neutral eye
All florid August from the sky
Had watched the earth behave and seen
Strange traffic on her brown and green,
Obedient to some hidden force
A ship abruptly change her course,
A train make an unwonted stop,
A little crowd smash up a shop,
Suspended hatreds crystallize
In visible hostilities,
Vague concentrations shrink to take
The sharp crude patterns generals make,
The very morning that the war
Took action on the Polish floor,
Lit up America and on
A cottage in Long Island shone
Where Buxtehude as we played
One of his *passacaglias* made
Our minds a *civitas* of sound
Where nothing but assent was found,
For art had set in order sense
And feeling and intelligence,
And from its ideal order grew
Our local understanding too.

To set in order—that's the task
Both Eros and Apollo ask;
For Art and Life agree in this

That each intends a synthesis,
That order which must be the end
That all self-loving things intend
Who struggle for their liberty,
Who use, that is, their will to be.
Though order never can be willed
But is the state of the fulfilled,
For will but wills its opposite
And not the whole in which they fit,
The symmetry disorders reach
When both are equal each to each,
Yet in intention all are one,
Intending that their wills be done
Within a peace where all desires
Find each in each what each requires,
A true *Gestalt* where indiscrete
Perceptions and extensions meet.
Art in intention is mimesis
But, realized, the resemblance ceases;
Art is not life and cannot be
A midwife to society,
For art is a *fait accompli*.
What they should do, or how or when
Life-order comes to living men
It cannot say, for it presents
Already lived experience
Through a convention that creates
Autonomous completed states.
Though their particulars are those
That each particular artist knows,
Unique events that once took place
Within a unique time and space,
In the new field they occupy,
The unique serves to typify,
Becomes, though still particular,

An algebraic formula,
An abstract model of events
Derived from dead experience,
And each life must itself decide
To what and how it be applied.

Great masters who have shown mankind
An order it has yet to find,
What if all pedants say of you
As personalities be true?
All the more honour to you then
If, weaker than some other men,
You had the courage that survives
Soiled, shabby, egotistic lives,
If poverty or ugliness,
Ill-health or social unsuccess
Hunted you out of life to play
At living in another way;
Yet the live quarry all the same
Were changed to huntsmen in the game,
And the wild furies of the past,
Tracked to their origins at last,
Trapped in a medium's artifice,
To charity, delight, increase.
Now large, magnificent, and calm,
Your changeless presences disarm
The sullen generations, still
The fright and fidget of the will,
And to the growing and the weak
Your final transformations speak,
Saying to dreaming 'I am deed.'
To striving 'Courage. I succeed.'
To mourning 'I remain. Forgive,'
And to becoming 'I am. Live,'

They challenge, warn and witness. Who
That ever has the rashness to
Believe that he is one of those
The greatest of vocations chose,
Is not perpetually afraid
That he's unworthy of his trade,
As round his tiny homestead spread
The grand constructions of the dead,
Nor conscious, as he works, of their
Complete uncompromising stare,
And the surveillance of a board
Whose warrant cannot be ignored?
O often, often must he face,
Whether the critics blame or praise,
Young, high-brow, popular or rich,
That summary tribunal which
In a perpetual session sits,
And answer, if he can, to its
Intense interrogation. Though
Considerate and mild and low
The voices of the questioners,
Although they delegate to us
Both prosecution and defence,
Accept our rules of evidence
And pass no sentence but our own,
Yet, as he faces them alone,
O who can show convincing proof
That he is worthy of their love?
Who ever rose to read aloud
Before that quiet attentive crowd
And did not falter as he read,
Stammer, sit down, and hang his head?
Each one, so liberal is the law,
May choose whom he appears before,
Pick any influential ghost

From those whom he admires the most.
So, when my name is called, I face,
Presiding coldly on my case,
That lean hard-bitten pioneer
Who spoiled a temporal career
And to the supernatural brought
His passion, senses, will and thought,
By *Amor Rationalis* led
Through the three kingdoms of the dead,
In concrete detail saw the whole
Environment that keeps the soul,
And grasped in its complexity
The Catholic ecology,
Described the savage fauna he
In Malebolge's fissure found,
And fringe of blessed flora round
A juster nucleus than Rome,
Where love had its creative home.
Upon his right appears, as I
Reluctantly must testify
And weigh the sentence to be passed,
A choleric enthusiast,
Self-educated WILLIAM BLAKE
Who threw his spectre in the lake,
Broke off relations in a curse
With the Newtonian Universe,
But even as a child would pet
The tigers Voltaire never met,
Took walks with them through Lambeth, and
Spoke to Isaiah in the Strand,
And heard inside each mortal thing
Its holy emanation sing,
While to his left upon the bench,
Muttering that terror is not French,
Frowns the young RIMBAUD guilt demands,

The adolescent with red hands,
Skilful, intolerant and quick,
Who strangled an old rhetoric.
The court is full; I catch the eyes
Of several I recognize,
For as I look up from the dock
Embarrassed glances interlock.
There DRYDEN sits with modest smile,
The master of the middle style,
Conscious CATULLUS who made all
His gutter-language musical,
Black TENNYSON whose talents were
For an articulate despair,
Trim, dualistic BAUDELAIRE,
Poet of cities, harbours, whores,
Acedia, gaslight and remorse,
HARDY whose Dorset gave much joy
To one unsocial English boy,
And RILKE whom *die Dinge* bless,
The Santa Claus of loneliness.
And many others, many times,
For I relapse into my crimes,
Time and again have slubbered through
With slip and slapdash what I do,
Adopted what I would disown,
The preacher's loose immodest tone;
Though warned by a great sonneteer
Not to sell cheap what is most dear,
Though horrible old KIPLING cried
'One instant's toil to Thee denied
Stands all eternity's offence,'
I would not give them audience.
Yet still the weak offender must
Beg still for leniency and trust
His power to avoid the sin

Peculiar to his discipline.
The situation of our time
Surrounds us like a baffling crime.
There lies the body half-undressed,
We all had reason to detest,
And all are suspects and involved
Until the mystery is solved
And under lock and key the cause
That makes a nonsense of our laws.
O Who is trying to shield Whom?
Who left a hairpin in the room?
Who was the distant figure seen
Behaving oddly on the green?
Why did the watchdog never bark?
Why did the footsteps leave no mark?
Where were the servants at that hour?
How did a snake get in the tower?
Delayed in the democracies
By departmental vanities,
The rival sergeants run about
But more to squabble than find out,
Yet where the Force has been cut down
To one inspector dressed in brown,
He makes the murderer whom he pleases
And all investigation ceases.
Yet our equipment all the time
Extends the area of the crime
Until the guilt is everywhere,
And more and more we are aware,
However miserable may be
Our parish of immediacy,
How small it is, how, far beyond,
Ubiquitous within the bond
Of an impoverishing sky,
Vast spiritual disorders lie.

Who, thinking of the last ten years,
Does not hear howling in his ears
The Asiatic cry of pain,
The shots of executing Spain
See stumbling through his outraged mind
The Abyssinian, blistered, blind,
The dazed uncomprehending stare
Of the Danubian despair,
The Jew wrecked in the German cell,
Flat Poland frozen into hell,
The silent dumps of unemployed
Whose *areté* has been destroyed,
And will not feel blind anger draw
His thoughts towards the Minotaur,
To take an early boat for Crete
And rolling, silly, at its feet
Add his small tidbit to the rest?
It lures us all; even the best,
Les hommes de bonne volonté, feel
Their politics perhaps unreal
And all they have believed untrue,
Are tempted to surrender to
The grand apocalyptic dream
In which the persecutors scream
As on the evil Aryan lives
Descends the night of the long knives;
The bleeding tyrant dragged through all
The ashes of his capitol.

Though language may be useless, for
No words men write can stop the war
Or measure up to the relief
Of its immeasurable grief,
Yet truth, like love and sleep, resents
Approaches that are too intense,

And often when the searcher stood
Before the Oracle, it would
Ignore his grown-up earnestness
But not the child of his distress,
For through the Janus of a joke
The candid psychopompos spoke.
May such heart and intelligence
As huddle now in conference
Whenever an impasse occurs
Use the good offices of verse;
May an Accord be reached, and may
This *aide-mémoire* on what they say,
This private minute for a friend,
Be the dispatch that I intend;
Although addressed to a Whitehall,
Be under Flying Seal to all
Who wish to read it anywhere,
And, if they open it, *En Clair*.

PART TWO

Tonight a scrambling decade ends,
And strangers, enemies and friends
Stand once more puzzled underneath
The signpost on the barren heath
Where the rough mountain track divides
To silent valleys on all sides,
Endeavouring to decipher what
Is written on it but cannot,
Nor guess in what direction lies
The overhanging precipice.
Through the pitch-darkness can be heard
Occasionally a muttered word,
And intense in the mountain frost
The heavy breathing of the lost;
Far down below them whence they came
Still flickers feebly a red flame,
A tiny glow in the great void
Where an existence was destroyed;
And now and then a nature turns
To look where her whole system burns
And with a last defiant groan
Shudders her future into stone.

How hard it is to set aside
Terror, concupiscence and pride,

Learn who and where and how we are,
The children of a modest star,
Frail, backward, clinging to the granite
Skirts of a sensible old planet,
Our placid and suburban nurse
In SITTER's swelling universe,
How hard to stretch imagination
To live according to our station.
For we are all insulted by
The mere suggestion that we die
Each moment and that each great I
Is but a process in a process
Within a field that never closes;
As proper people find it strange
That we are changed by what we change,
That no event can happen twice
And that no two existences
Can ever be alike; we'd rather
Be perfect copies of our father,
Prefer our *idées fixes* to be
True of a fixed Reality.
No wonder, then, we lose our nerve
And blubber when we should observe
The patriots of an old idea
No longer sovereign this year,
Get angry like LABELLIÈRE,
Who, finding no invectives hurled
Against a topsy-turvy world
Would right it, earned a quaint renown
By being buried upside-down:
Unwilling to adjust belief,
Go mad in a fantastic grief
Where no adjustment need be done,
Like SARAH WHITEHEAD, the Bank Nun,
For, loving a live brother, she

90

Wed an impossibility,
Pacing Threadneedle Street in tears,
She watched one door for twenty years,
Expecting, what she dared not doubt,
Her hanged embezzler to walk out.

But who, though, is the Prince of Lies
If not the Spirit-that-denies,
The shadow just behind the shoulder
Claiming it's wicked to grow older,
Though we are damned if we turn round
Thinking salvation has been found?
Yet in his very effort to
Prevent the actions we could do,
He has to make the here and now
As marvellous as he knows how
And so engrossing we forget
To drop attention for regret;
Defending relaxation, he
Must show impassioned energy,
And all through tempting us to doubt
Point us the way to find truth out.
Poor cheated MEPHISTOPHELES,
Who think you're doing as you please
In telling us by doing ill
To prove that we possess free will,
Yet do not will the will you do,
For the Determined uses you,
Creation's errand-boy creator,
Diabolus egredietur
Ante pedes ejus–foe,
But so much more effective, though,
Than our well-meaning stupid friends
In driving us towards good ends
Lame fallen shadow, *retro me,*

Retro but do not go away:
Although, for all your fond insistence,
You have no positive existence,
Are only a recurrent state
Of fear and faithlessness and hate,
That takes on from becoming me
A legal personality,
Assuming your existence is
A rule-of-thumb hypostasis,
For, though no person, you can damn,
So, *credo ut intelligam.*
For how could we get on without you
Who give the *savoir-faire* to doubt you
And keep you in your proper place,
Which is, to push us into grace?

Against his paralysing smile
And honest realistic style
Our best protection is that we
In fact live in eternity.
The sleepless counter of our breaths
That chronicles the births and deaths
Of pious hopes, the short careers
Of dashing promising ideas,
Each congress of the Greater Fears,
The emigration of beliefs,
The voyages of hopes and griefs,
Has no direct experience
Of discontinuous events,
And all our intuitions mock
The formal logic of the clock.
All real perception, it would seem,
Has shifting contours like a dream,
Nor have our feelings ever known
Any discretion but their own.

Suppose we love, not friends or wives,
But certain patterns in our lives,
Effects that take the cause's name,
Love cannot part them all the same;
If in this letter that I send
I write 'Elizabeth's my friend,'
I cannot but express my faith
That I is Not-Elizabeth.
For though the intellect in each
Can only think in terms of speech
We cannot practise what we preach.
The cogitations of DESCARTES
Are where all sound semantics start;
In Ireland the great BERKELEY rose
To add new glories to our prose,
But when in the pursuit of knowledge,
Risking the future of his college,
The bishop hid his anxious face,
'Twas more by grammar than by grace
His modest Church-of-England God
Sustained the fellows and the quad.

But the Accuser would not be
In his position, did not he,
Unlike the big-shots of the day,
Listen to what his victims say.
Observing every man's desire
To warm his bottom by the fire
And state his views on Education,
Art, Women, and The Situation,
Has learnt what every woman knows,
The wallflower can become the rose,
Penelope the homely seem
The Helen of Odysseus' dream
If she will look as if she were

A fascinated listener,
Since men will pay large sums to whores
For telling them they are not bores.
So when with overemphasis
We contradict a lie of his,
The great Denier won't deny
But purrs: 'You're cleverer than I;
Of course you're absolutely right,
I never saw it in that light.
I see it now: The intellect
That parts the Cause from the Effect
And thinks in terms of Space and Time
Commits a legalistic crime,
For such an unreal severance
Must falsify experience.
Could one not almost say that the
Cold serpent on the poisonous tree
Was *l'esprit de géométrie*,
That Eve and Adam till the Fall
Were totally illogical,
But as they tasted of the fruit
The syllogistic sin took root?
Abstracted, bitter refugees,
They fought over their premises,
Shut out from Eden by the bar
And Chinese Wall of *Barbara*.
O foolishness of man to seek
Salvation in an *ordre logique*!
O cruel intellect that chills
His natural warmth until it kills
The roots of all togetherness!
Love's vigour shrinks to less and less,
On sterile acres governed by
Wage's abstract prudent tie
The hard self-conscious particles

Collide, divide like numerals
In knock-down drag-out *laissez-faire*,
And build no order anywhere.
O when will men show common sense
And throw away intelligence,
That killjoy which discriminates,
Recover what appreciates,
The deep unsnobbish instinct which
Alone can make relation rich,
Upon the *Beischlaf* of the blood
Establish a real neighbourhood
Where art and industry and *mœurs*
Are governed by an *ordre du cœur*?'

The Devil, as is not surprising—
His business is self-advertising—
Is a first-rate psychologist
Who keeps a conscientious list,
To help him in his ticklish deals,
Of what each client thinks and feels,
His school, religion, birth and breeding,
Where he has dined and what he's reading,
By every name he makes a note
Of what quotations to misquote,
And flings at every author's head
Something a favourite author said.
'The Arts? Well, FLAUBERT didn't say
Of artists: "*Ils sont dans le vrai.*"
Democracy? Ask BAUDELAIRE:
"*Un esprit Belge,*" a soiled affair
Of gas and steam and table-turning.
Truth? ARISTOTLE was discerning:
"In crowds I am a friend of myth." '
Then, as I start protesting, with
The air of one who understands

He puts a RILKE in my hands.
'You know the *Elegies*, I'm sure –
O Seligkeit der Kreatur
Die immer bleibt im Schosse – womb,
In English, is a rhyme to tomb.'
He moves on tiptoe round the room,
Turns on the radio to mark
Isolde's *Sehnsucht* for the dark.

But all his tactics are dictated
By problems he himself created,
For as the great schismatic who
First split creation into two
He did what it could never do,
Inspired it with the wish to be
Diversity in unity,
An action which has put him in,
Pledged as he is to Rule-by-Sin,
As ambiguous a position
As any Irish politician,
For, torn between conflicting needs,
He's doomed to fail if he succeeds,
And his neurotic longing mocks
Him with its self-made paradox
To be both god and dualist.
For, if dualities exist,
What happens to the god? If there
Are any cultures anywhere
With other values than his own,
How can it possibly be shown
That his are not subjective or
That all life is a state of war?
While, if the monist view be right,
How is it possible to fight?
If love has been annihilated

There's only hate left to be hated.
To say two different things at once,
To wage offensives on two fronts,
And yet to show complete conviction,
Requires the purpler kinds of diction
And none appreciate as he
Polysyllabic oratory.
All vague idealistic art
That coddles the uneasy heart
Is up his alley, and his pigeon
The woozier species of religion,
Even a novel, play or song,
If loud, lugubrious and long;
He knows the bored will not unmask him
But that he's lost if someone ask him
To come the hell in off the links
And say exactly what he thinks.
To win support of any kind
He has to hold before the mind
Amorphous shadows it can hate,
Yet constantly postpone the date
Of what he's made The Grand Attraction,
Putting an end to them by action,
Because he knows, were he to win,
Man could do evil but not sin.
To sin is to act consciously
Against what seems necessity,
A possibility cut out
In any world that excludes doubt.
So victory could do no more
Than make us what we were before,
Beasts with a Rousseauistic charm
Unconscious we were doing harm.
Politically, then, he's right
To keep us shivering all night,

Watching for dawn from Pisgah's height,
And to sound earnest as he paints
The new Geneva of the saints,
To strike the poses as he speaks
Of David's too too Empire Greeks,
Look forward with the cheesecake air
Of one who crossed the Delaware.
A realist, he has always said:
'It is Utopian to be dead,
For only on the Other Side
Are Absolutes all satisfied
Where, at the bottom of the graves,
Low Probability behaves.'

The False Association is
A favourite strategy of his:
Induce men to associate
Truth with a lie, then demonstrate
The lie and they will, in truth's name,
Treat babe and bath-water the same,
A trick that serves him in good stead
At all times. It was thus he led
The early Christians to believe
All Flesh unconscious on the eve
Of the Word's temporal interference
With the old Adam of Appearance;
That almost any moment they
Would see the trembling consuls pray,
Knowing that as their hope grew less
So would their heavenly worldliness,
Their early agape decline
To a late lunch with Constantine.
Thus WORDSWORTH fell into temptation
In France during a long vacation,
Saw in the fall of the Bastille

The Parousia of liberty,
And weaving a platonic dream
Round a provisional régime
That sloganized the Rights of Man,
A liberal fellow-traveller ran
With Sans-culotte and Jacobin,
Nor guessed what circles he was in,
But ended as the Devil knew
An earnest Englishman would do,
Left by Napoleon in the lurch,
Supporting the Established Church,
The Congress of Vienna and
The Squire's paternalistic hand.

Like his, our lives have been coeval
With a political upheaval,
Like him, we had the luck to see
A rare discontinuity,
Old Russia suddenly mutate
Into a proletarian state,
The odd phenomenon, the strange
Event of qualitative change.
Some dreamed, as students always can,
It realized the potential Man,
A higher species brought to birth
Upon a sixth part of the earth,
While others settled down to read
The theory that forecast the deed
And found their humanistic view
In question from the German who,
Obscure in gaslit London, brought
To human consciousness a thought
It thought unthinkable, and made
Another consciousness afraid.
What if his hate distorted? Much

Was hateful that he had to touch.
What if he erred? He flashed a light
On facts where no one had been right.
The father-shadow that he hated
Weighed like an Alp; his love, frustrated,
Negating as it was negated,
Burst out in boils; his animus
Outlawed him from himself; but thus,
And only thus, perhaps, could he
Have come to his discovery.
Heroic charity is rare;
Without it, what except despair
Can shape the hero who will dare
The desperate catabasis
Into the snarl of the abyss
That always lies just underneath
Our jolly picnic on the heath
Of the agreeable, where we bask,
Agreed on what we will not ask,
Bland, sunny and adjusted by
The light of the accepted lie?
As he explored the muttering tomb
Of a museum reading room,
The Dagon of the General Will
Fell in convulsions and lay still;
The tempting Contract of the rich,
Revealed as an abnormal witch,
Fled with a shriek, for as he spoke
The justifying magic broke;
The garden of the Three Estates
Turned desert, and the Ivory Gates
Of Pure Idea to gates of horn
Through which the Governments are born.
But his analysis reveals
The other side to Him-who-steals

Is He-who-makes-what-is-of-use,
Since, to consume, man must produce;
By Man the Tough Devourer sets
The nature his despair forgets
Of Man Prolific since his birth,
A race creative on the earth,
Whose love of money only shows
That in his heart of hearts he knows
His love is not determined by
A personal or tribal tie
Or colour, neighbourhood, or creed,
But universal, mutual need;
Loosed from its shroud of temper, his
Determinism comes to this:
None shall receive unless they give;
All must co-operate to live.
Now he is one with all of those
Who brought an epoch to a close,
With him who ended as he went
Past an archbishop's monument
The slaveowners' mechanics, one
With the ascetic farmer's son
Who, while the Great Plague ran its course,
Drew up a Roman code of Force,
One with the naturalist, who fought
Pituitary headaches, brought
Man's pride to heel at last and showed
His kinship with the worm and toad,
And Order as one consequence
Of the unfettered play of Chance.

Great sedentary Caesars who
Have pacified some dread tabu,
Whose wits were able to withdraw
The *numen* from some local law

And with a single concept brought
Some ancient rubbish heap of thought
To rational diversity,
You are betrayed unless we see
No *codex gentium* we make
Is difficult for Truth to break;
The *Lex Abscondita* evades
The vigilantes in the glades;
Now here, now there, one leaps and cries
'I've got her and I claim the prize,'
But when the rest catch up, he stands
With just a torn blouse in his hands.

We hoped; we waited for the day
The State would wither clean away,
Expecting the Millennium
That theory promised us would come,
It didn't. Specialists must try
To detail all the reasons why;
Meanwhile at least the layman knows
That none are lost so soon as those
Who overlook their crooked nose,
That they grow small who imitate
The mannerisms of the great,
Afraid to be themselves, or ask
What acts are proper to their task,
And that a tiny trace of fear
Is lethal in man's atmosphere.
The rays of Logos take effect,
But not as theory would expect,
For, sterile and diseased by doubt,
The dwarf mutations are thrown out
From Eros' weaving centrosome.

O Freedom still is far from home,

For MOSCOW is as far as ROME
Or PARIS. Once again we wake
With swimming heads and hands that shake
And stomachs that keep nothing down.
Here's where the devil goes to town,
Who knows that nothing suits his book
So well as the hang-over look,
That few drunks feel more awful than
The Simon-pure Utopian.
He calls at breakfast in the role
Of blunt but sympathetic soul:
'Well, how's our Socialist this morning?
I could say "Let this be a warning,"
But no, why should I? Students must
Sow their wild oats at times or bust.
Such things have happened in the lives
Of all the best Conservatives.
I'll fix you something for your liver.'
And thus he sells us down the river.
Repenting of our last infraction
We seek atonement in reaction
And cry, nostalgic like a whore,
'I was a virgin still at four.'
Perceiving that by sailing near
The Hegelian whirlpool of Idea
Some foolish aliens have gone down,
Lest our democracy should drown
We'd wreck her on the solid rock
Of genteel anarchists like LOCKE,
Wave at the mechanized barbarian
The vorpal sword of an Agrarian.

O how the devil who controls
The moral asymmetric souls
The either-ors, the mongrel halves

Who find truth in a mirror, laughs.
Yet time and memory are still
Limiting factors on his will;
He cannot always fool us thrice,
For he may never tell us lies,
Just half-truths we can synthesize.
So, hidden in his hocus-pocus,
There lies the gift of double focus,
That magic lamp which looks so dull
And utterly impractical
Yet, if Aladdin use it right,
Can be a sesame to light.

PART THREE

Across East River in the night
Manhattan is ablaze with light.
No shadow dares to criticize
The popular festivities,
Hard liquor causes everywhere
A general *détente*, and Care
For this state function of Good Will
Is diplomatically ill:
The Old Year dies a noisy death.

Warm in your house, Elizabeth,
A week ago at the same hour
I felt the unexpected power
That drove our ragged egos in
From the dead-ends of greed and sin
To sit down at the wedding feast,
Put shining garments on the least,
Arranged us so that each and all,
The erotic and the logical,
Each felt the *placement* to be such
That he was honoured overmuch,
And SCHUBERT sang and MOZART played
And GLUCK and food and friendship made
Our privileged community
That real republic which must be

The State all politicians claim,
Even the worst, to be their aim.

O but it happens every day
To someone. Suddenly the way
Leads straight into their native lands,
The *temenos'* small wicket stands
Wide open, shining at the centre
The well of life, and they may enter.
Though compasses and stars cannot
Direct to that magnetic spot,
Nor Will nor willing-not-to-will,
For there is neither good nor ill,
But free rejoicing energy.
Yet anytime, how casually,
Out of his organized distress
An accidental happiness,
Catching man off his guard, will blow him
Out of his life in time to show him
The field of Being where he may,
Unconscious of Becoming, play
With the Eternal Innocence
In unimpeded utterance.
But perfect Being has ordained
It must be lost to be regained,
And in its orchards grow the tree
And fruit of human destiny,
And man must eat it and depart
At once with gay and grateful heart,
Obedient, reborn, re-aware;
For, if he stop an instant there,
The sky grows crimson with a curse,
The flowers change colour for the worse,
He hears behind his back the wicket
Padlock itself, from the dark thicket

The chuckle with no healthy cause,
And, helpless, sees the crooked claws
Emerging into view and groping
For handholds on the low round coping,
As Horror clambers from the well:
For he has sprung the trap of Hell.

Hell is the being of the lie
That we become if we deny
The laws of consciousness and claim
Becoming and Being are the same,
Being in time, and man discrete
In will, yet free and self-complete;
Its fire the pain to which we go
If we refuse to suffer, though
The one unnecessary grief
Is the vain craving for relief,
When to the suffering we could bear
We add intolerable fear,
Absconding from remembrance, mocked
By our own partial senses, locked
Each in a stale uniqueness, lie
Time-conscious for eternity.

We cannot, then, will Heaven where
Is perfect freedom; our wills there
Must lose the will to operate.
But will is free not to negate
Itself in Hell; we're free to will
Ourselves to Purgatory still,
Consenting parties to our lives,
To love them like attractive wives
Whom we adore but do not trust,
We cannot love without their lust,
And need their stratagems to win

Truth out of Time. In Time we sin.
But Time is sin and can forgive;
Time is the life with which we live
At least three quarters of our time,
The purgatorial hill we climb,
Where any skyline we attain
Reveals a higher ridge again.
Yet since, however much we grumble,
However painfully we stumble,
Such mountaineering all the same
Is, it would seem, the only game
At which we show a natural skill,
The hardest exercises still
Just those our muscles are the best
Adapted to, its grimmest test
Precisely what our fear suspected,
We have no cause to look dejected
When, wakened from a dream of glory,
We find ourselves in Purgatory,
Back on the same old mountain side
With only guessing for a guide.
To tell the truth, although we stifle
The feeling, are we not a trifle
Relieved to wake on its damp earth?
It's been our residence since birth,
Its inconveniences are known,
And we have made its flaws our own.
Is it not here that we belong,
Where everyone is doing wrong,
And normal our freemartin state,
Half angel and half *petite bête*?
So, perched upon the sharp *arête*,
When if we do not move we fall,
Yet movement is heretical,
Since over its ironic rocks

No route is truly orthodox,
O once again let us set out,
Our faith well balanced by our doubt,
Admitting every step we make
Will certainly be a mistake,
But still believing we can climb
A little higher every time,
And keep in order, that we may
Ascend the penitential way
That forces our wills to be free,
A reverent frivolity
That suffers each unpleasant test
With scientific interest,
And finds romantic, *faute de mieux*,
Its sad *nostalgie des adieux*.

Around me, pausing as I write,
A tiny object in the night,
Whichever way I look, I mark
Importunate along the dark
Horizon of immediacies
The flares of desperation rise
From signallers who justly plead
Their cause is piteous indeed:
Bewildered, how can I divine
Which is my true Socratic Sign,
Which of these calls to conscience is
For me the *casus fœderis*,
From all the tasks submitted, choose
The *athlon* I must not refuse?
A particle, I must not yield
To particles who claim the field,
Nor trust the demagogue who raves,
A quantum speaking for the waves,
Nor worship blindly the ornate

Grandezza of the Sovereign State.
Whatever wickedness we do
Need not be, orators, for you;
We can at least serve other ends,
Can love the *polis* of our friends
And pray that loyalty may come
To serve mankind's *imperium*.

But where to serve and when and how?
O none escape these questions now:
The future which confronts us has
No likeness to that age when, as
Rome's huggermugger unity
Was slowly knocked to pieces by
The unco-ordinated blows
Of artless and barbaric foes,
The stressed and rhyming measures rose;
The cities we abandon fall
To nothing primitive at all;
This lust in action to destroy
Is not the pure instinctive joy
Of animals, but the refined
Creation of machines and mind.
As out of Europe comes a voice,
Compelling all to make their choice
A theologian who denies
What more than twenty centuries
Of Europe have assumed to be
The basis of civility,
Our evil *Daimon* to express
In all its ugly nakedness
What none before dared say aloud,
The metaphysics of the Crowd,
The Immanent Imperative
By which the lost and injured live

In mechanized societies
Where natural intuition dies,
The international result
Of Industry's *Quicunque vult*,
The hitherto-unconscious creed
Of little men who half succeed.

Yet maps and languages and names
Have meaning and their proper claims.
There are two atlases: the one
The public space where acts are done,
In theory common to us all,
Where we are needed and feel small,
The *agora* of work and news
Where each one has the right to choose
His trade, his corner and his way,
And can, again in theory, say
For whose protection he will pay,
And loyalty is help we give
The place where we prefer to live;
The other is the inner space
Of private ownership, the place
That each of us is forced to own,
Like his own life from which it's grown,
The landscape of his will and need
Where he is sovereign indeed,
The state created by his acts
Where he patrols the forest tracts
Planted in childhood, farms the belt
Of doings memorized and felt,
And even if he find it hell
May neither leave it nor rebel.
Two worlds describing their rewards,
That one in tangents, this in chords;
Each lives in one, all in the other,

III

Here all are kings, there each a brother:
In politics the Fall of Man
From natural liberty began
When, loving power or sloth, he came
Like BURKE to think them both the same.

England to me is my own tongue,
And what I did when I was young.
If now, two aliens in New York,
We meet, Elizabeth, and talk
Of friends who suffer in the torn
Old Europe where we both were born,
What this refutes or that confirms,
I can but think our talk in terms
Of images that I have seen,
And England tells me what we mean.
Thus, squalid beery BURTON stands
For shoddy thinking of all brands;
The wreck of RHONDDA for the mess
We make when for a short success
We split our symmetry apart,
Deny the Reason or the Heart;
YE OLDE TUDOR TEA-SHOPPE for
The folly of dogmatic law,
While graceless BOURNEMOUTH is the sloth
Of men or bureaucrats or both.

No matter where, or whom I meet,
Shop-gazing in a Paris street,
Bumping through Iceland in a bus,
At teas when clubwomen discuss
The latest Federation Plan,
In Pullman washrooms, man to man,
Hearing how circumstance has vexed
A broker who is oversexed,

In houses where they do not drink,
Whenever I begin to think
About the human creature we
Must nurse to sense and decency,
An English area comes to mind,
I see the nature of my kind
As a locality I love,
Those limestone moors that stretch from BROUGH
To HEXHAM and the ROMAN WALL,
There is my symbol of us all.
There, where the EDEN leisures through
Its sandstone valley, is my view
Of green and civil life that dwells
Below a cliff of savage fells
From which original address
Man faulted into consciousness.
Along the line of lapse the fire
Of life's impersonal desire
Burst through his sedentary rock
And, as at DUFTON and at KNOCK,
Thrust up between his mind and heart
Enormous cones of myth and art.
Always my boy of wish returns
To those peat-stained deserted burns
That feed the WEAR and TYNE and TEES,
And, turning states to strata, sees
How basalt long oppressed broke out
In wild revolt at CAULDRON SNOUT,
And from the relics of old mines
Derives his algebraic signs
For all in man that mourns and seeks,
For all of his renounced techniques,
Their tramways overgrown with grass,
For lost belief, for all Alas,
The derelict lead-smelting mill,

Flued to its chimney up the hill,
That smokes no answer any more
But points, a landmark on BOLTS LAW,
The finger of all questions. There
In ROOKHOPE I was first aware
Of Self and Not-self, Death and Dread:
Adits were entrances which led
Down to the Outlawed, to the Others,
The Terrible, the Merciful, the Mothers;
Alone in the hot day I knelt
Upon the edge of shafts and felt
The deep *Urmutterfurcht* that drives
Us into knowledge all our lives,
The far interior of our fate
To civilize and to create,
Das Weibliche that bids us come
To find what we're escaping from.
There I dropped pebbles, listened, heard
The reservoir of darkness stirred;
'*O deine Mutter kehrt dir nicht*
Wieder. Du selbst bin ich, dein' Pflicht
Und Liebe. Brach sie nun mein Bild.'
And I was conscious of my guilt.

But such a bond is not an Ought,
Only a given mode of thought,
Whence my imperatives were taught.
Now in that other world I stand
Of fully alienated land,
An earth made common by the means
Of hunger, money, and machines,
Where each determined nature must
Regard that nature as a trust
That, being chosen, he must choose,
Determined to become of use;

For we are conscripts to our age
Simply by being born; we wage
The war we are, and may not die
With POLYCARP's despairing cry,
Desert or become ill: but how
To be the patriots of the Now?
Here all, by rights, are volunteers,
And anyone who interferes
With how another wills to fight
Must base his action, not on right,
But on the power to compel;
Only the 'Idiot' can tell
For which state office he should run,
Only the Many make the One.

Eccentric, wrinkled, and ice-capped,
Swarming with parasites and wrapped
In a peculiar atmosphere,
Earth wobbles on down her career
With no ambition in her heart;
Her loose land-masses drift apart,
Her zone of shade and silence crawls
Steadily westward. Daylight falls
On Europe's frozen soldiery
And millions brave enough to die
For a new day; for each one knows
A day is drawing to a close.
Yes, all of us at least know that,
All from the seasoned diplomat
Used to the warm Victorian summers
Down to the juveniles and drummers.
Whatever nonsense we believe,
Whomever we can still deceive,
Whatever language angers us,
Whoever seems the poisonous

Old dragon to be killed if men
Are ever to be rich again,
We know no fuss or pain or lying
Can stop the moribund from dying,
That all the special tasks begun
By the Renaissance have been done.

When unity has come to grief
Upon professional belief
Another unity was made
By equal amateurs in trade.
Out of the noise and horror, the
Opinions of artillery,
The barracks chatter and the yell
Of charging cavalry, the smell
Of poor opponents roasting, out
Of LUTHER's faith and MONTAIGNE's doubt,
The epidemic of translations,
The Councils and the navigations,
The confiscations and the suits,
The scholars' scurrilous disputes
Over the freedom of the Will
And right of Princes to do ill,
Emerged a new *Anthropos*, an
Empiric Economic Man,
The urban, prudent, and inventive,
Profit his rational incentive
And Work his whole *exercitus*,
The individual let loose
To guard himself, at liberty
To starve or be forgotten, free
To feel in splendid isolation
Or drive himself about creation
In the closed cab of Occupation.

He did what he was born to do,
Proved some assumptions were untrue.
He had his half-success; he broke
The silly and unnatural yoke
Of famine and disease that made
A false necessity obeyed;
A Protestant, he found the key
To Catholic economy,
Subjected earth to the control
And moral choices of the soul;
And in the training of each sense
To serve with joy its evidence
He founded a new discipline
To fight an intellectual sin,
Reason's depravity that takes
The useful concepts that she makes
As universals, as the *kitsch*,
But worshipped statues upon which
She leaves her effort and her crown,
And if his half-success broke down,
All failures have one good result:
They prove the Good is difficult.

He never won complete support;
However many votes he bought.
He could not silence all the cliques,
And no miraculous techniques
Could sterilize all discontent
Or dazzle it into assent,
But at the very noon and arch
Of his immense triumphal march
Stood prophets pelting him with curses
And sermons and satiric verses,
And ostentatious beggars slept.
BLAKE shouted insults, ROUSSEAU wept,

Ironic KIERKEGAARD stared long
And muttered 'All are in the wrong,'
While BAUDELAIRE went mad protesting
That progress is not interesting
And thought he was an albatross,
The great Erotic on the cross
Of Science, crucified by fools
Who sit all day on office stools,
Are fairly faithful to their wives
And play for safety all their lives,
For whose *Verbürgerlichung* of
All joy and suffering and love
Let the grand pariah atone
By dying hated and alone.

The World ignored them; they were few.
The careless victor never knew
Their grapevine rumour would grow true,
Their alphabet of warning sounds
The common grammar all have grounds
To study; for their guess is proved:
It is the Mover that is moved.
Whichever way we turn, we see
Man captured by his liberty,
The measurable taking charge
Of him who measures, set at large
By his own actions, useful facts
Become the user of his acts,
And Chance the choices of his soul;
The beggar put out by his bowl,
Boys trained by factories for leading
Unusual lives as nurses, feeding
Helpless machines, girls married off
To typewriters, old men in love
With prices they can never get,

Homes blackmailed by a radio set,
Children inherited by slums
And idiots by enormous sums.
We see, we suffer, we despair:
The well-armed children everywhere
Who envy the self-governed beast
Now know that they are bound at least,
Die Aufgeregten without pity
Destroying the historic city,
The ruined showering with honours
The blind Christs and the mad Madonnas,
The Gnostics in the brothels treating
The flesh as secular and fleeting,
The *dialegesthai* of the rich
At cocktail parties as to which
Technique is most effective in
Enforcing labour discipline,
What Persian Apparatus will
Protect their privileges still
And safely keep the living dead
Entombed, hilarious, and fed,
The Disregarded in their shacks
Upon the wrong side of the tracks,
Poisoned by reasonable hate,
Are symptoms of one common fate.
All in their morning mirrors face
A member of a governed race.
Each recognizes what LEAR saw,
And he and THURBER like to draw,
The neuter outline that's the plan
And icon of Industrial Man,
The Unpolitical afraid
Of all that has to be obeyed.

But still each private citizen
Thanks God he's not as other men:
O all too easily we blame
The politicians for our shame
And the hired officers of state
For all those customs that frustrate
Our own intention to fulfil
Eros's legislative will.
Yet who must not, if he reflect,
See how unserious the effect
That he to love's volition gives,
On what base compromise he lives?
Even true lovers on some bed
The graceful god has visited
Find faults at which to hang the head,
And know the morphon full of guilt
Whence all community is built,
The cryptozoön with two backs
Whose sensibility that lacks
True reverence contributes much
Towards the soldier's violent touch.
For, craving language and a myth
And hands to shape their purpose with,
In shadow round the fond and warm
The possible societies swarm,
Because their freedom as their form
Upon our sense of style depends,
Whose eyes alone can seek their ends,
And they are impotent if we
Decline responsibility.
O what can love's intention do
If all his agents are untrue?
The politicians we condemn
Are nothing but our L. C. M.
The average of the average man
Becomes the dread Leviathan,

Our million individual deeds,
Omissions, vanities, and creeds,
Put through the statistician's hoop
The gross behaviour of a group:
Upon each English conscience lie
Two decades of hypocrisy,
And not a German can be proud
Of what his apathy allowed.

The flood of tyranny and force
Arises at a double source:
In PLATO's lie of intellect
That all are weak but the Elect
Philosophers who must be strong,
For, knowing Good, they will no Wrong,
United in the abstract Word
Above the low anarchic herd;
Or ROUSSEAU's falsehood of the flesh
That stimulates our pride afresh
To think all men identical
And strong in the Irrational.
And yet, although the social lie
Looks double to the dreamer's eye,
The rain to fill the mountain streams
That water the opposing dreams
By turns in favour with the crowd
Is scattered from one common cloud.
Up in the Ego's atmosphere
And higher altitudes of fear
The particles of error form
The shepherd-killing thunderstorm,
And our political distress
Descends from her self-consciousness,
Her cold *concupiscence d'esprit*
That looks upon her liberty

Not as a gift from life with which
To serve, enlighten, and enrich
The total creature that could use
Her function of free-will to choose
The actions that this world requires
To educate its blind desires,
But as the right to lead alone
An attic life all on her own,
Unhindered, unrebuked, unwatched,
Self-known, self-praising, self-attached.
All happens as she wishes till
She ask herself why she should will
This more than that, or who would care
If she were dead or gone elsewhere,
And on her own hypothesis
Is powerless to answer this.
Then panic seizes her; the glance
Of mirrors shows a countenance
Of wretched empty-brilliance. How
Can she escape self-loathing now?
What is there left for pride to do
Except plunge headlong *vers la boue*,
For freedom except suicide,
The self-asserted self-denied?
A witch self-tortured as she spins
Her whole devotion widdershins,
She worships in obscene delight
The Not, the Never, and the Night,
The formless Mass without a Me,
The Midnight Women and the Sea.
The genius of the loud Steam Age,
Loud WAGNER, put it on the stage:
The mental hero who has swooned
With sensual pleasure at his wound,
His intellectual life fulfilled

In knowing that his doom is willed,
Exists to suffer; borne along
Upon a timeless tide of song,
The huge doll roars for death or mother,
Synonymous with one another;
And Woman, passive as in dreams,
Redeems, redeems, redeems, redeems.

Delighted with their takings, bars
Are closing under fading stars;
The revellers go home to change
Back into something far more strange,
The tightened self in which they may
Walk safely through their bothered day,
With formal purpose up and down
The crowded fatalistic town,
And dawn sheds its calm candour now
On monasteries where they vow
An economic abstinence.
Modern in their impenitence,
Blonde, naked, paralysed, alone,
Like rebel angels turned to stone
The secular cathedrals stand
Upon their valuable land,
Frozen forever in a lie,
Determined always to deny
That man is weak and has to die,
And hide the huge phenomena
Which must decide America,
That culture that had worshipped no
Virgin before the Dynamo,
Held no Nicea nor Canossa,
Hat keine verfallenen Schlösser,
Keine Basalte, the great Rome
To all who lost or hated home.

A long time since it seems to-day
The Saints in Massachusetts Bay
Heard theocratic COTTON preach
And legal WINTHROP's Little Speech;
Since MISTRESS HUTCHINSON was tried
By those her Inner Light defied,
And WILLIAMS questioned Moses' law
But in Rhode Island waited for
The Voice of the Beloved to free
Himself and the Democracy;
Long since inventive JEFFERSON
Fought realistic HAMILTON,
Pelagian versus Jansenist;
But the same heresies exist.
Time makes old formulas look strange,
Our properties and symbols change,
But round the freedom of the Will
Our disagreements centre still,
And now as then the voter hears
The battle cries of two ideas.
Here, as in Europe, is dissent,
This raw untidy continent
Where the Commuter can't forget
The Pioneer; and even yet
A *Völkerwanderung* occurs:
Resourceful manufacturers
Trek southward by progressive stages
For sites with no floor under wages,
No ceiling over hours; and by
Artistic souls in towns that lie
Out in the weed and pollen belt
The need for sympathy is felt,
And east to hard New York they come;
And self-respect drives Negroes from
The one-crop and race-hating delta

To northern cities helter-skelter;
And in jalopies there migrates
A rootless tribe from windblown states
To suffer further westward where
The tolerant Pacific air
Makes logic seem so silly, pain
Subjective, what he seeks so vain
The wanderer may die; and kids,
When their imagination bids,
Hitch-hike a thousand miles to find
The Hesperides that's on their mind,
Some Texas where real cowboys seem
Lost in a movie-cowboy's dream.
More even than in Europe, here
The choice of patterns is made clear
Which the machine imposes, what
Is possible and what is not,
To what conditions we must bow
In building the Just City now.

However we decide to act,
Decision must accept the fact
That the machine has now destroyed
The local customs we enjoyed,
Replaced the bonds of blood and nation
By personal confederation.
No longer can we learn our good
From chances of a neighbourhood
Or class or party, or refuse
As individuals to choose
Our loves, authorities, and friends,
To judge our means and plan our ends;
For the machine has cried aloud
And publicized among the crowd
The secret that was always true

But known once only to the few,
Compelling all to the admission,
Aloneness is man's real condition,
That each must travel forth alone
In search of the Essential Stone,
'The Nowhere-without-No' that is
The justice of societies.
Each salesman now is the polite
Adventurer, the landless knight
GAWAINE-QUIXOTE, and his goal
The *Frauendienst* of his weak soul;
Each biggie in the Canning Ring
An unrobust lone FISHER-KING;
Each subway face the PEQUOD of
Some ISHMAEL hunting his lost love,
To harpoon his unhappiness
And turn the whale to a princess;
In labs the puzzled KAFKAS meet
The inexplicable defeat:
The odd behaviour of the law,
The facts that suddenly withdraw,
The path that twists away from the
Near-distant CASTLE they can see,
The Truth where they will be denied
Permission ever to reside;
And all the operatives know
Their factory is the *champ-clos*
And drawing-room of HENRY JAMES,
Where the *débat* decides the claims
Of liberty and justice; where,
Like any Jamesian character,
They learn to draw the careful line,
Develop, understand, refine.

A weary Asia out of sight
Is tugging gently at the night,
Uncovering a restless race;
Clocks shoo the childhood from its face,
And accurate machines begin
To concentrate its adults in
A narrow day to exercise
Their gifts in some cramped enterprise.
How few pretend to like it: O
Three quarters of these people know
Instinctively what ought to be
The nature of society
And how they'd live there if they could.
If it were easy to be good,
And cheap, and plain as evil how,
We all would be its members now:
How readily would we become
The seamless live continuum
Of supple and coherent stuff,
Whose form is truth, whose content love,
Its pluralist interstices
The homes of happiness and peace,
Where in a unity of praise
The largest *publicum's* a *res*,
And the least *res* a *publicum*;
How grandly would our virtues bloom
In a more conscionable dust
Where Freedom dwells because it must,
Necessity because it can,
And men confederate in Man.

But wishes are not horses, this
Annus is not *mirabilis*;
Day breaks upon the world we know
Of war and wastefulness and woe;
Ashamed civilians come to grief

In brotherhoods without belief,
Whose good intentions cannot cure
The actual evils they endure,
Nor smooth their practical career,
Nor bring the far horizon near.
The New Year brings an earth afraid,
Democracy a ready-made
And noisy tradesman's slogan, and
The poor betrayed into the hand
Of lackeys with ideas, and truth
Whipped by their elders out of youth,
The peaceful fainting in their tracks
With martyrs' tombstones on their backs,
And culture on all fours to greet
A butch and criminal *élite*,
While in the vale of silly sheep
Rheumatic old patricians weep.

Our news is seldom good: the heart,
As ZOLA said, must always start
The day by swallowing its toad
Of failure and disgust. Our road
Gets worse and we seem altogether
Lost as our theories, like the weather,
Veer round completely every day,
And all that we can always say
Is: true democracy begins
With free confession of our sins.
In this alone are all the same,
All are so weak that none dare claim
'I have the right to govern,' or
'Behold in me the Moral Law,'
And all real unity commences
In consciousness of differences,
That all have wants to satisfy

And each a power to supply.
We need to love all since we are
Each a unique particular
That is no giant, god, or dwarf,
But one odd human isomorph;
We can love each because we know
All, all of us, that this is so:
Can live since we are lived, the powers
That we create with are not ours.

O Unicorn among the cedars,
To whom no magic charm can lead us,
White childhood moving like a sigh
Through the green woods unharmed in thy
Sophisticated innocence,
To call thy true love to the dance,
O Dove of science and of light,
Upon the branches of the night,
O Ichthus playful in the deep
Sea-lodges that forever keep
Their secret of excitement hidden,
O sudden Wind that blows unbidden,
Parting the quiet reeds, O Voice
Within the labyrinth of choice
Only the passive listener hears,
O Clock and Keeper of the years,
O Source of equity and rest,
Quando non fuerit, non est,
It without image, paradigm
Of matter, motion, number, time,
The grinning gap of Hell, the hill
Of Venus and the stairs of Will,
Disturb our negligence and chill,
Convict our pride of its offence
In all things, even penitence,

Instruct us in the civil art
Of making from the muddled heart
A desert and a city where
The thoughts that have to labour there
May find locality and peace,
And pent-up feelings their release,
Send strength sufficient for our day,
And point out knowledge on its way,
O *da quod jubes, Domine.*

Dear friend Elizabeth, dear friend
These days have brought me, may the end
I bring to the grave's dead-line be
More worthy of your sympathy
Than the beginning; may the truth
That no one marries lead my youth
Where you already are and bless
Me with your learned peacefulness,
Who on the lives about you throw
A calm *solificatio,*
A warmth throughout the universe
That each for better or for worse
Must carry round with him through life,
A judge, a landscape, and a wife.
We fall down in the dance, we make
The old ridiculous mistake,
But always there are such as you
Forgiving, helping what we do.
O every day in sleep and labour
Our life and death are with our neighbour,
And love illuminates again
The city and the lion's den,
The world's great rage, the travel of young men.

For the Time Being

A Christmas Oratorio

IN MEMORIAM
CONSTANCE ROSALIE AUDEN
1870–1941

*What shall we say then? Shall we continue
in sin, that grace may abound? God forbid.*
Romans VI

Advent

I

Darkness and snow descend;
The clock on the mantelpiece
Has nothing to recommend,
Nor does the face in the glass
Appear nobler than our own
As darkness and snow descend
On all personality.
Huge crowds mumble—'Alas,
Our angers do not increase,
Love is not what she used to be;'
Portly Caesar yawns—'I know;'
He falls asleep on his throne,
They shuffle off through the snow:
Darkness and snow descend.

SEMI-CHORUS

Can great Hercules keep his
Extraordinary promise
To reinvigorate the Empire?
Utterly lost, he cannot
Even locate his task but
Stands in some decaying orchard
Or the irregular shadow
Of a ruined temple, aware of

Being watched from the horrid mountains
By fanatical eyes yet
Seeing no one at all, only hearing
The silence softly broken
By the poisonous rustle
Of famishing Arachne.

CHORUS

Winter completes an age
With its thorough levelling;
Heaven's tourbillions of rage
Abolish the watchman's tower
And delete the cedar grove.
As winter completes an age,
The eyes huddle like cattle, doubt
Seeps into the pores and power
Ebbs from the heavy signet ring;
The prophet's lantern is out
And gone the boundary stone,
Cold the heart and cold the stove,
Ice condenses on the bone:
Winter completes an age.

SEMI-CHORUS

Outside the civil garden
Of every day of love there
Crouches a wild passion
    To destroy and be destroyed.
O who to boast their power
Have challenged it to charge? Like
Wheat our souls are sifted
    And cast into the void.

CHORUS

The evil and armed draw near;
The weather smells of their hate
And the houses smell of our fear;
Death has opened his white eye
And the black hole calls the thief
As the evil and armed draw near.
Ravens alight on the wall,
Our plans have all gone awry,
The rains will arrive too late,
Our resourceful general
Fell down dead as he drank
And his horses died of grief,
Our navy sailed away and sank;
The evil and armed draw near.

II

NARRATOR

If, on account of the political situation,
There are quite a number of homes without roofs, and men
Lying about in the countryside neither drunk nor asleep,
If all sailings have been cancelled till further notice,
If it's unwise now to say much in letters, and if,
Under the subnormal temperatures prevailing,
The two sexes are at present the weak and the strong,
That is not at all unusual for this time of year.
If that were all we should know how to manage. Flood, fire,
The desiccation of grasslands, restraint of princes,
Piracy on the high seas, physical pain and fiscal grief,
These after all are our familiar tribulations,
And we have been through them all before, many, many times.
As events which belong to the natural world where
The occupation of space is the real and final fact
And time turns round itself in an obedient circle,

135

They occur again and again but only to pass
Again and again into their formal opposites,
From sword to ploughshare, coffin to cradle, war to work,
So that, taking the bad with the good, the pattern composed
By the ten thousand odd things that can possibly happen
Is permanent in a general average way.

    Till lately we knew of no other, and between us we seemed
To have what it took—the adrenal courage of the tiger,
The chameleon's discretion, the modesty of the doe,
Or the fern's devotion to spatial necessity:
To practise one's peculiar civic virtue was not
So impossible after all; to cut our losses
And bury our dead was really quite easy: That was why
We were always able to say: 'We are children of God,
And our Father has never forsaken His people.'

    But then we were children: That was a moment ago,
Before an outrageous novelty had been introduced
Into our lives. Why were we never warned? Perhaps we were.
Perhaps that mysterious noise at the back of the brain
We noticed on certain occasions—sitting alone
In the waiting room of the country junction, looking
Up at the toilet window—was not indigestion
But this Horror starting already to scratch Its way in?
Just how, just when It succeeded we shall never know:
We can only say that now It is there and that nothing
We learnt before It was there is now of the slightest use,
For nothing like It has happened before. It's as if
We had left our house for five minutes to mail a letter,
And during that time the living room had changed places
With the room behind the mirror over the fireplace;
It's as if, waking up with a start, we discovered
Ourselves stretched out flat on the floor, watching our shadow
Sleepily stretching itself at the window. I mean

That the world of space where events re-occur is still there,
Only now it's no longer real; the real one is nowhere
Where time never moves and nothing can ever happen:
I mean that although there's a person we know all about
Still bearing our name and loving himself as before,
That person has become a fiction; our true existence
Is decided by no one and has no importance to love.

   That is why we despair; that is why we would welcome
The nursery bogey or the winecellar ghost, why even
The violent howling of winter and war has become
Like a juke-box tune that we dare not stop. We are afraid
Of pain but more afraid of silence; for no nightmare
Of hostile objects could be as terrible as this Void.
This is the Abomination. This is the wrath of God.

III

CHORUS

Alone, alone, about a dreadful wood
Of conscious evil runs a lost mankind,
Dreading to find its Father lest it find
The Goodness it has dreaded is not good:
Alone, alone, about our dreadful wood.

Where is that Law for which we broke our own,
Where now that Justice for which Flesh resigned
Her hereditary right to passion, Mind
His will to absolute power? Gone. Gone.
Where is that Law for which we broke our own?

The Pilgrim Way has led to the Abyss.
Was it to meet such grinning evidence
We left our richly odoured ignorance?
Was the triumphant answer to be this?
The Pilgrim Way has led to the Abyss.

We who must die demand a miracle.
How could the Eternal do a temporal act,
The Infinite become a finite fact?
Nothing can save us that is possible:
We who must die demand a miracle.

IV

RECITATIVE

If the muscle can feel repugnance, there is still a false move to be
    made;
If the mind can imagine tomorrow, there is still a defeat to
    remember;
As long as the self can say 'I', it is impossible not to rebel;
As long as there is an accidental virtue, there is a necessary vice:
And the garden cannot exist, the miracle cannot occur.

For the garden is the only place there is, but you will not find it
Until you have looked for it everywhere and found nowhere that
    is not a desert;
The miracle is the only thing that happens, but to you it will not be
    apparent,
Until all events have been studied and nothing happens that you
    cannot explain;
And life is the destiny you are bound to refuse until you have
    consented to die.

Therefore, see without looking, hear without listening, breathe
    without asking:
The Inevitable is what will seem to happen to you purely by chance;
The Real is what will strike you as really absurd;
Unless you are certain you are dreaming, it is certainly a dream of
    your own;
Unless you exclaim—'There must be some mistake'—you must be
    mistaken.

V

CHORUS

O where is that immortal and nameless Centre from which our
  points of
  Definition and death are all equi-distant? Where
The well of our wish to wander, the everlasting fountain
  Of the waters of joy that our sorrow uses for tears?
O where is the garden of Being that is only known in Existence
  As the command to be never there, the sentence by which
Alephs of throbbing fact have been banished into position,
  The clock that dismisses the moment into the turbine of time?

O would I could mourn over Fate like the others, the resolute
  creatures,
  By seizing my chance to regret. The stone is content
With a formal anger and falls and falls; the plants are indignant
  With one dimension only and can only doubt
Whether light or darkness lies in the worse direction; and the subtler
  Exiles who try every path are satisfied
With proving that none have a goal: why must Man also
  acknowledge
  It is not enough to bear witness, for even protest is wrong?

Earth is cooled and fire is quenched by his unique excitement,
  All answers expire in the clench of his questioning hand,
His singular emphasis frustrates all possible order:
  Alas, his genius is wholly for envy; alas,
The vegetative sadness of lakes, the locomotive beauty
  Of choleric beasts of prey, are nearer than he
To the dreams that deprive him of sleep, the powers that compel him
  to idle,
  To his amorous nymphs and his sanguine athletic gods.

How can his knowledge protect his desire for truth from illusion?
  How can he wait without idols to worship, without
Their overwhelming persuasion that somewhere, over the high hill,
  Under the roots of the oak, in the depths of the sea,
Is a womb or a tomb wherein he may halt to express some
    attainment?
  How can he hope and not dream that his solitude
Shall disclose a vibrating flame at last and entrust him forever
  With its magic secret of how to extemporize life?

The Annunciation

I

THE FOUR FACULTIES
Over the life of Man
We watch and wait,
The Four who manage
His fallen estate:
We who are four were
Once but one,
Before his act of
Rebellion;
We were himself when
His will was free,
His error became our
Chance to be.
Powers of air and fire,
Water and earth,
Into our hands is given
Man from his birth:

INTUITION
As a dwarf in the dark of
His belly I rest;

FEELING
A nymph, I inhabit
The heart in his breast;

SENSATION
A giant, at the gates of
His body I stand;

THOUGHT
His dreaming brain is
My fairyland.

TUTTI
Invisible phantoms,
The forms we assume are
Adapted to each
Individual humour,
Beautiful facts or true
Generalizations,
Test cases in Law or
Market quotations:
As figures and formulae
Chemists have seen us,
Who to true lovers were
Putti of Venus.

Ambiguous causes
Of all temptation,
We lure men either
To death or salvation:
We alone may look over
The wall of that hidden
Garden whose entrance
To him is forbidden;
Must truthfully tell him
What happens inside,
But what it may mean he
Alone must decide.

142

II

THOUGHT

The garden is unchanged, the silence is unbroken.
Truth has not yet intruded to possess
Its empty morning nor the promised hour
Shaken its lasting May.

INTUITION

       The human night,
Whose messengers we are, cannot dispel
Its wanton dreams, and they are all we know.

SENSATION

My senses are still coarse
From late engrossment in a fair. Old tunes
Reiterated, lights with repeated winks,
Were fascinating like a tic and brought
Whole populations running to a plain,
Making its lush alluvial meadows
One boisterous preposter. By the river
A whistling crowd had waited many hours
To see a naked woman swim upstream;
Honours and reckless medicines were served
In booths where interest was lost
As easily as money; at the back,
In a wet vacancy among the ash cans,
A waiter coupled sadly with a crow.

FEELING

I have but now escaped a raging landscape:
There woods were in a tremor from the shouts
Of hunchbacks hunting a hermaphrodite;
A burning village scampered down a lane;
Insects with ladders stormed a virgin's house;

On a green knoll littered with picnics
A mob of horses kicked a gull to death.

INTUITION

Remembrance of the moment before last
Is like a yawning drug. I have observed
The sombre valley of an industry
In dereliction. Conduits, ponds, canals,
Distressed with weeds; engines and furnaces
At rust in rotting sheds; and their strong users
Transformed to spongy heaps of drunken flesh.
Deep among dock and dusty nettle lay
Each ruin of a will; manors of mould
Grew into empires as a westering sun
Left the air chilly; not a sound disturbed
The autumn dusk except a stertorous snore
That over their drowned condition like a sea
Wept without grief.

THOUGHT

         My recent company
Was worse than your three visions. Where I was,
The haunting ghosts were figures with no ground,
Areas of wide omission and vast regions
Of passive colour; higher than any squeak,
One note went on for ever; an embarrassed sum
Stuck on the stutter of a decimal,
And points almost coincident already
Approached so slowly they could never meet.
There nothing could be stated or constructed:
To Be was an archaic nuisance.

INTUITION

Look. There is someone in the garden.

FEELING

The garden is unchanged, the silence is unbroken
For she is still walking in her sleep of childhood:
Many before
Have wandered in, like her, then wandered out
Unconscious of their visit and unaltered,
The garden unchanged, the silence unbroken:
None may wake there but One who shall be woken.

THE ANGEL GABRIEL

Wake.

III

GABRIEL

Mary, in a dream of love
Playing as all children play,
For unsuspecting children may
Express in comic make-believe
The wish that later they will know
Is tragic and impossible;
Hear, child, what I am sent to tell:
Love wills your dream to happen, so
Love's will on earth may be, through you,
No longer a pretend but true.

MARY

What dancing joy would whirl
My ignorance away?
Light blazes out of the stone,
The taciturn water
Burst into music,
And warm wings throb within
The motionless rose:
What sudden rush of Power
Commands me to command?

GABRIEL

When Eve, in love with her own will,
Denied the will of Love and fell,
She turned the flesh Love knew so well
To knowledge of her love until
Both love and knowledge were of sin:
What her negation wounded, may
Your affirmation heal today;
Love's will requires your own, that in
The flesh whose love you do not know,
Love's knowledge into flesh may grow.

MARY

My flesh in terror and fire
Rejoices that the Word
Who utters the world out of nothing,
As a pledge of His word to love her
Against her will, and to turn
Her desperate longing to love,
Should ask to wear me,
From now to their wedding day,
For an engagement ring.

GABRIEL

Since Adam, being free to choose,
Chose to imagine he was free
To choose his own necessity,
Lost in his freedom, Man pursues
The shadow of his images:
Today the Unknown seeks the known;
What I am willed to ask, your own
Will has to answer; child, it lies
Within your power of choosing to
Conceive the Child who chooses you.

146

IV

SOLO AND CHORUS

Let number and weight rejoice
In this hour of their translation
Into conscious happiness:
For the whole in every part,
The truth at the proper centre
(*There's a Way. There's a Voice.*)
Of language and distress
Is recognized in her heart
Singing and dancing.

Let even the great rejoice.
Though buffeted by admirers
And arrogant as noon,
The rich and the lovely have seen
For an infinitesimal moment
(*There's a Way. There's a Voice.*)
In another's eye till their own
Reflection came between,
Singing and dancing.

Let even the small rejoice
Though threatened from purple rostra
And dazed by the soldier's drum
Proclaiming total defeat,
The general loquacious Public
(*There's a Way. There's a Voice.*)
Have been puzzled and struck dumb,
Hearing in every street
Singing and dancing.

147

Let even the young rejoice
Lovers at their betrayal
Weeping alone in the night,
Have fallen asleep as they heard,
Though too far off to be certain
(*There's a Way. There's a Voice.*)
They had not imagined it,
Sounds that made grief absurd,
Singing and dancing.

Let even the old rejoice
The Bleak and the Dim, abandoned
By impulse and regret,
Are startled out of their lives;
For to footsteps long expected
(*There's a Way. There's a Voice.*)
Their ruins echo, yet
The Demolisher arrives
Singing and dancing.

The Temptation of St. Joseph

I

JOSEPH
My shoes were shined, my pants were
          cleaned and pressed,
And I was hurrying to meet
  My own true Love:
But a great crowd grew and grew
Till I could not push my way through,
  Because
A star had fallen down the street;
  When they saw who I was,
The police tried to do their best.

    CHORUS [*off*]
    Joseph, you have heard
    What Mary says occurred;
    Yes, it may be so.
    Is it likely? No.

    JOSEPH
The bar was gay, the lighting well-designed,
And I was sitting down to wait
  My own true Love:
A voice I'd heard before, I think,
Cried: 'This is on the House. I drink
  To him

149

Who does not know it is too late;'
    When I asked for the time,
Everyone was very kind.

    CHORUS [*off*]
    Mary may be pure,
    But, Joseph, are you sure?
    How is one to tell?
    Suppose, for instance. . . Well . . .

    JOSEPH
Through cracks, up ladders, into waters deep,
I squeezed, I climbed, I swam to save
    My own true Love:
Under a dead apple tree
I saw an ass; when it saw me
    It brayed;
A hermit sat in the mouth of a cave:
    When I asked him the way,
He pretended to be asleep.

    CHORUS [*off*]
    Maybe, maybe not.
    But, Joseph, you know what
    Your world, of course, will say
    About you anyway.

    JOSEPH
Where are you, Father, where?
Caught in the jealous trap
Of an empty house I hear
As I sit alone in the dark
Everything, everything,
The drip of the bathroom tap,
The creak of the sofa spring,

The wind in the air-shaft, all
Making the same remark
Stupidly, stupidly,
Over and over again.
Father, what have I done?
Answer me, Father, how
Can I answer the tactless wall
Or the pompous furniture now?
Answer them . . .

GABRIEL
No, you must.

JOSEPH
How then am I to know,
Father, that you are just?
Give me one reason.

GABRIEL
No.

JOSEPH
All I ask is one
Important and elegant proof
That what my Love had done
Was really at your will
And that your will is Love.

GABRIEL
No, you must believe;
Be silent, and sit still.

II

    For the perpetual excuse
Of Adam for his fall – 'My little Eve,
God bless her, did beguile me and I ate,'
    For his insistence on a nurse,
All service, breast, and lap, for giving Fate
Feminine gender to make girls believe
That they can save him, you must now atone,
    Joseph, in silence and alone;
While she who loves you makes you shake with fright,
Your love for her must tuck you up and kiss good night.

    For likening Love to war, for all
The pay-off lines of limericks in which
The weak resentful bar-fly shows his sting,
    For talking of their spiritual
Beauty to chorus-girls, for flattering
The features of old gorgons who are rich,
For the impudent grin and Irish charm
    That hides a cold will to do harm,
Today the roles are altered; you must be
The Weaker Sex whose passion is passivity.

    For those delicious memories
Cigars and sips of brandy can restore
To old dried boys, for gallantry that scrawls
    In idolatrous detail and size
A symbol of aggression on toilet walls,
For having reasoned – 'Woman is naturally pure
Since she has no moustache,' for having said,
    'No woman has a business head,'
You must learn now that masculinity,
To Nature, is a non-essential luxury.

Lest, finding it impossible
To judge its object now or throatily
Forgive it as eternal God forgives,
　Lust, tempted by this miracle
To more ingenious evil, should contrive
A heathen fetish from Virginity
To soothe the spiritual petulance
　Of worn-out rakes and maiden aunts,
Forgetting nothing and believing all,
You must behave as if this were not strange at all.

　Without a change in look or word,
You both must act exactly as before;
Joseph and Mary shall be man and wife
　Just as if nothing had occurred.
There is one World of Nature and one Life;
Sin fractures the Vision, not the Fact; for
The Exceptional is always usual
　And the Usual exceptional.
To choose what is difficult all one's days
As if it were easy, that is faith. Joseph, praise.

III

SEMI-CHORUS
Joseph, Mary, pray for those
　Misled by moonlight and the rose,
For all in our perplexity.
Lovers who hear a distant bell
That tolls from somewhere in their head
Across the valley of their dream—
'All those who love excessively
Foot or thigh or arm or face
Pursue a louche and fatuous fire

153

And stumble into Hell'–
Yet what can such foreboding seem
But intellectual talk
So long as bodies walk
An earth where Time and Space
Turn Heaven to a finite bed
And Love into desire?
Pray for us, enchanted with
The green Bohemia of that myth
Where knowledge of the flesh can take
The guilt of being born away,
Simultaneous passions make
One eternal chastity:
Pray for us romantics, pray.

BOYS' SEMI-CHORUS

Joseph, Mary, pray for us,
Independent embryos who,
Unconscious in another, do
Evil as each creature does
In every definite decision
To improve; for even in
The germ-cell's primary division
Innocence is lost and sin,
Already given as a fact,
Once more issues as an act.

SEMI-CHORUS

Joseph, Mary, pray for all
The proper and conventional
Of whom this world approves.
Pray for us whose married loves
Acquire so readily
The indolent fidelity

Of unaired beds, for us to whom
Domestic hatred can become
A habit-forming drug, whose will
To civil anarchy
Uses disease to disobey
And makes our private bodies ill.
O pray for our salvation
Who take the prudent way,
Believing we shall be exempted
From the general condemnation
Because our self-respect is tempted
To incest not adultery:
O pray for us, the bourgeoisie.

BOYS' SEMI-CHORUS

Joseph, Mary, pray
For us children as in play
Upon the nursery floor
We gradually explore
Our members till our jealous lives
Have worked through to a clear
But trivial idea
Of that whence each derives
A vague but massive feel
Of being individual.
O pray for our redemption; for
The will that occupies
Our sensual infancy
Already is mature
And could immediately
Beget upon our flesh far more
Expressions of its disbelief
Than we shall manage to conceive
In a long life of lies.

CHORUS
Blessed Woman,
Excellent Man,
Redeem for the dull the
Average Way,
That common ungifted
Natures may
Believe that their normal
Vision can
Walk to perfection.

The Summons

I

STAR OF THE NATIVITY

I am that star most dreaded by the wise,
For they are drawn against their will to me,
Yet read in my procession through the skies
The doom of orthodox sophrosyne:
I shall discard their major preservation,
All that they know so long as no one asks;
I shall deprive them of their minor tasks
In free and legal households of sensation,
Of money, picnics, beer, and sanitation.

Beware. All those who follow me are led
Onto that Glassy Mountain where are no
Footholds for logic, to that Bridge of Dread
Where knowledge but increases vertigo:
Those who pursue me take a twisting lane
To find themselves immediately alone
With savage water or unfeeling stone,
In labyrinths where they must entertain
Confusion, cripples, tigers, thunder, pain.

THE FIRST WISE MAN

To break down Her defences
    And profit from the vision
That plain men can predict through an

157

Ascesis of their senses,
With rack and screw I put Nature through
A thorough inquisition:
But She was so afraid that if I were disappointed
I should hurt Her more that Her answers were disjointed –
I did. I didn't. I will. I won't.
She is just as big a liar, in fact, as we are.
To discover how to be truthful now
Is the reason I follow this star.

THE SECOND WISE MAN

My faith that in Time's constant
Flow lay real assurance
Broke down on this analysis –
At any given instant
All solids dissolve, no wheels revolve,
And facts have no endurance –
And who knows if it is by design or pure inadvertence
That the Present destroys its inherited self-importance?
With envy, terror, rage, regret,
We anticipate or remember but never are.
To discover how to be living now
Is the reason I follow this star.

THE THIRD WISE MAN

Observing how myopic
Is the Venus of the Soma,
The concept Ought would make, I thought,
Our passions philanthropic,
And rectify in the sensual eye
Both lens-flare and lens-coma:
But arriving at the Greatest Good by introspection
And counting the Greater Number, left no time for affection,
Laughter, kisses, squeezing, smiles:
And I learned why the learned are as despised as they are.

To discover how to be loving now
Is the reason I follow this star.

THE THREE WISE MEN

The weather has been awful,
    The countryside is dreary,
Marsh, jungle, rock; and echoes mock,
    Calling our hope unlawful;
But a silly song can help along
    Yours ever and sincerely:
At least we know for certain that we are three old sinners,
That this journey is much too long, that we want our dinners,
    And miss our wives, our books, our dogs,
But have only the vaguest idea why we are what we are.
    To discover how to be human now
    Is the reason we follow this star.

STAR OF THE NATIVITY

Descend into the fosse of Tribulation,
Take the cold hand of Terror for a guide;
Below you in its swirling desolation
Hear tortured Horror roaring for a bride:
O do not falter at the last request
But, as the huge deformed head rears to kill,
Answer its craving with a clear I Will;
Then wake, a child in the rose-garden, pressed
Happy and sobbing to your lover's breast.

II

NARRATOR

Now let the wife look up from her stove, the husband
Interrupt his work, the child put down its toy,
That His voice may be heard in our Just Society

Who under the sunlight
Of His calm, possessing the good earth, do well. Pray
Silence for Caesar: stand motionless and hear
In a concourse of body and concord of soul
  His proclamation.

RECITATIVE

CITIZENS OF THE EMPIRE, GREETING. ALL MALE PERSONS
WHO SHALL HAVE ATTAINED THE AGE OF TWENTY-ONE
YEARS OR OVER MUST PROCEED IMMEDIATELY TO THE VIL-
LAGE, TOWNSHIP, CITY, PRECINCT OR OTHER LOCAL AD-
MINISTRATIVE AREA IN WHICH THEY WERE BORN AND
THERE REGISTER THEMSELVES AND THEIR DEPENDANTS IF
ANY WITH THE POLICE. WILFUL FAILURE TO COMPLY WITH
THIS ORDER IS PUNISHABLE BY CONFISCATION OF GOODS
AND LOSS OF CIVIL RIGHTS.

NARRATOR

You have been listening to the voice of Caesar
Who overcame implacable Necessity
By His endurance and by His skill has subdued the
  Welter of Fortune.
It is meet, therefore, that, before dispersing
In pious equanimity to obey His orders,
With well-tuned instruments and grateful voices
  We should praise Caesar.

III

FUGAL-CHORUS

Great is Caesar: He has conquered Seven Kingdoms.
The First was the Kingdom of Abstract Idea:
Last night it was Tom, Dick and Harry; to-night it is S's with P's;
Instead of inflexions and accents
There are prepositions and word-order;

Instead of aboriginal objects excluding each other
There are specimens reiterating a type;
Instead of wood-nymphs and river-demons,
There is one unconditioned ground of Being.
Great is Caesar: God must be with Him.

Great is Caesar: He has conquered Seven Kingdoms.
The Second was the Kingdom of Natural Cause:
Last night it was Sixes and Sevens; to-night it is One and Two;
Instead of saying, 'Strange are the whims of the Strong,'
We say, 'Harsh is the Law but it is certain;'
Instead of building temples, we build laboratories;
Instead of offering sacrifices, we perform experiments;
Instead of reciting prayers, we note pointer-readings;
Our lives are no longer erratic but efficient.
Great is Caesar: God must be with Him.

Great is Caesar; He has conquered Seven Kingdoms.
The Third was the Kingdom of Infinite Number:
Last night it was Rule-of-Thumb, to-night it is To-a-T;
Instead of Quite-a-lot, there is Exactly-so-many;
Instead of Only-a-few, there is Just-these;
Instead of saying, 'You must wait until I have counted,'
We say, 'Here you are. You will find this answer correct;'
Instead of a nodding acquaintance with a few integers,
The Transcendentals are our personal friends.
Great is Caesar: God must be with Him.

Great is Caesar: He has conquered Seven Kingdoms.
The Fourth was the Kingdom of Credit Exchange:
Last night it was Tit-for-Tat, to-night it is C.O.D.;
When we have a surplus, we need not meet someone with a deficit;
When we have a deficit, we need not meet someone with a surplus;
Instead of heavy treasures, there are paper symbols of value;
Instead of Pay at Once, there is Pay when you can;

Instead of My Neighbour, there is Our Customers;
Instead of Country Fair, there is World Market.
Great is Caesar: God must be with Him.

Great is Caesar; He has conquered Seven Kingdoms.
The Fifth was the Kingdom of Inorganic Giants:
Last night it was Heave-Ho, to-night it is Whee-Spree;
When we want anything, They make it;
When we dislike anything, They change it;
When we want to go anywhere, They carry us;
When the Barbarian invades us, They raise immovable shields;
When we invade the Barbarian, They brandish irresistible swords;
Fate is no longer a fiat of Matter, but a freedom of Mind.
Great is Caesar: God must be with Him.

Great is Caesar: He has conquered Seven Kingdoms.
The Sixth was the Kingdom of Organic Dwarfs:
Last night it was Ouch-Ouch, to-night it is Yum-Yum;
When diseases waylay us, They strike them dead;
When worries intrude on us, They throw them out;
When pain accosts us, They save us from embarrassment;
When we feel like sheep, They make us lions;
When we feel like geldings, They make us stallions;
Spirit is no longer under Flesh, but on top.
Great is Caesar: God must be with Him.

Great is Caesar: He has conquered Seven Kingdoms.
The Seventh was the Kingdom of Popular Soul:
Last night it was Order-Order, to-night it is Hear-Hear;
When he says, You are happy, we laugh;
When he says, You are wretched, we cry;
When he says, It is true, everyone believes it;
When he says, It is false, no one believes it;
When he says, This is good, this is loved;
When he says, That is bad, that is hated.
Great is Caesar: God must be with Him.

IV

These are stirring times for the editors of newspapers:
History is in the making; Mankind is on the march.
The longest aqueduct in the world is already
Under construction; the Committees on Fen-Drainage
And Soil-Conservation will issue very shortly
Their Joint Report; even the problems of Trade Cycles
And Spiralling Prices are regarded by the experts
As practically solved; and the recent restrictions
Upon aliens and free-thinking Jews are beginning
To have a salutary effect upon public morale.
True, the Western seas are still infested with pirates,
And the rising power of the Barbarian in the North
Is giving some cause for uneasiness; but we are fully
Alive to these dangers; we are rapidly arming; and both
Will be taken care of in due course: then, united
In a sense of common advantage and common right,
Our great Empire shall be secure for a thousand years.

  If we were never alone or always too busy,
Perhaps we might even believe what we know is not true:
But no one is taken in, at least not all of the time;
In our bath, or the subway, or the middle of the night,
We know very well we are not unlucky but evil,
That the dream of a Perfect State or No State at all,
To which we fly for refuge, is a part of our punishment.

  Let us therefore be contrite but without anxiety,
For Powers and Times are not gods but mortal gifts from God;
Let us acknowledge our defeats but without despair,
For all societies and epochs are transient details,
Transmitting an everlasting opportunity
That the Kingdom of Heaven may come, not in our present
And not in our future, but in the Fullness of Time.
Let us pray.

V

CHORALE

Our Father, whose creative Will
   Asked Being for us all,
Confirm it that Thy Primal Love
May weave in us the freedom of
The actually deficient on
   The justly actual.

Though written by Thy children with
   A smudged and crooked line,
Thy Word is ever legible,
Thy Meaning unequivocal,
And for Thy Goodness even sin
   Is valid as a sign.

Inflict Thy promises with each
   Occasion of distress,
That from our incoherence we
May learn to put our trust in Thee,
And brutal fact persuade us to
   Adventure, Art, and Peace.

The Vision of the Shepherds

I

THE FIRST SHEPHERD

The winter night requires our constant attention,
   Watching that water and good-will,
Warmth and well-being, may still be there in the morning.

THE SECOND SHEPHERD

  For behind the spontaneous joy of life
There is always a mechanism to keep going,

THE THIRD SHEPHERD

  And someone like us is always there.

THE FIRST SHEPHERD

We observe that those who assure us their education
   And money would do us such harm,
How real we are just as we are, and how they envy us,
   For it is the centreless tree
And the uncivilized robin who are the truly happy,
   Have done pretty well for themselves:

THE SECOND SHEPHERD

Nor can we help noticing how those who insist that
   We ought to stand up for our rights,
And how important we are, keep insisting also
   That it doesn't matter a bit
If one of us gets arrested or injured, for
   It is only our numbers that count.

THE THIRD SHEPHERD
In a way they are right,

THE FIRST SHEPHERD
But to behave like a cogwheel
When one knows one is no such thing,

THE SECOND SHEPHERD
Merely to add to a crowd with one's passionate body,
Is not a virtue.

THE THIRD SHEPHERD
What is real
About us all is that each of us is waiting.

THE FIRST SHEPHERD
That is why we are able to bear
Ready-made clothes, second-hand art and opinions
And being washed and ordered about;

THE SECOND SHEPHERD
That is why you should not take our conversation
Too seriously, nor read too much
Into our songs;

THE THIRD SHEPHERD
Their purpose is mainly to keep us
From watching the clock all the time.

THE FIRST SHEPHERD
For, though we cannot say why, we know that something
Will happen:

THE SECOND SHEPHERD
What we cannot say,

THE THIRD SHEPHERD
Except that it will not be a reporter's item
  Of unusual human interest;

THE FIRST SHEPHERD
That always means something unpleasant.

THE SECOND SHEPHERD
                    But one day or
The next we shall hear the Good News.

II

THE THREE SHEPHERDS
Levers nudge the aching wrist;
  'You are free
  Not to be,
  Why exist?'
Wheels a thousand times a minute
  Mutter, stutter,
'End the self you cannot mend,
Did you, friend, begin it?'
  And the streets
  Sniff at our defeats.
Then who is the Unknown
Who answers for our fear
As if it were His own,
So that we reply
Till the day we die;
'No, I don't know why,
But I'm glad I'm here?'

III

Unto you a Child,
A Son is given.
Praising, proclaiming
The ingression of Love,
Earth's darkness invents
The blaze of Heaven,
And frigid silence
Meditates a song;
For great joy has filled
The narrow and the sad,
While the emphasis
Of the rough and big,
The abiding crag
And wandering wave,
Is on forgiveness:
Sing Glory to God
And good-will to men,
All, all, all of them.
Run to Bethlehem.

SHEPHERDS
Let us run to learn
How to love and run;
Let us run to Love.

CHORUS
How all things living,
Domestic or wild,
With whom you must share
Light, water, and air,
And suffer and shake
In physical need,

The sullen limpet,
The exuberant weed,
The mischievous cat,
And the timid bird,
Are glad for your sake
As the new-born Word
Declares that the old
Authoritarian
Constraint is replaced
By His Covenant,
And a city based
On love and consent
Suggested to men,
All, all, all of them.
Run to Bethlehem.

SHEPHERDS

Let us run to learn
How to love and run;
Let us run to Love.

CHORUS

The primitive dead
Progress in your blood,
And generations
Of the unborn, all
Are leaping for joy
In your reins today
When the Many shall,
Once in your common
Certainty of this
Child's lovableness,
Resemble the One,
That after today
The children of men

May be certain that
The Father Abyss
Is affectionate
To all Its creatures,
All, all, all of them.
Run to Bethlehem.

At the Manger

I

MARY

O shut your bright eyes that mine must endanger
With their watchfulness; protected by its shade
Escape from my care: what can you discover
From my tender look but how to be afraid?
Love can but confirm the more it would deny.
  Close your bright eye.

Sleep. What have you learned from the womb that bore you
But an anxiety your Father cannot feel?
Sleep. What will the flesh that I gave do for you,
Or my mother love, but tempt you from His will?
Why was I chosen to teach His Son to weep?
  Little One, sleep.

Dream. In human dreams earth ascends to Heaven
Where no one need pray nor ever feel alone.
In your first few hours of life here, O have you
Chosen already what death must be your own?
How soon will you start on the Sorrowful Way?
  Dream while you may.

II

FIRST WISE MAN

Led by the light of an unusual star,
We hunted high and low.

SECOND WISE MAN

                           Have travelled far,
For many days, a little group alone
With doubts, reproaches, boredom, the unknown.

THIRD WISE MAN

Through stifling gorges.

FIRST WISE MAN

                          Over level lakes,

SECOND WISE MAN

Tundras intense and irresponsive seas.

THIRD WISE MAN

In vacant crowds and humming silences,

FIRST WISE MAN

By ruined arches and past modern shops,

SECOND WISE MAN

Counting the miles,

THIRD WISE MAN

                    And the absurd mistakes.

THE THREE WISE MEN

O here and now our endless journey stops.

FIRST SHEPHERD

We never left the place where we were born,

SECOND SHEPHERD

Have only lived one day, but every day,

172

THIRD SHEPHERD

Have walked a thousand miles yet only worn
The grass between our work and home away.

FIRST SHEPHERD

Lonely we were though never left alone.

SECOND SHEPHERD

The solitude familiar to the poor
Is feeling that the family next door,
The way it talks, eats, dresses, loves, and hates,
Is indistinguishable from one's own.

THIRD SHEPHERD

Tonight for the first time the prison gates
Have opened.

FIRST SHEPHERD

               Music and sudden light

SECOND SHEPHERD

Have interrupted our routine tonight,

THIRD SHEPHERD

And swept the filth of habit from our hearts.

THE THREE SHEPHERDS

O here and now our endless journey starts.

WISE MEN

Our arrogant longing to attain the tomb,

SHEPHERDS

Our sullen wish to go back to the womb,

To have no past.

SHEPHERDS
No future,

TUTTI
                           Is refused.
And yet, without our knowledge, Love has used
  Our weakness as a guard and guide.
                         We bless

WISE MEN
Our lives' impatience.

SHEPHERDS
                    Our lives' laziness,

TUTTI
And bless each other's sin, exchanging here

WISE MEN
Exceptional conceit

SHEPHERDS
                    With average fear.

TUTTI
Released by Love from isolating wrong,
Let us for Love unite our various song,
Each with his gift according to his kind
Bringing this child his body and his mind.

III

Child, at whose birth we would do obsequy
For our tall errors of imagination,
Redeem our talents with your little cry.

SHEPHERDS

Clinging like sheep to the earth for protection,
We have not ventured far in any direction:
    Wean, Child, our ageing flesh away
    From its childish way.

WISE MEN

Love is more serious than Philosophy
Who sees no humour in her observation
That Truth is knowing that we know we lie.

SHEPHERDS

When, to escape what our memories are thinking,
We go out at nights and stay up drinking,
    Stay then with our sick pride and mind
    The forgetful mind.

WISE MEN

Love does not will enraptured apathy;
Fate plays the passive role of dumb temptation
To wills where Love can doubt, affirm, deny.

SHEPHERDS

When, chafing at the rule of old offences,
We run away to the sea of the senses,
    On strange beds then O welcome home
    Our horror of home.

WISE MEN

Love knows of no somatic tyranny;
For homes are built for Love's accommodation
By bodies from the void they occupy.

SHEPHERDS

When, exhausting our wills with our evil courses,
We demand the good-will of cards and horses,
  Be then our lucky certainty
  Of uncertainty.

WISE MEN

Love does not fear substantial anarchy,
But vividly expresses obligation
With movement and in spontaneity.

SHEPHERDS

When, feeling the great boots of the rich on our faces,
We live in the hope of one day changing places,
  Be then the truth of our abuse
  That we abuse.

WISE MEN

The singular is not Love's enemy;
Love's possibilities of realization
Require an Otherness that can say *I*.

SHEPHERDS

When in dreams the beasts and cripples of resentment
Rampage and revel to our hearts' contentment,
  Be then the poetry of hate
  That replaces hate.

WISE MEN

Not In but With our time Love's energy
Exhibits Love's immediate operation;
The choice to love is open till we die.

O Living Love, by your birth we are able
Not only, like the ox and ass of the stable,
   To love with our live wills, but love,
   Knowing we love.

O Living Love replacing phantasy,
O Joy of life revealed in Love's creation;
Our mood of longing turns to indication:
Space is the Whom our loves are needed by,
Time is our choice of How to love and Why.

The Meditation of Simeon

As long as the apple had not been entirely digested, as long as there remained the least understanding between Adam and the stars, rivers and horses with whom he had once known complete intimacy, as long as Eve could share in any way with the moods of the rose or the ambitions of the swallow, there was still a hope that the effects of the poison would wear off, that the exile from Paradise was only a bad dream, that the Fall had not occurred in fact.

CHORUS

When we woke, it was day; we went on weeping.

SIMEON

As long as there were any roads to amnesia and anaesthesia still to be explored, any rare wine or curiosity of cuisine as yet untested, any erotic variation as yet unimagined or unrealized, any method of torture as yet undevised, any style of conspicuous waste as yet unindulged, any eccentricity of mania or disease as yet unrepresented, there was still a hope that man has not been poisoned but transformed, that Paradise was not an eternal state from which he had been forever expelled, but a childish state which he had permanently outgrown, that the Fall had occurred by necessity.

CHORUS

We danced in the dark, but were not deceived.

As long as there were any experiments still to be undertaken in restoring that order in which desire had once rejoiced to be reflected, any code of equity and obligation upon which some society had not yet been founded, any species of property of which the value had not yet been appreciated, any talent that had not yet won private devotion and public honour, any rational concept of the Good or intuitive feeling for the Holy that had not yet found its precise and beautiful expression, any technique of contemplation or ritual of sacrifice and praise that had not yet been properly conducted, any faculty of mind or body that had not yet been thoroughly disciplined, there was still a hope that some antidote might be found, that the gates of Paradise had indeed slammed to, but with the exercise of a little patience and ingenuity could be unlocked, that the Fall had occurred by accident.

CHORUS

Lions came loping into the lighted city.

SIMEON

Before the Positive could manifest Itself specifically, it was necessary that nothing should be left that negation could remove; the emancipation of Time from Space had first to be complete, the Revolution of the Images, in which the memories rose up and cast into subjection the senses by Whom hitherto they had been enslaved, successful beyond their wildest dreams, the mirror in which the Soul expected to admire herself so perfectly polished that her natural consolation of vagueness should be utterly withdrawn.

CHORUS

We looked at our Shadow, and, Lo, it was lame.

SIMEON

Before the Infinite could manifest Itself in the finite, it was necessary that man should first have reached that point along his road to Knowledge where, just as it rises from the swamps of Confusion onto the sunny slopes of Objectivity, it forks in opposite directions towards the One and the Many; where, therefore, in order to proceed at all, he must decide which is Real and which only Appearance, yet at the same time cannot escape the knowledge that his choice is arbitrary and subjective.

CHORUS

Promising to meet, we parted forever.

SIMEON

Before the Unconditional could manifest Itself under the conditions of existence, it was necessary that man should first have reached the ultimate frontier of consciousness, the secular limit of memory beyond which there remained but one thing for him to know, his Original Sin, but of this it is impossible for him to become conscious because it is itself what conditions his will to knowledge. For as long as he was in Paradise he could not sin by any conscious intention or act: his as yet unfallen will could only rebel against the truth by taking flight into an unconscious lie; he could only eat of the Tree of Knowledge of Good and Evil by forgetting that its existence was a fiction of the Evil One, that there is only the Tree of Life.

CHORUS

The bravest drew back on the brink of the Abyss.

SIMEON

From the beginning until now God spoke through His prophets. The Word aroused the uncomprehending depths of their flesh to a witnessing fury, and their witness was this: that the Word should be made Flesh. Yet their witness could only be received as long as it was vaguely misunderstood, as long as it seemed either to be neither impossible nor necessary, or necessary but not impossible, or impossible but not necessary; and the prophecy could not therefore be fulfilled. For it could only be fulfilled when it was no longer possible to receive, because it was clearly understood as absurd. The Word could not be made Flesh until men had reached a state of absolute contradiction between clarity and despair in which they would have no choice but either to accept absolutely or to reject absolutely, yet in their choice there should be no element of luck, for they would be fully conscious of what they were accepting or rejecting.

CHORUS

The eternal spaces were congested and depraved.

SIMEON

But here and now the Word which is implicit in the Beginning and in the End is become immediately explicit, and that which hitherto we could only passively fear as the incomprehensible I AM, henceforth we may actively love with comprehension that THOU ART. Wherefore, having seen Him, not in some prophetic vision of what might be, but with the eyes of our own weakness as to what actually is, we are bold to say that we have seen our salvation.

CHORUS

Now and forever, we are not alone.

SIMEON

By the event of this birth the true significance of all other events is defined, for of every other occasion it can be said that it could have been different, but of this birth it is the case that it could in no way be other than it is. And by the existence of this Child, the proper value of all other existences is given, for of every other creature it can be said that it has extrinsic importance but of this Child it is the case that He is in no sense a symbol.

CHORUS

We have right to believe that we really exist.

By Him is dispelled the darkness wherein the fallen will cannot distinguish between temptation and sin, for in Him we become fully conscious of Necessity as our freedom to be tempted, and of Freedom as our necessity to have faith. And by Him is illuminated the time in which we execute those choices through which our freedom is realized or prevented, for the course of History is predictable in the degree to which all men love themselves, and spontaneous in the degree to which each man loves God and through Him his neighbour.

CHORUS

The distresses of choice are our chance to be blessed.

SIMEON

Because in Him the Flesh is united to the Word without magical transformation, Imagination is redeemed from promiscuous fornication with her own images. The tragic conflict of Virtue with Necessity is no longer confined to the Exceptional Hero; for disaster is not the impact of a curse upon a few great families, but issues continually from the hubris of every tainted will. Every invalid is Roland defending the narrow pass against hopeless odds, every stenographer Brünnhilde refusing to renounce her lover's ring which came into existence through the renunciation of love.

Nor is the Ridiculous a species any longer of the Ugly; for since of themselves all men are without merit, all are ironically assisted to their comic bewilderment by the Grace of God. Every Cabinet Minister is the woodcutter's simple-minded son to whom the fishes and the crows are always whispering the whereabouts of the Dancing Water or the Singing Branch, every heiress the washerwoman's butter-fingered daughter on whose pillow the fairy keeps laying the herb that could cure the Prince's mysterious illness.

Nor is there any situation which is essentially more or less interesting than another. Every tea-table is a battlefield littered with old catastrophes and haunted by the vague ghosts of vast issues, every martyrdom an occasion for flip cracks and sententious oratory.

Because in Him all passions find a logical In-Order-That, by Him is the perpetual recurrence of Art assured.

CHORUS

Safe in His silence, our songs are at play.

SIMEON

Because in Him the Word is united to the Flesh without loss of perfection, Reason is redeemed from incestuous fixation on her own Logic, for the One and the Many are simultaneously revealed as real. So that we may no longer, with the Barbarians, deny the Unity, asserting that there are as many gods as there are creatures, nor, with the philosophers, deny the Multiplicity, asserting that God is One who has no need of friends and is indifferent to a World of Time and Quantity and Horror which He did not create, nor, with Israel, may we limit the co-inherence of the One and the Many to a special case, asserting that God is only concerned with and of concern to that People whom out of all that He created He has chosen for His own.

For the Truth is indeed One, without which is no salvation, but the possibilities of real knowledge are as many as are the creatures in the very real and most exciting universe that God creates with and for His love, and it is not Nature which is one public illusion, but we who have each our many private illusions about Nature.

Because in Him abstraction finds a passionate For-The-Sake-Of, by Him is the continuous development of Science assured.

CHORUS

Our lost Appearances are saved by His love.

SIMEON

And because of His visitation, we may no longer desire God as if He were lacking: our redemption is no longer a question of pursuit

183

but of surrender to Him who is always and everywhere present. Therefore at every moment we pray that, following Him, we may depart from our anxiety into His peace.

CHORUS

Its errors forgiven, may our Vision come home.

The Massacre of the Innocents

I

HEROD

Because I am bewildered, because I must decide, because my decision must be in conformity with Nature and Necessity, let me honour those through whom my nature is by necessity what it is.

To Fortune—that I have become Tetrarch, that I have escaped assassination, that at sixty my head is clear and my digestion sound.

To my Father—for the means to gratify my love of travel and study.

To my Mother—for a straight nose.

To Eva, my coloured nurse—for regular habits.

To my brother, Sandy, who married a trapeze-artist and died of drink—for so refuting the position of the Hedonists.

To Mr. Stewart, nicknamed The Carp, who instructed me in the elements of geometry through which I came to perceive the errors of the tragic poets.

To Professor Lighthouse—for his lectures on The Peloponnesian War.

To the stranger on the boat to Sicily—for recommending to me Brown on Resolution.

To my secretary, Miss Button—for admitting that my speeches were inaudible.

There is no visible disorder. No crime—what could be more

innocent than the birth of an artisan's child? Today has been one of those perfect winter days, cold, brilliant, and utterly still, when the bark of the shepherd's dog carries for miles, and the great wild mountains come up quite close to the city walls, and the mind feels intensely awake, and this evening as I stand at this window high up in the citadel there is nothing in the whole magnificent panorama of plain and mountains to indicate that the Empire is threatened by a danger more dreadful than any invasion of Tartars on racing camels or conspiracy of the Praetorian Guard.

Barges are unloading soil fertilizer at the river wharves. Soft drinks and sandwiches may be had in the inns at reasonable prices. Allotment gardening has become popular. The highway to the coast goes straight up over the mountains and the truck-drivers no longer carry guns. Things are beginning to take shape. It is a long time since anyone stole the park benches or murdered the swans. There are children in this province who have never seen a louse, shopkeepers who have never handled a counterfeit coin, women of forty who have never hidden in a ditch except for fun. Yes, in twenty years I have managed to do a little. Not enough, of course. There are villages only a few miles from here where they still believe in witches. There isn't a single town where a good bookshop would pay. One could count on the fingers of one hand the people capable of solving the problem of Achilles and the Tortoise. Still it is a beginning. In twenty years the darkness has been pushed back a few inches. And what, after all, is the whole Empire, with its few thousand square miles on which it is possible to lead the Rational Life, but a tiny patch of light compared with those immense areas of barbaric night that surround it on all sides, that incoherent wilderness of rage and terror, where Mongolian idiots are regarded as sacred and mothers who give birth to twins are instantly put to death, where malaria is treated by yelling, where warriors of superb courage obey the commands of hysterical female impersonators, where the best cuts of meat are reserved for the dead, where, if a white blackbird has been seen, no more work may be done that day, where it is firmly believed that the world was created by a giant with three heads or that the motions of the stars are controlled from the liver of a rogue elephant?

Yet even inside this little civilized patch itself, where, at the cost of heaven knows how much grief and bloodshed, it has been made unnecessary for anyone over the age of twelve to believe in fairies or that First Causes reside in mortal and finite objects, so many are still homesick for that disorder wherein every passion formerly enjoyed a frantic licence. Caesar flies to his hunting lodge pursued by ennui; in the faubourgs of the Capital, Society grows savage, corrupted by silks and scents, softened by sugar and hot water, made insolent by theatres and attractive slaves; and everywhere, including this province, new prophets spring up every day to sound the old barbaric note.

I have tried everything. I have prohibited the sale of crystals and ouija-boards; I have slapped a heavy tax on playing cards; the courts are empowered to sentence alchemists to hard labour in the mines; it is a statutory offence to turn tables or feel bumps. But nothing is really effective. How can I expect the masses to be sensible when, for instance, to my certain knowledge, the captain of my own guard wears an amulet against the Evil Eye, and the richest merchant in the city consults a medium over every important transaction?

Legislation is helpless against the wild prayer of longing that rises, day in, day out, from all these households under my protection: 'O God, put away justice and truth for we cannot understand them and do not want them. Eternity would bore us dreadfully. Leave Thy heavens and come down to our earth of waterclocks and hedges. Become our uncle. Look after Baby, amuse Grandfather, escort Madam to the Opera, help Willy with his home-work, introduce Muriel to a handsome naval officer. Be interesting and weak like us, and we will love you as we love ourselves.'

Reason is helpless, and now even the Poetic Compromise no longer works, all those lovely fairy tales in which Zeus, disguising himself as a swan or a bull or a shower of rain or what-have-you, lay with some beautiful woman and begot a hero. For the Public has grown too sophisticated. Under all the charming metaphors and symbols, it detects the stern command, 'Be and act heroically;' behind the myth of divine origin, it senses the real human excellence that is a reproach to its own baseness. So, with a bellow of rage, it kicks Poetry downstairs and sends for Prophecy. 'Your sister has just insulted me. I asked for a God who should be as like me as possible. What use to me is a God whose divinity consists in doing difficult things that I cannot do or saying clever things that I cannot understand? The God I want and intend to get must be someone I can recognize immediately without having to wait and see what he says or does. There must be nothing in the least extraordinary about him. Produce him at once, please. I'm sick of waiting.'

Today, apparently, judging by the trio who came to see me this morning with an ecstatic grin on their scholarly faces, the job has been done. 'God has been born,' they cried, 'we have seen him ourselves. The World is saved. Nothing else matters.'

One needn't be much of a psychologist to realize that if this rumour is not stamped out now, in a few years it is capable of diseasing the whole Empire, and one doesn't have to be a prophet to predict the consequences if it should.

Reason will be replaced by Revelation. Instead of Rational Law, objective truths perceptible to any who will undergo the necessary intellectual discipline, and the same for all, Knowledge will degenerate into a riot of subjective visions—feelings in the solar plexus induced by undernourishment, angelic images generated by fevers or drugs, dream warnings inspired by the sound of falling water. Whole cosmogonies will be created out of some forgotten personal resentment, complete epics written in private languages, the daubs of school children ranked above the greatest masterpieces.

Idealism will be replaced by Materialism. Priapus will only have to move to a good address and call himself Eros to become the darling of middle-aged women. Life after death will be an eternal dinner party where all the guests are twenty years old. Diverted from its normal and wholesome outlet in patriotism and civic or family pride, the need of the materialistic Masses for some visible Idol to worship will be driven into totally unsocial channels where no education can reach it. Divine honours will be paid to silver tea-pots, shallow depressions in the earth, names on maps, domestic pets, ruined windmills, even in extreme cases, which will become increasingly common, to headaches, or malignant tumours, or four o'clock in the afternoon.

Justice will be replaced by Pity as the cardinal human virtue, and all fear of retribution will vanish. Every cornerboy will congratulate himself: 'I'm such a sinner that God had to come down in person to save me. I must be a devil of a fellow.' Every crook will argue: 'I like committing crimes. God likes forgiving them. Really the world is admirably arranged.' And the ambition of every young cop will be to secure a death-bed repentance. The New Aristocracy will consist exclusively of hermits, bums, and permanent invalids. The Rough Diamond, the Consumptive Whore, the bandit who is good to his mother, the epileptic girl who has a way with animals will be the heroes and heroines of the New Tragedy when the general, the statesman, and the philosopher have become the butt of every farce and satire.

Naturally this cannot be allowed to happen. Civilization must be saved even if this means sending for the military, as I suppose it does. How dreary. Why is it that in the end civilization always has to call in these professional tidiers to whom it is all one whether it be Pythagoras or a homicidal lunatic that they are instructed to exter-minate. O dear, Why couldn't this wretched infant be born some-where else? Why can't people be sensible? I don't want to be horrid. Why can't they see that the notion of a finite God is absurd? Because it is. And suppose, just for the sake of argument, that it isn't, that this story is true, that this child is in some inexplicable manner both God and Man, that he grows up, lives, and dies, without committing a single sin? Would that make life any better? On the contrary it would make it far, far worse. For it could only mean this; that once having shown them how, God would expect every man, whatever his fortune, to lead a sinless life in the flesh and on earth. Then indeed would the human race be plunged into madness and despair. And for me personally at this moment it would mean that God had

given me the power to destroy Himself. I refuse to be taken in. He
could not play such a horrible practical joke. Why should He dislike
me so? I've worked like a slave. Ask anyone you like. I read all
official dispatches without skipping. I've taken elocution lessons. I've
hardly ever taken bribes. How dare He allow me to decide? I've
tried to be good. I brush my teeth every night. I haven't had sex for
a month. I object. I'm a liberal. I want everyone to be happy. I wish
I had never been born.

II

SOLDIERS

When the Sex War ended with the slaughter of the Grandmothers,
They found a bachelor's baby suffocating under them;
Somebody called him George and that was the end of it:
   They hitched him up to the Army.
   Gearge, you old debutante,
   How did you get in the Army?

In the Retreat from Reason he deserted on his rocking-horse
And lived on a fairy's kindness till he tired of kicking her;
He smashed her spectacles and stole her cheque-book and
    mackintosh
   Then cruised his way back to the Army.
   Gearge, you old numero,
   How did you get in the Army?

Before the Diet of Sugar he was using razor-blades
And exited soon after with an allergy to maidenheads;
He discovered a cure of his own, but no one would patent it,
   So he showed up again in the Army.
   Gearge, you old flybynight,
   How did you get in the Army?

When the Vice Crusades were over he was hired by some
    Muscovites
Prospecting for deodorants among the Eskimos;
He was caught by a common cold and condemned to the whiskey
    mines,
   But schemozzled back to the Army.
   Gearge, you old Emperor,
   How did you get in the Army?

Since Peace was signed with Honour he's been minding his
    business;
But, whoops, here comes His Idleness, buttoning his uniform;
Just in tidy time to massacre the Innocents;
   He's come home to roost in the Army.
   Gearge, you old matador,
   Welcome back to the Army.

III

RACHEL

On the Left are grinning dogs, peering down into a solitude too
    deep to fill with roses.
On the Right are sensible sheep, gazing up at a pride where no dream
    can grow.
Somewhere in these unending wastes of delirium is a lost child,
    speaking of Long Ago in the language of wounds.
Tomorrow, perhaps, he will come to himself in Heaven.
But here Grief turns her silence, neither in this direction, nor in that,
    nor for any reason.
And her coldness now is on the earth forever.

The Flight into Egypt

I

JOSEPH

Mirror, let us through the glass
No authority can pass.

MARY

Echo, if the strong should come,
Tell a white lie or be dumb.

VOICES OF THE DESERT

It was visitors' day at the vinegar works
In Tenderloin Town when I tore my time;
A sorrowful snapshot was my sinful wage:
Was that why you left me, elusive bones?
  Come to our bracing desert
  Where eternity is eventful,
    For the weather-glass
    Is set at Alas,
  The thermometer at Resentful.

MARY

The Kingdom of the Robbers lies
Between Time and our memories;

JOSEPH

Fugitives from Space must cross
The waste of the Anonymous.

How should he figure my fear of the dark?
The moment he can he'll remember me,
The silly, he locked in the cellar for fun,
And his dear little doggie shall die in his arms.
  Come to our old-world desert
  Where everyone goes to pieces;
    You can pick up tears
    For souvenirs
  Or genuine diseases.

                    JOSEPH
Geysers and volcanoes give
Sudden comical relief;

                    MARY

And the vulture is a boon
On a dull hot afternoon.

            VOICES OF THE DESERT
All Father's nightingales knew their place,
The gardens were loyal: look at them now.
The roads are so careless, the rivers so rude,
My studs have been stolen; I must speak to the sea.
  Come to our well-run desert
  Where anguish arrives by cable,
    And the deadly sins
    May be bought in tins
  With instructions on the label.

                    MARY
Skulls recurring every mile
Direct the thirsty to the Nile;

JOSEPH

And the jackal's eye at night
Forces Error to keep right.

VOICES OF THE DESERT

In the land of lilies I lost my wits,
Nude as a number all night I ran
With a ghost for a guest along green canals;
By the waters of waking I wept for the weeds.
  Come to our jolly desert
  Where even the dolls go whoring;
    Where cigarette-ends
    Become intimate friends,
  And it's always three in the morning.

JOSEPH AND MARY

Safe in Egypt we shall sigh
For lost insecurity;
Only when her terrors come
Does our flesh feel quite at home.

II

RECITATIVE

Fly, Holy Family, from our immediate rage,
That our future may be freed from our past; retrace
    The footsteps of law-giving
  Moses, back through the sterile waste,

Down to the rotten kingdom of Egypt, the damp
Tired delta where in her season of glory our
    Forefathers sighed in bondage;
  Abscond with the Child to the place

That their children dare not revisit, to the time
    They do not care to remember; hide from our pride
        In our humiliation;
    Fly from our death with our new life.

III

Well, so that is that. Now we must dismantle the tree,
Putting the decorations back into their cardboard boxes—
Some have got broken—and carrying them up into the attic.
The holly and the mistletoe must be taken down and burnt,
And the children got ready for school. There are enough
Left-overs to do, warmed-up, for the rest of the week—
Not that we have much appetite, having drunk such a lot,
Stayed up so late, attempted—quite unsuccessfully—
To love all of our relatives, and in general
Grossly overestimated our powers. Once again
As in previous years we have seen the actual Vision and failed
To do more than entertain it as an agreeable
Possibility, once again we have sent Him away,
Begging though to remain His disobedient servant,
The promising child who cannot keep His word for long.
The Christmas Feast is already a fading memory,
And already the mind begins to be vaguely aware
Of an unpleasant whiff of apprehension at the thought
Of Lent and Good Friday which cannot, after all, now
Be very far off. But, for the time being, here we all are,
Back in the moderate Aristotelian city
Of darning and the Eight-Fifteen, where Euclid's geometry
And Newton's mechanics would account for our experience,
And the kitchen table exists because I scrub it.
It seems to have shrunk during the holidays. The streets
Are much narrower than we remembered; we had forgotten

The office was as depressing as this. To those who have seen
The Child, however dimly, however incredulously
The Time Being is, in a sense, the most trying time of all.
For the innocent children who whispered so excitedly
Outside the locked door where they knew the presents to be
Grew up when it opened. Now, recollecting that moment
We can repress the joy, but the guilt remains conscious;
Remembering the stable where for once in our lives
Everything became a You and nothing was an It.
And craving the sensation but ignoring the cause,
We look round for something, no matter what, to inhibit
Our self-reflection, and the obvious thing for that purpose
Would be some great suffering. So, once we have met the Son,
We are tempted ever after to pray to the Father:
'Lead us into temptation and evil for our sake'.
They will come, all right, don't worry; probably in a form
That we do not expect, and certainly with a force
More dreadful than we can imagine. In the meantime
There are bills to be paid, machines to keep in repair,
Irregular verbs to learn, the Time Being to redeem
From insignificance. The happy morning is over,
The night of agony still to come; the time is noon:
When the Spirit must practise his scales of rejoicing
Without even a hostile audience, and the Soul endure
A silence that is neither for nor against her faith
That God's Will will be done, that, in spite of her prayers,
God will cheat no one, not even the world of its triumph.

IV

CHORUS

He is the Way.
Follow Him through the Land of Unlikeness;
You will see rare beasts, and have unique adventures.

He is the Truth.
Seek Him in the Kingdom of Anxiety;
You will come to a great city that has expected your return for
     years.

He is the Life.
Love Him in the World of the Flesh;
And at your marriage all its occasions shall dance for joy.

The Sea and the Mirror

A Commentary on Shakespeare's The Tempest

TO JAMES AND TANIA STERN

And am I wrong to worship where
Faith cannot doubt nor Hope despair
Since my own soul can grant my prayer?
Speak, God of Visions, plead for me
And tell why I have chosen thee.

Emily Brontë

Preface

(*The* STAGE MANAGER *to the Critics*)

The aged catch their breath,
For the nonchalant couple go
Waltzing across the tightrope
As if there were no death
Or hope of falling down;
The wounded cry as the clown
Doubles his meaning, and O
How the dear little children laugh
When the drums roll and the lovely
Lady is sawn in half.

O what authority gives
Existence its surprise?
Science is happy to answer
That the ghosts who haunt our lives
Are handy with mirrors and wire,
That song and sugar and fire,
Courage and come-hither eyes
Have a genius for taking pains.
But how does one think up a habit?
Our wonder, our terror remains.

Art opens the fishiest eye
To the Flesh and the Devil who heat
The Chamber of Temptation
Where heroes roar and die.

We are wet with sympathy now;
Thanks for the evening; but how
Shall we satisfy when we meet,
Between Shall-I and I-Will,
The lion's mouth whose hunger
No metaphors can fill?

Well, who in his own backyard
Has not opened his heart to the smiling
Secret he cannot quote?
Which goes to show that the Bard
Was sober when he wrote
That this world of fact we love
Is unsubstantial stuff:
All the rest is silence
On the other side of the wall;
And the silence ripeness,
And the ripeness all.

I

Prospero to Ariel

Stay with me, Ariel, while I pack, and with your first free act
　　Delight my leaving; share my resigning thoughts
As you have served my revelling wishes: then, brave spirit,
　　Ages to you of song and daring, and to me
Briefly Milan, then earth. In all, things have turned out better
　　Than I once expected or ever deserved;
I am glad that I did not recover my dukedom till
　　I do not want it; I am glad that Miranda
No longer pays me any attention; I am glad I have freed you,
　　So at last I can really believe I shall die.
For under your influence death is inconceivable:
　　On walks through winter woods, a bird's dry carcass
Agitates the retina with novel images,
　　A stranger's quiet collapse in a noisy street
Is the beginning of much lively speculation,
　　And every time some dear flesh disappears
What is real is the arriving grief; thanks to your service,
　　The lonely and unhappy are very much alive.
But now all these heavy books are no use to me any more, for
　　Where I go, words carry no weight: it is best,
Then, I surrender their fascinating counsel
　　To the silent dissolution of the sea
Which misuses nothing because it values nothing;
　　Whereas man overvalues everything
Yet, when he learns the price is pegged to his valuation,
　　Complains bitterly he is being ruined which, of course, he is.

So kings find it odd they should have a million subjects
    Yet share in the thoughts of none, and seducers
Are sincerely puzzled at being unable to love
    What they are able to possess; so, long ago,
In an open boat, I wept at giving a city,
    Common warmth and touching substance, for a gift
In dealing with shadows. If age, which is certainly
    Just as wicked as youth, look any wiser,
It is only that youth is still able to believe
    It will get away with anything, while age
Knows only too well that it has got away with nothing:
    The child runs out to play in the garden, convinced
That the furniture will go on with its thinking lesson,
    Who, fifty years later, if he plays at all,
Will first ask its kind permission to be excused.

    When I woke into my life, a sobbing dwarf
Whom giants served only as they pleased, I was not what I seemed;
    Beyond their busy backs I made a magic
To ride away from a father's imperfect justice,
    Take vengeance on the Romans for their grammar,
Usurp the popular earth and blot for ever
    The gross insult of being a mere one among many:
Now, Ariel, I am that I am, your late and lonely master,
    Who knows now what magic is;—the power to enchant
That comes from disillusion. What the books can teach one
    Is that most desires end up in stinking ponds,
But we have only to learn to sit still and give no orders,
    To make you offer us your echo and your mirror;
We have only to believe you, then you dare not lie;
    To ask for nothing, and at once from your calm eyes,
With their lucid proof of apprehension and disorder,
    All we are not stares back at what we are. For all things,
In your company, can be themselves: historic deeds
    Drop their hauteur and speak of shabby childhoods

When all they longed for was to join in the gang of doubts
    Who so tormented them; sullen diseases
Forget their dreadful appearance and make silly jokes;
    Thick-headed goodness for once is not a bore.
No one but you had sufficient audacity and eyesight
    To find those clearings where the shy humiliations
Gambol on sunny afternoons, the waterhole to which
    The scarred rogue sorrow comes quietly in the small hours:
And no one but you is reliably informative on hell;
    As you whistle and skip past, the poisonous
Resentments scuttle over your unrevolted feet,
    And even the uncontrollable vertigo,
Because it can scent no shame, is unobliged to strike.

Could he but once see Nature as
    In truth she is for ever,
What oncer would not fall in love?
Hold up your mirror, boy, to do
    Your vulgar friends this favour:
One peep, though, will be quite enough;
    To those who are not true,
A statue with no figleaf has
    A pornographic flavour.

Inform my hot heart straight away
    Its treasure loves another,
But turn to neutral topics then,
Such as the pictures in this room,
    Religion or the Weather;
Pure scholarship in Where and When,
    How Often and With Whom,
Is not for Passion that must play
    The Jolly Elder Brother.

Be frank about our heathen foe,
  For Rome will be a goner
If you soft-pedal the loud beast;
Describe in plain four-letter words
  This dragon that's upon her:
But should our beggars ask the cost,
  Just whistle like the birds;
Dare even Pope or Caesar know
  The price of faith and honour?

Today I am free and no longer need your freedom:
You, I suppose, will be off now to look for likely victims;
  Crowds chasing ankles, lone men stalking glory,
Some feverish young rebel among amiable flowers
  In consultation with his handsome envy,
A punctual plump judge, a fly-weight hermit in a dream
  Of gardens that time is for ever outside—
To lead absurdly by their self-important noses.
  Are you malicious by nature? I don't know.
Perhaps only incapable of doing nothing or of
  Being by yourself, and, for all your wry faces
May secretly be anxious and miserable without
  A master to need you for the work you need.
Are all your tricks a test? If so, I hope you find, next time,
  Someone in whom you cannot spot the weakness
Through which you will corrupt him with your charm. Mine you
    did
  And me you have: thanks to us both, I have broken
Both of the promises I made as an apprentice;—
  To hate nothing and to ask nothing for its love.
All by myself I tempted Antonio into treason;
  However that could be cleared up; both of us know
That both were in the wrong, and neither need be sorry:
  But Caliban remains my impervious disgrace.

We did it, Ariel, between us; you found on me a wish
   For absolute devotion; result–his wreck
That sprawls in the weeds and will not be repaired:
   My dignity discouraged by a pupil's curse,
I shall go knowing and incompetent into my grave.

   The extravagant children, who lately swaggered
Out of the sea like gods, have, I think, been soundly hunted
   By their own devils into their human selves:
To all, then, but me, their pardons. Alonso's heaviness
   Is lost; and weak Sebastian will be patient
In future with his slothful coinscience–after all, it pays;
   Stephano is contracted to his belly, a minor
But a prosperous kingdom; stale Trinculo receives,
   Gratis, a whole fresh repertoire of stories, and
Our younger generation its independent joy.
   Their eyes are big and blue with love; its lighting
Makes even us look new: yes, today it all looks so easy.
   Will Ferdinand be as fond of a Miranda
Familiar as a stocking? Will a Miranda who is
   No longer a silly lovesick little goose,
When Ferdinand and his brave world are her profession,
   Go into raptures over existing at all?
Probably I over-estimate their difficulties;
   Just the same, I am very glad I shall never
Be twenty and have to go through the business again,
   The hours of fuss and fury, the conceit, the expense.

> Sing first that green remote Cockagne
>   Where whiskey-rivers run,
> And every gorgeous number may
>   Be laid by anyone;
> For medicine and rhetoric
>   Lie mouldering on shelves,
> While sad young dogs and stomach-aches
>   Love no one but themselves.

Tell then of witty angels who
  Come only to the beasts,
Of Heirs Apparent who prefer
  Low dives to formal feasts;
For shameless Insecurity
  Prays for a boot to lick,
And many a sore bottom finds
  A sorer one to kick.

Wind up, though, on a moral note; –
  That Glory will go bang,
Schoolchildren shall co-operate,
  And honest rogues must hang;
Because our sound committee man
  Has murder in his heart:
But should you catch a living eye,
  Just wink as you depart.

Now our partnership is dissolved, I feel so peculiar:
  As if I had been on a drunk since I was born
And suddenly now, and for the first time, am cold sober,
  With all my unanswered wishes and unwashed days
Stacked up all round my life; as if through the ages I had
    dreamed
  About some tremendous journey I was taking,
Sketching imaginary landscapes, chasms and cities,
  Cold walls, hot spaces, wild mouths, defeated backs,
Jotting down fictional notes on secrets overheard
  In theatres and privies, banks and mountain inns,
And now, in my old age, I wake, and this journey really exists,
  And I have actually to take it, inch by inch,
Alone and on foot, without a cent in my pocket,
  Through a universe where time is not foreshortened,
No animals talk, and there is neither floating nor flying.

When I am safely home, oceans away in Milan, and
Realize once and for all I shall never see you again,
   Over there, maybe, it won't seem quite so dreadful
Not to be interesting any more, but an old man
   Just like other old men, with eyes that water
Easily in the wind, and a head that nods in the sunshine,
   Forgetful, maladroit, a little grubby,
And to like it. When the servants settle me into a chair
   In some well-sheltered corner of the garden,
And arrange my muffler and rugs, shall I ever be able
   To stop myself from telling them what I am doing,—
Sailing alone, out over seventy thousand fathoms—?
   Yet if I speak, I shall sink without a sound
Into unmeaning abysses. Can I learn to suffer
   Without saying something ironic or funny
On suffering? I never suspected the way of truth
   Was a way of silence where affectionate chat
Is but a robbers' ambush and even good music
   In shocking taste; and you, of course, never told me.
If I peg away at it honestly every moment,
   And have luck, perhaps by the time death pounces
His stumping question, I shall just be getting to know
   The difference between moonshine and daylight. . . .
I see you starting to fidget. I forgot. To you
   That doesn't matter. My dear, here comes Gonzalo
With a solemn face to fetch me. O Ariel, Ariel,
   How I shall miss you. Enjoy your element. Good-bye.

       Sing, Ariel, sing,
       Sweetly, dangerously
       Out of the sour
       And shiftless water,
       Lucidly out
       Of the dozing tree,

Entrancing, rebuking
The raging heart
With a smoother song
Than this rough world,
Unfeeling god.

O brilliantly, lightly,
Of separation,
Of bodies and death,
Unanxious one, sing
To man, meaning me,
As now, meaning always,
In love or out,
Whatever that mean,
Trembling he takes
The silent passage
Into discomfort.

II

The Supporting Cast, Sotto Voce

ANTONIO
As all the pigs have turned back into men
And the sky is auspicious and the sea
Calm as a clock, we can all go home again.

Yes, it undoubtedly looks as if we
Could take life as easily now as tales
Write ever-after: not only are the

Two heads silhouetted against the sails
–And kissing, of course–well-built, but the lean
Fool is quite a person, the fingernails

Of the dear old butler for once quite clean,
And the royal passengers quite as good
As rustics, perhaps better, for they mean

What they say, without, as a rustic would,
Casting reflections on the courtly crew.
Yes, Brother Prospero, your grouping could

Not be more effective: given a few
Incomplete objects and a nice warm day,
What a lot a little music can do.

Dotted about the deck they doze or play,
Your loyal subjects all, grateful enough
To know their place and believe what you say.

Antonio, sweet brother, has to laugh.
How easy you have made it to refuse
Peace to your greatness! Break your wand in half,

The fragments will join; burn your books or lose
Them in the sea, they will soon reappear,
Not even damaged: as long as I choose

To wear my fashion, whatever you wear
Is a magic robe; while I stand outside
Your circle, the will to charm is still there.

As I exist so you shall be denied,
Forced to remain our melancholy mentor,
The grown-up man, the adult in his pride,

Never have time to curl up at the centre
Time turns on when completely reconciled,
Never become and therefore never enter
The green occluded pasture as a child.
>   *Your all is partial, Prospero;*
>   *My will is all my own:*
>   *Your need to love shall never know*
>   *Me: I am I, Antonio,*
>   *By choice myself alone.*

FERDINAND

Flesh, fair, unique, and you, warm secret that my kiss
Follows into meaning Miranda, solitude
Where my omissions are, still possible, still good,
Dear Other at all times, retained as I do this,

From moment to moment as you enrich them so
Inherit me, my cause, as I would cause you now
With mine your sudden joy, two wonders as one vow
Pre-empting all, here, there, for ever, long ago.

I would smile at no other promise than touch, taste, sight,
Were there not, my enough, my exaltation, to bless
As world is offered world, as I hear it tonight

Pleading with ours for us, another tenderness
That neither without either could or would possess,
The Right Required Time, The Real Right Place, O Light.

> *One bed is empty, Prospero,*
> *My person is my own;*
> *Hot Ferdinand will never know*
> *The flame with which Antonio*
> *Burns in the dark alone.*

STEPHANO

Embrace me, belly, like a bride;
Dear daughter, for the weight you drew
From humble pie and swallowed pride,
Believe the boast in which you grew:
Where mind meets matter, both should woo;
Together let us learn that game
The high play better than the blue:
A lost thing looks for a lost name.

Behind your skirts your son must hide
When disappointments bark and boo;
Brush my heroic ghosts aside,
Wise nanny, with a vulgar pooh:
Exchanging cravings we pursue
Alternately a single aim:
Between the bottle and the 'loo'

A lost thing looks for a lost name.
Though in the long run satisfied,
The will of one by being two
At every moment is denied;
Exhausted glasses wonder who
Is self and sovereign, I or You?
We cannot both be what we claim,
The real Stephano – Which is true?
A lost thing looks for a lost name.

Child? Mother? Either grief will do;
The need for pardon is the same,
The contradiction is not new:
A lost thing looks for a lost name.

One glass is untouched, Prospero,
  My nature is my own;
Inert Stephano does not know
The feast at which Antonio
  Toasts One and One alone.

GONZALO
Evening, grave, immense, and clear,
Overlook our ship whose wake
Lingers undistorted on
Sea and silence; I look back
For the last time as the sun
Sets behind that island where
All our loves were altered: yes,
My prediction came to pass,
Yet I am not justified,
And I weep but not with pride.
Not in me the credit for
Words I uttered long ago
Whose glad meaning I betrayed;

Truths today admitted, owe
Nothing to the councillor
In whose booming eloquence
Honesty became untrue.
Am I not Gonzalo who
By his self-reflection made
Consolation an offence?

There was nothing to explain:
Had I trusted the Absurd
And straightforward note by note
Sung exactly what I heard,
Such immediate delight
Would have taken there and then
Our common welkin by surprise,
All would have begun to dance
Jigs of self-deliverance.
It was I prevented this,
Jealous of my native ear,
Mine the art which made the song
Sound ridiculous and wrong,
I whose interference broke
The gallop into jog-trot prose
And by speculation froze
Vision into an idea,
Irony into a joke,
Till I stood convicted of
Doubt and insufficient love.

Farewell, dear island of our wreck:
All have been restored to health,
All have seen the Commonwealth,
There is nothing to forgive.
Since a storm's decision gave
His subjective passion back
To a meditative man,

Even reminiscence can
Comfort ambient troubles like
Some ruined tower by the sea
Whence boyhoods growing and afraid
Learn a formula they need
In solving their mortality,
Even rusting flesh can be
A simple locus now, a bell
The Already There can lay
Hands on if at any time
It should feel inclined to say
To the lonely–'Here I am',
To the anxious–'All is well'.

One tongue is silent. Prospero,
My language is my own;
Decayed Gonzalo does not know
The shadow that Antonio
Talks to, at noon, alone.

ADRIAN *and* FRANCISCO

Good little sunbeams must learn to fly,
But it's madly ungay when the goldfish die.

One act is censored, Prospero,
My audience is my own;
Nor Adrian nor Francisco know
The drama that Antonio
Plays in his head alone.

ALONSO

Dear Son, when the warm multitudes cry,
Ascend your throne majestically,
But keep in mind the waters where fish
See sceptres descending with no wish
To touch them; sit regal and erect,

But imagine the sands where a crown
Has the status of a broken-down
Sofa or mutilated statue:
Remember as bells and cannon boom
The cold deep that does not envy you,
The sunburnt superficial kingdom
Where a king is an object.

Expect no help from others, for who
Talk sense to princes or refer to
The scorpion in official speeches
As they unveil some granite Progress
Leading a child and holding a bunch
Of lilies? In their Royal Zoos the
Shark and the octopus are tactfully
Omitted; synchronized clocks march on
Within their powers: without, remain
The ocean flats where no subscription
Concerts are given, the desert plain
Where there is nothing for lunch.

Only your darkness can tell you what
A prince's ornate mirror dare not,
Which you should fear more—the sea in which
A tyrant sinks entangled in rich
Robes while a mistress turns a white back
Upon his splutter, or the desert
Where an emperor stands in his shirt
While his diary is read by sneering
Beggars, and far off he notices
A lean horror flapping and hopping
Toward him with inhuman swiftness:
Learn from your dreams what you lack,

For as your fears are, so must you hope.
The Way of Justice is a tightrope
Where no prince is safe for one instant
Unless he trust his embarrassment,
As in his left ear the siren sings
Meltingly of water and a night
Where all flesh had peace, and on his right
The efreet offers a brilliant void
Where his mind could be perfectly clear
And all his limitations destroyed:
Many young princes soon disappear
To join all the unjust kings.

So, if you prosper, suspect those bright
Mornings when you whistle with a light
Heart. You are loved; you have never seen
The harbour so still, the park so green,
So many well-fed pigeons upon
Cupolas and triumphal arches,
So many stags and slender ladies
Beside the canals. Remember when
Your climate seems a permanent home
For marvellous creatures and great men,
What griefs and convulsions startled Rome,
Ecbatana, Babylon.

How narrow the space, how slight the chance
For civil pattern and importance
Between the watery vagueness and
The triviality of the sand,
How soon the lively trip is over
From loose craving to sharp aversion,
Aimless jelly to paralysed bone:
At the end of each successful day

Remember that the fire and the ice
Are never more than one step away
From the temperate city; it is
But a moment to either.

But should you fail to keep your kingdom
And, like your father before you, come
Where thought accuses and feeling mocks,
Believe your pain: praise the scorching rocks
For their desiccation of your lust,
Thank the bitter treatment of the tide
For its dissolution of your pride,
That the whirlwind may arrange your will
And the deluge release it to find
The spring in the desert, the fruitful
Island in the sea, where flesh and mind
Are delivered from mistrust.

Blue the sky beyond her humming sail
As I sit today by our ship's rail
Watching exuberant porpoises
Escort us homeward and writing this
For you to open when I am gone:
Read it, Ferdinand, with the blessing
Of Alonso, your father, once King
Of Naples, now ready to welcome
Death, but rejoicing in a new love,
A new peace, having heard the solemn
Music strike and seen the statue move
To forgive our illusion.

> One crown is lacking, Prospero,
>   My empire is my own;
> Dying Alonso does not know
> The diadem Antonio
>   Wears in his world alone.

MASTER *and* BOATSWAIN

At Dirty Dick's and Sloppy Joe's
   We drank our liquor straight,
Some went upstairs with Margery,
   And some, alas, with Kate;
And two by two like cat and mouse
The homeless played at keeping house.

There Wealthy Meg, the Sailor's Friend,
   And Marion, cow-eyed,
Opened their arms to me but I
   Refused to step inside;
I was not looking for a cage
In which to mope in my old age.

The nightingales are sobbing in
   The orchards of our mothers,
And hearts that we broke long ago
   Have long been breaking others;
Tears are round, the sea is deep:
Roll them overboard and sleep.

   One gaze points elsewhere, Prospero,
     My compass is my own;
   Nostalgic sailors do not know
   The waters where Antonio
     Sails on and on alone.

SEBASTIAN

My rioters all disappear, my dream
Where Prudence flirted with a naked sword,
Securely vicious, crumbles; it is day;
Nothing has happened; we are all alive:
I am Sebastian, wicked still, my proof
Of mercy that I wake without a crown.

What sadness signalled to our children's day
Where each believed all wishes wear a crown
And anything pretended is alive,
That one by one we plunged into that dream
Of solitude and silence where no sword
Will ever play once it is called a proof?

The arrant jewel singing in his crown
Persuaded me my brother was a dream
I should not love because I had no proof,
Yet all my honesty assumed a sword;
To think his death I thought myself alive
And stalked infected through the blooming day.

The lie of Nothing is to promise proof
To any shadow that there is no day
Which cannot be extinguished with some sword,
To want and weakness that the ancient crown
Envies the childish head, murder a dream
Wrong only while its victim is alive,

O blessed be bleak Exposure on whose sword,
Caught unawares, we prick ourselves alive!
Shake Failure's bruising fist! Who else would crown
Abominable error with a proof?
I smile because I tremble, glad today
To be ashamed, not anxious, not a dream.

Children are playing, brothers are alive,
And not a heart or stomach asks for proof
That all this dearness is no lovers' dream;
Just Now is what it might be every day,
Right Here is absolute and needs no crown,
Ermine or trumpets, protocol or sword.

In dream all sins are easy, but by day
It is defeat gives proof we are alive;
The sword we suffer is the guarded crown.

One face cries nothing, Prospero,
    My conscience is my own;
Pallid Sebastian does not know
The dream in which Antonio
    Fights the white bull alone.

TRINCULO

Mechanic, merchant, king,
Are warmed by the cold clown
Whose head is in the clouds
And never can get down.

Into a solitude
Undreamed of by their fat
Quick dreams have lifted me;
The north wind steals my hat,

On clear days I can see
Green acres far below,
And the red roof where I
Was Little Trinculo.

There lies that solid world
These hands can never reach;
My history, my love,
Is but a choice of speech.

A terror shakes my tree,
A flock of words fly out,
Whereat a laughter shakes
The busy and devout.

Wild images, come down
Out of your freezing sky,
That I, like shorter men,
May get my joke and die.

One note is jarring, Prospero,
  My humour is my own;
Tense Trinculo will never know
The paradox Antonio
  Laughs at, in woods, alone.

MIRANDA

My Dear One is mine as mirrors are lonely,
As the poor and sad are real to the good king,
And the high green hill sits always by the sea.

Up jumped the Black Man behind the elder tree,
Turned a somersault and ran away waving;
My Dear One is mine as mirrors are lonely.

The Witch gave a squawk; her venomous body
Melted into light as water leaves a spring,
And the high green hill sits always by the sea.

At the crossroads, too, the Ancient prayed for me;
Down his wasted cheeks tears of joy were running:
My Dear One is mine as mirrors are lonely.

He kissed me awake, and no one was sorry;
The sun shone on sails, eyes, pebbles, anything,
And the high green hill sits always by the sea.

So, to remember our changing garden, we
Are linked as children in a circle dancing:
My Dear One is mine as mirrors are lonely,
And the high greeen hill sits always by the sea.

> One link is missing, Prospero,
>   My magic is my own;
> Happy Miranda does not know
> The figure that Antonio,
> The Only One, Creation's O
>   Dances for Death alone.

III

Caliban to the Audience

If now, having dismissed your hired impersonators with verdicts ranging from the laudatory orchid to the disgusted and disgusting egg, you ask and, of course, notwithstanding the conscious fact of his irrevocable absence, you instinctively *do* ask for our so good, so great, so dead author to stand before the finally lowered curtain and take his shyly responsible bow for this, his latest, ripest production, it is I—my reluctance is, I can assure you, co-equal with your dismay—who will always loom thus wretchedly into your confused picture, for, in default of the all-wise, all-explaining master you would speak *to*, who else at least can, who else indeed must respond to your bewildered cry, but its very echo, the begged question you would speak to him *about*.

*   *   *

We must own [*for the present I speak your echo*] to a nervous perplexity not unmixed, frankly, with downright resentment. How *can* we grant the indulgence for which in his epilogue your personified type of the creative so lamely, tamely pleaded? Imprisoned, by you, in the mood doubtful, loaded, by you, with distressing embarrassments, we are, we submit, in no position to set *anyone* free.

Our native Muse, heaven knows and heaven be praised, is not exclusive. Whether out of the innocence of a childlike heart to whom all things are pure, or with the serenity of a status so majestic that the mere keeping up of tones and appearances, the suburban wonder as to what the strait-laced Unities might possibly think, or sad sour Probability possibly say, are questions for which she doesn't because she needn't, she hasn't in her lofty maturity any longer, to care a rap, she invites, dear generous-hearted creature that she is, just *tout le monde* to drop in at any time so that her famous, memorable, sought-after evenings present to the speculative eye an ever-shining, never-tarnished proof of her amazing unheard-of power to combine and happily contrast, to make *every* shade of the social and moral palette contribute to the general richness, of the skill, unapproached and unattempted by Grecian aunt or Gallic sister, with which she can skate full tilt toward the forbidden incoherence and then, in the last split second, on the shuddering edge of the bohemian standard-less abyss, effect her breathtaking triumphant turn.

No timid segregation by rank or taste for her, no prudent listing into those who will, who might, who certainly would not get on, no nicely graded scale of invitations to heroic formal Tuesdays, young comic Thursdays, al fresco farcical Saturdays. No, the real, the only, test of the theatrical as of the gastronomic, her practice confidently wagers, is the mixed perfected brew.

As he looks in on her, so marvellously at home with all her cosy swarm about her, what accents will not assault the new arrival's ear, the magnificent tropes of tragic defiance and despair, the repartee of the high humour, the pun of the very low, cultured drawl and manly illiterate bellow, yet all of them gratefully doing their huge or tiny best to make the party go?

And if, assured by her smiling wave that of course he may, he should presently set out to explore her vast and rambling mansion, to do honour to its dear odd geniuses of local convenience and proportion, its multiplied deities of mysterious stair and interesting alcove, not one of the laughing groups and engrossed warmed couples that he keeps 'surprising' – the never-ending surprise for him is that he doesn't seem to – but affords some sharper instance of relations he would have been the last to guess at, choleric prince at his ease with lymphatic butler, moist hand taking so to dry, youth getting on quite famously with stingy cold old age, some stranger vision of the large loud liberty violently rocking yet never, he is persuaded, finally upsetting the jolly crowded boat.

What, he may well ask, has the gracious goddess done to all these people that, at her most casual hint, they should so trustingly, so immediately take off those heavy habits one thinks of them as having for their health and happiness day and night to wear, without in this unfamiliar unbuttoned state—the notable absence of the slightest shiver or not-quite-inhibited sneeze is indication positive—for a second feeling the draught? Is there, could there be, *any* miraculous suspension of the wearily historic, the dingily geographic, the dully drearily sensible beyond her faith, her charm, her love, to command? Yes, there could be, yes, alas, indeed yes, O there is, right here, right now before us, the situation present.

How *could* you, you who are one of the oldest habitués at these delightful functions, one, possibly the closest, of her trusted inner circle, how could you be guilty of the incredible unpardonable treachery of bringing along the one creature, as you above all men must have known, whom she cannot and will not under any circumstances stand, the solitary exception she is not at any hour of the day or night at home to, the unique case that her attendant spirits have absolute instructions never, neither at the front door nor at the back, to admit?

At Him and at Him only does she draw the line, not because there are any limits to her sympathy but precisely because there are none. Just because of all she is and all she means to be, she cannot conceivably tolerate in her presence the represented principle of *not* sympathizing, *not* associating, *not* amusing, the only child of her Awful Enemy, the rival whose real name she will never sully her lips with—'that envious witch' is sign sufficient—who does not rule but defiantly is the unrectored chaos.

All along and only too well she has known what would happen if, by any careless mischance—of conscious malice she never dreamed till now—He should ever manage to get in. She foresaw what He would do to the conversation, lying in wait for its vision of private love or public justice to warm to an Egyptian brilliance and then

227

with some fishlike odour or *bruit insolite* snatching the visionaries back tongue-tied and blushing to the here and now; she foresaw what He would do to the arrangements, breaking, by a refusal to keep in step, the excellent order of the dancing ring, and ruining supper by knocking over the loaded appetising tray; worst of all, she foresaw, she dreaded, what He would end up by doing to her, that, not content with upsetting her guests, with spoiling their fun, His progress from outrage to outrage would not relent before the gross climax of His making, horror unspeakable, a pass at her virgin self.

Let us suppose, even, that in your eyes she is by no means as we have always fondly imagined, your dear friend, that what we have just witnessed was not what it seemed to us, the inexplicable betrayal of a life-long sacred loyalty, but your long-premeditated just revenge, the final evening up of some ancient never-forgotten score, then even so, why make us suffer who have never, in all conscience, done you harm? Surely the theatrical relation, no less than the marital is governed by the sanely decent general law that, before visitors, in front of the children or the servants, there shall be no indiscreet revelation of animosity, no 'scenes', that, no matter to what intolerable degrees of internal temperature and pressure restraint may raise both the injured and the guilty, nevertheless such restraint is applied to tones and topics, the exhibited picture must be still as always the calm and smiling one the most malicious observer can see nothing wrong with, and not until the last of those whom manifested anger or mistrust would embarrass or amuse or not be good for have gone away or out or up, is the voice raised, the table thumped, the suspicious letter snatched at or the outrageous bill furiously waved.

For we, after all – you cannot have forgotten this – are strangers to her. We have never claimed her acquaintance, knowing as well as she that we do not and never could belong on her side of the curtain. All we have ever asked for is that for a few hours the curtain should be left undrawn, so as to allow our humble ragged selves the privilege of craning and gaping at the splendid goings-on inside. We most emphatically do *not* ask that she should speak to us, or try to understand us; on the contrary our one desire has always been that she should preserve for ever her old high strangeness, for what delights us about her world is just that it neither is nor possibly could become one in which we could breathe or behave, that in her house the right of innocent passage should remain so universal that the same neutral space accommodates the conspirator and his victim; the generals of both armies, the chorus of patriots and the choir of nuns, palace and farmyard, cathedral and smugglers' cave, that time should never revert to that intransigent element we are so ineluctably and only too familiarly in, but remain the passive good-natured creature she and her friends can by common consent do anything they like with–(it is not surprising that they should take advantage of their strange power and so frequently skip hours and days and even years: the dramatic mystery is that they should always so unanimously agree upon exactly how many hours and days and years to skip)–that upon their special constitutions the moral law should continue to operate so exactly that the timid not only deserve but actually win the fair, and it is the socially and physically unemphatic David who lays low the gorilla-chested Goliath with one well-aimed custard pie, that in their blessed climate, the manifestation of the inner life should always remain so easy and habitual that a sudden eruption of musical and metaphorical power is instantly recognized as standing for grief and disgust, an elegant *contrapposto* for violent death, and that consequently the picture which they in there present to us out here is always that of the perfectly tidiable case of disorder, the beautiful and serious problem exquisitely set without a single superfluous datum and insoluble with less, the expert landing of all the passengers with all their luggage safe and sound in the best of health and spirits and without so much as a scratch or a bruise.

Into that world of freedom without anxiety, sincerity without loss of vigour, feeling that loosens rather than ties the tongue, we are not, we reiterate, so blinded by presumption to our proper status and interest as to expect or even wish at any time to enter, far less to dwell there.

Must we–it seems oddly that we must–remind you that our existence does not, like hers, enjoy an infinitely indicative mood, an eternally present tense, a limitlessly active voice, for in our shambling, slovenly makeshift world any two persons, whether domestic first or neighbourly second, require and necessarily presuppose in both their numbers and in all their cases, the whole inflected gamut of an alien third, since, without a despised or dreaded Them to turn the back *on*, there could be no intimate or affectionate Us to turn the eye *to*; that, *chez nous*, space is never the whole uninhibited circle but always some segment, its eminent domain upheld by two co-ordinates. There always has been and always will be not only the vertical boundary, the river on this side of which initiative and honesty stroll arm in arm wearing sensible clothes, and beyond which is a savage elsewhere swarming with contagious diseases, but also its horizontal counterpart, the railroad above which houses stand in their own grounds, each equipped with a garage and a beautiful woman, sometimes with several, and below which huddled shacks provide a squeezing shelter to collarless herds who eat blancmange and have never said anything witty. Make the case as special as you please; take the tamest congregation or the wildest faction; take, say, a college. What river and railroad did for the grosser instance, lawn and corridor do for the more refined, dividing the tender who value from the tough who measure, the superstitious who still sacrifice to causation from the heretics who have already reduced the worship of truth to bare description, and so creating the academic fields to be guarded with umbrella and learned periodical against the trespass of any unqualified stranger not a whit less jealously than the game-preserve is protected from the poacher by the unamiable shot-gun. For without these prohibitive frontiers we should never know who we were or what we wanted. It is they who donate to neighbourhood all its accuracy and vehemence. It is thanks to them that we do know with whom to associate, make love, exchange recipes and jokes, go mountain climbing or sit side by side fishing from piers. It is thanks to them, too, that we know against whom to rebel. We *can* shock our parents by visiting the dives below the railroad tracks, we *can* amuse ourselves on what would otherwise have been a very dull evening indeed, in plotting to seize the post office across the river.

Of course, these several private regions must together comprise one public whole – we would never deny that logic and instinct require that. Of course, We and They are united in the candid glare of the same commercial hope by day, and the soft refulgence of the same erotic nostalgia by night but – and this is our point – without our privacies of situation, our local idioms of triumph and mishap, our different doctrines concerning the transubstantiation of the larger pinker bun on the terrestrial dish for which the mature sense may reasonably water and the adult fingers furtively or unabashedly go for, our specific choices of which hill it would be romantic to fly away over or what sea it would be exciting to run away to, our peculiar visions of the absolute stranger with a spontaneous longing for the lost who will adopt our misery not out of desire but pure compassion, without, in short, our devoted pungent expression of the partial and contrasted, the Whole would have no importance and its Day and Night no interest.

So, too, with Time who, in our auditorium, is not her dear old buffer so anxious to please everybody, but a prim magistrate whose court never adjourns, and from whose decisions, as he laconically sentences one to loss of hair and talent, another to seven days' chastity, and a third to boredom for life, there is no appeal. We should not be sitting here now, washed, warm, well-fed, in seats we have paid for, unless there were others who are not here; our liveliness and good-humour, such as they are, are those of survivors, conscious that there are others who have not been so fortunate, others who did not succeed in navigating the narrow passage or to whom the natives were not friendly, others whose streets were chosen by the explosion or through whose country the famine turned aside from ours to go, others who failed to repel the invasion of bacteria or to crush the insurrection of their bowels, others who lost their suit against their parents or were ruined by wishes they could not adjust or murdered by resentments they could not control; aware of some who were better and bigger but from whom, only the other day, Fortune withdrew her hand in sudden disgust, now nervously playing chess with drunken sea-captains in sordid cafés on the equator or the Arctic Circle, or lying, only a few blocks away, strapped and screaming on iron beds or dropping to naked pieces in damp graves. And shouldn't you too, dear master, reflect – forgive us for mentioning it – that we might very well not have been attending a production of yours this evening, had not some other and maybe – who can tell? – brighter talent married a barmaid or turned religious and shy or gone down in a liner with all his manuscripts, the loss recorded only in the corner of some country newspaper below A Poultry Lover's Jottings?

You yourself, we seem to remember, have spoken of the conjured spectacle as 'a mirror held up to nature', a phrase misleading in its aphoristic sweep but indicative at least of one aspect of the relation between the real and the imagined, their mutual reversal of value, for isn't the essential artistic strangeness to which your citation of the sinisterly biassed image would point just this: that on the far side of the mirror the general will to compose, to form at all costs a felicitous pattern becomes the *necessary cause* of any particular effort to live or act or love or triumph or vary, instead of being as, in so far as it emerges at all, it is on this side, their *accidental effect*?

Does Ariel – to nominate the spirit of reflection in your terms – call for manifestation? Then neither modesty nor fear of reprisals excuses the one so called on from publicly confessing that she cheated at croquet or that he committed incest in a dream. Does He demand concealment? Then their nearest and dearest must be deceived by disguises of sex and age which anywhere else would at once attract the attentions of the police or the derisive whistle of the awful schoolboy. That is the price asked, and how promptly and gladly paid, for universal reconciliation and peace, for the privilege of all galloping together past the finishing post neck and neck.

How then, we continue to wonder, knowing all this, could you act as if you did not, as if you did not realize that the embarrassing compresence of the absolutely natural, incorrigibly right-handed,

232

and, to any request for co-operation, utterly negative, with the enthusiastically self-effacing would be a simultaneous violation of both worlds, as if you were not perfectly well aware that the magical musical condition, the orphic spell that turns the fierce dumb greedy beasts into grateful guides and oracles who will gladly take one anywhere and tell one everything free of charge, is precisely and simply that of his finite immediate note *not*, under any circumstances, being struck, of its not being tentatively whispered, far less positively banged.

Are we not bound to conclude, then, that, whatever snub to the poetic you may have intended incidentally to administer, your profounder motive in so introducing Him to them among whom, because He doesn't belong, He couldn't appear as anything but His distorted parody, a deformed and savage slave, was to deal a mortal face-slapping insult to us among whom He does and is, moreover, all grossness turned to glory, no less a person than the nude august elated archer of our heaven, the darling single son of Her who, in her right milieu, is certainly no witch but the most sensible of all the gods, whose influence is as sound as it is pandemic, on the race-track no less than in the sleeping cars of the Orient Express, our great white Queen of Love herself?

But even that is not the worst we suspect you of. If your words have not buttered any parsnips, neither have they broken any bones. He, after all, can come back to us now to be comforted and respected, perhaps, after the experience of finding Himself for a few hours and for the first time in His life not wanted, more fully and freshly appreciative of our affection than He has always been in the past; as for His dear mother, She is far too grand and far too busy to hear or care what you say or think. If only we were certain that your malice was confined to the verbal affront, we should long ago have demanded our money back and gone whistling home to bed. Alas, in addition to resenting what you have openly said, we fear even more what you may secretly have done. Is it possible that, not content with inveigling Caliban into Ariel's kingdom, you have also let loose Ariel in Caliban's? We note with alarm that when the other members of the final tableau were dismissed, He was not returned to His arboreal confinement as He should have been. Where is He now? For if the intrusion of the real has disconcerted and incommoded the poetic, that is a mere bagatelle compared to the damage which the poetic would inflict if it ever succeeded in intruding upon the real. We want no Ariel here, breaking down our picket fences in the name of fraternity, seducing our wives in the name of romance, and robbing us of our sacred pecuniary deposits in the name of justice. Where is Ariel? What have you done with Him? For we won't, we daren't leave until you give us a satisfactory answer.

*   *   *

Such (*let me cease to play your echo and return to my officially natural role*) – such are your questions, are they not, but before I try to deal with them, I must ask for your patience, while I deliver a special message for our late author to those few among you, if indeed there be any – I have certainly heard no comment yet from them – who have come here, not to be entertained but to learn; that is, to any gay apprentice in the magical art who may have chosen this specimen of the prestidigitatory genus to study this evening in the hope of grasping more clearly just how the artistic contraption works, of observing some fresh detail in the complex process by which the heady wine of amusement is distilled from the grape of composition. The rest of you I must beg for a little while to sit back and relax as the remarks I have now to make do not concern you; your turn will follow later.

*   *   *

So, strange young man, – it is at his command, remember, that I say this to you; whether I agree with it or not is neither here nor there – you have decided on the conjurer's profession. Somewhere, in the middle of a salt marsh or at the bottom of a kitchen garden or on the top of a bus, you heard imprisoned Ariel call for help, and it is now a liberator's face that congratulates you from your shaving

234

mirror every morning. As you walk the cold streets hatless, or sit over coffee and doughnuts in the corner of a cheap restaurant, your secret has already set you apart from the howling merchants and transacting multitudes to watch with fascinated distaste the bellowing barging banging passage of the awkward profit-seeking elbow, the dazed eye of the gregarious acquisitive condition. Lying awake at night in your single bed you are conscious of a power by which you will survive the wallpaper of your boardinghouse or the expensive bourgeois horrors of your home. Yes, Ariel is grateful; He does come when you call, He does tell you all the gossip He overhears on the stairs, all the goings-on He observes through the keyhole; He really is willing to arrange anything you care to ask for, and you are rapidly finding out the right orders to give—who should be killed in the hunting accident, which couple to send into the cast-iron shelter, what scent will arouse a Norwegian engineer, how to get the young hero from the country lawyer's office to the Princess' reception, when to mislay the letter, where the cabinet minister should be reminded of his mother, why the dishonest valet must be a martyr to indigestion but immune from the common cold.

As the gay productive months slip by, in spite of fretful discouraged days, of awkward moments of misunderstanding or rather, seen retrospectively as happily cleared up and got over, verily because of them, you are definitely getting the hang of this, at first so novel and bewildering, relationship between magician and familiar, whose duty it is to sustain your infinite conceptual appetite with vivid concrete experiences. And, as the months turn into years, your wonder-working romance into an economic habit, the encountered case of good or evil in our wide world of property and boredom which leaves you confessedly and unsympathetically at a loss, the aberrant phase in the whole human cycle of ecstasy and exhaustion with which you are imperfectly familiar, become increasingly rare. No perception however *petite*, no notion however subtle, escapes your attention or baffles your understanding: on entering any room you immediately distinguish the wasters who throw away their fruit half-eaten from the preservers who bottle all the summer; as the passengers file down the ship's gangway you unerringly guess which suitcase contains indecent novels; a five-minute chat about the weather or the coming elections is all you require to diagnose any distemper, however self-assured, for by then your eye has already spotted the tremor of the lips in that infinitesimal moment while the lie was getting its balance, your ear already picked up the heart's low whimper which the capering legs were determined to stifle, your nose detected on love's breath the trace of ennui which foretells his early death, or the despair just starting to smoulder at the base of the scholar's brain which years hence will suddenly blow it up with one appalling laugh: in every case you can prescribe the saving treatment called for, knowing at once when it may be gentle and remedial when all that is needed is soft music and a pretty girl, and when it must be drastic and surgical, when nothing will do any good but political disgrace or financial and erotic failure. If I seem to attribute these powers to you when the eyes, the ears, the nose, the putting two and two together are, of course, all His, and yours only the primitive wish to know, it is a rhetorical habit I have caught from your, in the main juvenile and feminine, admirers whose naïve unawareness of whom they ought properly to thank and praise you see no point in, for mere accuracy's stuffy sake, correcting.

Anyway, the partnership is a brilliant success. On you go together to ever greater and faster triumphs; ever more major grows the accumulated work, ever more masterly the manner, sound even at its pale sententious worst, and at its best the rich red personal flower of the grave and grand, until one day which you can never either at the time or later identify exactly, your strange fever reaches its crisis and from now on begins, ever so slowly, maybe to subside. At first you cannot tell what or why is the matter; you have only a vague feeling that it is no longer between you so smooth and sweet as it used to be. Sour silences appear, at first only for an occasional moment, but progressively more frequently and more prolonged, curdled moods in which you cannot for the life of you think of any request to make, and His dumb standing around, waiting for orders gets inexplicably but maddeningly on your nerves, until presently, to your amazement, you hear yourself asking Him if He wouldn't like a vacation and are shocked by your feeling of intense disappointment when He who has always hitherto so immediately and recklessly taken your slightest hint, says gauchely 'No'. So it goes on from exasperated bad to desperate worst until you realize in despair that there is nothing for it but you two to part. Collecting all your strength for the distasteful task, you finally manage to stammer or shout 'You are free. Good-bye', but to your dismay He whose obedience through all the enchanted years has never been less than perfect, now refuses to budge. Striding up to Him in fury, you glare into His unblinking eyes and stop dead, transfixed with horror at seeing reflected there, not what you had always expected to see, a conqueror smiling at a conqueror, both promising mountains and marvels, but a gibbering fist-clenched creature with which you are all too unfamiliar, for this is the first time indeed that you have met the only subject that you have, who is not a dream amenable to magic but the all too solid flesh you must acknowledge as your own; at last you have come face to face with me, and are appalled to learn how far I am from being, in any sense, your dish; how completely lacking in that poise and calm and all-forgiving because all-understanding good nature which to the critical eye is so wonderfully and domestically present on every page of your published inventions.

But where, may I ask, should I have acquired them, when, like a society mother who, although she is, of course, as she tells everyone, absolutely *devoted* to her child, simply *cannot* leave the dinner table just now and really *must* be in Le Touquet tomorrow, and so leaves him in charge of servants she doesn't know or boarding schools she has never seen, you have never in all these years taken the faintest personal interest in me? 'Oh!' you protestingly gasp, 'but how can you say such a thing, after I've toiled and moiled and worked my fingers to the bone, trying to give you a good home, after all the hours I've spent planning wholesome nourishing meals for you, after all the things I've gone without so that you should have swimming lessons and piano lessons and a new bicycle. Have I ever let you go out in summer without your sun hat, or come in in winter without feeling your stockings and insisting, if they were the least bit damp, on your changing them at once? Haven't you always been allowed to do everything, in reason, that you liked?'

Exactly: even deliberate ill-treatment would have been less unkind. Gallows and battlefields are, after all, no less places of mutual concern than sofa and bridal-bed; the dashing flirtations of fighter pilots and the coy tactics of twirled moustache and fluttered fan, the gasping mudcaked wooing of the coarsest foes and the reverent rage of the highest-powered romance, the lover's nip and the grip of the torturer's tongs are all,–ask Ariel,–variants of one common type, the bracket within which life and death with such passionate gusto cohabit, to be distinguished solely by the plus or minus sign which stands before them, signs which He is able at any time and in either direction to switch, but the one exception, the sum no magic of His can ever transmute, is the indifferent zero. Had you tried to destroy me, had we wrestled through long dark hours, we might by daybreak have learnt something from each other; in some panting pause to recover breath for further more savage blows or in the moment before your death or mine, we might both have heard together that music which explains and pardons all.

Had you, on the other hand, really left me alone to go my whole free-wheeling way to disorder, to be drunk every day before lunch, to jump stark naked from bed to bed, to have a fit every week or a major operation every other year, to forge checks or water the widow's stock, I might, after countless skids and punctures, have come by the bumpy third-class road of guilt and remorse smack into that very same truth which you were meanwhile admiring from your distant comfortable veranda but would never point out to me.

Such genuine escapades, though, might have disturbed the master at his meditations and even involved him in trouble with the police. The strains of oats, therefore, that you prudently permitted me to sow were each and all of an unmitigatedly minor wildness: a quick cold clasp now and then in some *louche* hotel to calm me down while you got on with the so thorough documentation of your great un-happy love for one who by being bad or dead or married provided you with the Good Right Subject that would never cease to bristle with importance; one bout of flu per winter, an occasional twinge of toothache, and enough tobacco to keep me in a good temper while you composed your melting eclogues of rustic piety; licence to break my shoelaces, spill soup on my tie, burn cigarette holes in the tablecloth, lose letters and borrowed books, and generally keep myself busy while you polished to a perfection your lyric praises of the more candid, more luxurious world to come.

Can you wonder then, when, as was bound to happen sooner or later, your charms, because they no longer amuse you, have cracked and your spirits, because you are tired of giving orders, have ceased to obey, and you are left alone with me, the dark thing you could never abide to be with, if I do not yield you kind answer or admire you for the achievements I was never allowed to profit from, if I resent hearing you speak of your neglect of me as your 'exile', of the pains you never took with me as 'all lost'?

But why continue? From now on we shall have, as we both know only too well, no company but each other's, and if I have had, as I consider, a good deal to put up with from you, I must own that, after all, I am not just the person I would have chosen for a life companion myself; so the only chance, which in any case is slim enough, of my getting a tolerably new master and you a tolerably new man, lies in our both learning, if possible and as soon as possible, to forgive and forget the past, and to keep our respective hopes for the future, within moderate, very moderate, limits.

*   *   *

And now at last it is you, assorted, consorted specimens of the general popular type, the major flock who have trotted trustingly hither but found, you reproachfully baah, no grazing, that I turn to and address on behalf of Ariel and myself. To your questions I shall attempt no direct reply, for the mere fact that you have been able so anxiously to put them is in itself sufficient proof that you possess their answers. All your clamour signifies is this: that your first big crisis, the breaking of the childish spell in which, so long as it enclosed you, there was, for you, no mirror, no magic, for everything that happened was a miracle–it was just as extraordinary for a chair to be a chair as for it to turn into a horse; it was no more absurd that the girding on of coal-scuttle and poker should transform you into noble Hector than that you should have a father and mother who called you Tommy–and it was therefore only necessary for you to presuppose one genius, one unrivalled I to wish these wonders in all their endless plenitude and novelty to be, is, in relation to your present, behind, that your singular transparent globes of enchantment have shattered one by one, and you have now all come together in the larger colder emptier room on this side of the mirror which *does* force your eyes to recognize and reckon with the two of us, your ears to detect the irreconcilable difference between my reiterated affirmation of what your furnished circumstances categorically are, and His successive propositions as to everything else which they conditionally might be. You have, as I say, taken your first step.

The Journey of life–the down-at-heels disillusioned figure can still put its characterization across–is infinitely long and its possible destinations infinitely distant from one another, but the time spent in actual travel is infinitesimally small. The hours the traveller measures are those in which he is at rest between the three or four decisive instants of transportation which are all he needs and all he gets to carry him the whole of his way; the scenery he observes is the view, gorgeous or drab, he glimpses from platform and siding; the incidents he thrills or blushes to remember take place in waiting and washrooms, ticket queues and parcels offices: it is in those promiscuous places of random association, in that air of anticipatory fidget, that he makes friends and enemies, that he promises, confesses, kisses, and betrays until, either because it is the one he has been expecting, or because, losing his temper, he has vowed to take the first to come along, or because he has been given a free ticket, or simply by misdirection or mistake, a train arrives which he does get into: it whistles – at least he thinks afterwards he remembers it whistling – but before he can blink, it has come to a standstill again and there he stands clutching his battered bags, surrounded by entirely strange smells and noises – yet in their smelliness and noisiness how familiar – one vast important stretch the nearer Nowhere, that still smashed terminus at which he will, in due course, be deposited, seedy and by himself.

Yes, you have made a definite start; you *have* left your homes way back in the farming provinces or way out in the suburban tundras, but whether you have been hanging around for years or have barely and breathlessly got here on one of those locals which keep arriving minute after minute, this is still only the main depot, the Grandly Average Place from which at odd hours the expresses leave seriously and sombrely for Somewhere, and where it is still possible for me to posit the suggestion that you go no farther. You will never, after all, feel better than in your present shaved and breakfasted state which there are restaurants and barber shops here indefinitely to preserve; you will never feel more secure than you do now in your knowledge that you *have* your ticket, your passport *is* in order, you have *not* forgotten to pack your pyjamas and an extra clean shirt; you will never have the same opportunity of learning about *all* the holy delectable spots of current or historic interest – an insistence on reaching *one* will necessarily exclude the others – than you have in these bepostered halls; you will never meet a jollier, more various crowd than you see around you here, sharing with you the throbbing, suppressed excitement of those to whom the exciting thing is still, perhaps, to happen. But once you leave, no matter in which direction, your next stop will be far outside this land of habit that so democratically stands up for your right to stagestruck hope, and well inside one of those, all equally foreign, uncomfortable and despotic, certainties of failure or success. Here at least I, and Ariel too, are free to warn you not, should we meet again there, to speak to either of us, not to engage either of us as your guide, but there we shall no longer be able to refuse you; then, unfortunately for you, we shall be compelled to say nothing and obey your fatal foolish commands. Here, whether you listen to me or not, and it's highly improbable that you will, I can at least warn you what will happen if at our next meeting you should insist—and that is all too probable—on putting one of us in charge.

*   *   *

'Release us,' you will beg, then, supposing it is I whom you make for,—oh how awfully uniform, once one translates them out of your private lingoes of expression, all your sorrows are and how awfully well I know them—'release us from our minor roles. Carry me back, Master, to the cathedral town where the canons run through the water meadows with butterfly nets and the old women keep sweet-shops in the cobbled side streets, or back to the upland mill town (gunpowder and plush) with its grope-movie and its poolroom lit by gas, carry me back to the days before my wife had put on weight, back to the years when beer was cheap and the rivers really froze in winter. Pity me, Captain, pity a poor old stranded sea-salt whom an unlucky voyage has wrecked on the desolate mahogany coast of this bar with nothing left him but his big moustache. Give me my passage home, let me see that harbour once again just as it was before I learned the bad words. Patriarchs wiser than Abraham mended their nets on the modest wharf; white and wonderful beings undressed on the sand-dunes; sunset glittered on the plate-glass windows of the Marine Biological Station; far off on the extreme horizon a whale spouted. Look, Uncle, look. They have broken my glasses and I have lost my silver whistle. Pick me up, Uncle, let little Johnny ride away on your massive shoulders to recover his green kingdom, where the steam rollers are as friendly as the farm dogs and it would never become necessary to look over one's left shoulder or clench one's right fist in one's pocket. You cannot miss it. Blackcurrant bushes hide the ruined opera house where badgers are said to breed in great numbers; an old horse-tramway winds away westward through suave foothills crowned with stone circles—follow it and by nightfall one would come to a large good-natured waterwheel—to the north, beyond a forest inhabited by charcoal burners, one can see the Devil's Bedposts quite distinctly, to the east the museum where for sixpence one can touch the ivory chessmen. O Cupid, Cupid, howls the whole dim chorus, take us home. We have never felt really well in this climate of distinct ideas; we have never been able to follow the regulations properly; Business, Science, Religion, Art, and all the other fictitious immortal persons who matter here have, frankly, not been very kind. We're so, so tired, the rewarding soup is stone cold, and over our blue wonders the grass grew long ago. O take us home with you, strong and swelling One, home to your promiscuous pastures where the minotaur of authority is just a roly-poly ruminant and nothing is at stake, those purring sites and amusing vistas where the fluctuating arabesques of sound, the continuous eruption of colours and scents, the whole rich incoherence of a nature made up of gaps and asymmetrical events plead beautifully and bravely for our undistress.'

And in that very moment when you so cry for deliverance from any and every anxious possibility, I shall have no option but to be faithful to my oath of service and instantly transport you, not indeed to any cathedral town or mill town or harbour or hillside or jungle or other specific Eden which your memory necessarily but falsely conceives of as the ultimately liberal condition, which in point of fact you have never known yet, but directly to that downright state itself. Here you are. This is it. Directly overhead a full moon casts a circle of dazzling light without any penumbra, exactly circumscribing its desolation in which every object is extraordinarily still and sharp. Cones of extinct volcanos rise up abruptly from the lava plateau fissured by chasms and pitted with hot springs from which steam rises without interruption straight up into the windless rarefied atmosphere. Here and there a geyser erupts without warning, spouts furiously for a few seconds and as suddenly subsides. Here, where the possessive note is utterly silent and all events are tautological repetitions and no decision will ever alter the secular stagnation, at long last you are, as you have asked to be, the only subject. Who, When, Why, the poor tired little historic questions fall wilting into a hush of utter failure. Your tears splash down upon clinkers which will never be persuaded to recognize a neighbour and there is really and truly no one to appear with tea and help. You have indeed come all the way to the end of your bachelor's journey where Liberty stands with her hands behind her back, not caring, not minding *anything*. Confronted by a straight and snubbing stare to which mythology is bosh, surrounded by an infinite passivity and purely arithmetical disorder which is only open to perception, and with nowhere to go on to, your existence is indeed free at last to choose its own meaning, that is, to plunge headlong into despair and fall through silence fathomless and dry, all fact your single drop, all value your pure alas.

★   ★   ★

But what of that other, smaller but doubtless finer group among you, important persons at the top of the ladder, exhausted lions of the season, local authorities with their tense tired faces, elderly hermits of both sexes living gloomily in the delta of a great fortune, whose *amour propre* prefers to turn for help to my more spiritual colleague.

'O yes,' you will sigh, 'we have had what once we would have called success. I moved the vices out of the city into a chain of re-conditioned lighthouses. I introduced statistical methods into the Liberal Arts. I revived the country dances and installed electric stoves in the mountain cottages. I saved democracy by buying steel. I gave the caesura its freedom. But this world is no better and it is now quite clear to us that there is nothing to be done with such a ship of fools, adrift on a sugarloaf sea in which it is going very soon and suitably to founder. Deliver us, dear Spirit, from the tantrums of our telephones and the whispers of our secretaries conspiring against Man; deliver us from these helpless agglomerations of dishevelled creatures with their bed-wetting, vomiting, weeping bodies, their giggling, fugitive, disappointing hearts, and scrawling, blotted, mis-spelt minds, to whom we have so foolishly tried to bring the light they did not want; deliver us from all the litter of *billets-doux*, empty beer bottles, laundry lists, directives, promissory notes and broken toys, the terrible mess that this particularized life, which we have so futilely attempted to tidy, sullenly insists on leaving behind it; translate us, bright Angel, from this hell of inert and ailing matter, growing steadily senile in a time for ever immature, to that blessed realm, so far above the twelve impertinent winds and the four unreliable seasons, that Heaven of the Really General Case where, tortured no longer by three dimensions and immune from temporal vertigo, Life turns into Light, absorbed for good into the permanently stationary, completely self-sufficient, absolutely reasonable One.'

Obliged by the terms of His contract to gratify this other request of yours, the wish for freedom to transcend *any* condition, for direct unentailed power without *any*, however secretly immanent, obligation to inherit or transmit, what can poor shoulder-shrugging Ariel do but lead you forthwith into a nightmare which has all the wealth of exciting action and all the emotional poverty of an adventure story for boys, a state of perpetual emergency and everlasting improvisation where all is need and change.

All the phenomena of an empirically ordinary world are given. Extended objects appear to which events happen – old men catch dreadful coughs, little girls get their arms twisted, flames run whooping through woods, round a river bend, as harmless looking as a dirty old bearskin rug, comes the gliding fury of a town-effacing wave, but these are merely elements in an allegorical land-scape to which mathematical measurement and phenomenological analysis have no relevance.

All the voluntary movements are possible – crawling through flues and old sewers, sauntering past shop-fronts, tiptoeing through quicksands and mined areas, running through derelict factories and across empty plains, jumping over brooks, diving into pools or swimming along between banks of roses, pulling at manholes or pushing at revolving doors, clinging to rotten balustrades, sucking at straws or wounds; all the modes of transport, letters, oxcarts, canoes, hansom cabs, trains, trolleys, cars, aeroplanes, balloons, are available, but any sense of direction, any knowledge of where on earth one has come from or where on earth one is going to is completely absent.

Religion and culture seem to be represented by a catholic belief that something is lacking which must be found, but as to what that something is, the keys of heaven, the missing heir, genius, the smells of childhood, or a sense of humour, why it is lacking, whether it has been deliberately stolen, or accidentally lost or just hidden for a lark, and who is responsible, our ancestors, ourselves, the social structure, or mysterious wicked powers, there are as many faiths as there are searchers, and clues can be found behind every clock, under every stone, and in every hollow tree to support all of them.

Again, other selves undoubtedly exist, but though everyone's pocket is bulging with birth certificates, insurance policies, passports and letters of credit, there is no way of proving whether they are genuine or planted or forged, so that no one knows whether another is his friend disguised as an enemy or his enemy disguised as a friend (there is probably no one whose real name is Brown), or whether the police who here as elsewhere are grimly busy, are crushing a criminal revolt or upholding a vicious tyranny, any more than he knows whether he himself is a victim of the theft, or the thief, or a rival thief, a professionally interested detective or a professionally impartial journalist.

Even the circumstances of the tender passion, the long-distance calls, the assignation at the aquarium, the farewell embrace under the fish-tail burner on the landing, are continually present, but since, each time it goes through its performance, it never knows whether it is saving a life, or obtaining secret information, or forgetting or spiting its real love, the heart feels nothing but a dull percussion of conceptual forboding. Everything, in short, suggests Mind but, surrounded by an infinite extension of the adolescent difficulty, a rising of the subjective and subjunctive to ever steeper, stormier heights, the panting frozen expressive gift has collapsed under the strain of its communicative anxiety, and contributes nothing by way of meaning but a series of staccato barks or a delirious gush of glossolalia.

And from this nightmare of public solitude, this everlasting Not

Yet, what relief have you but in an ever giddier collective gallop, with bisson eye and bevel course, toward the grey horizon of the bleaker vision, what landmarks but the four dead rivers, the Joyless, the Flaming, the Mournful, and the Swamp of Tears, what goal but the Black Stone on which the bones are cracked, for only there in its cry of agony can your existence find at last an unequivocal meaning and your refusal to be yourself become a serious despair, the love nothing, the fear all?

*   *   *

Such are the alternative routes, the facile glad-handed highway or the virtuous averted track, by which the human effort to make its own fortune arrives all eager at its abruptly dreadful end. I have tried – the opportunity was not to be neglected – to raise the admonitory forefinger, to ring the alarming bell, but with so little confidence of producing the right result, so certain that the open eye and attentive ear will always interpret any sight and any sound to their advantage, every rebuff as a consolation, every prohibition as a rescue – that is what they open and attend for – that I find myself almost hoping, for your sake, that I have had the futile honour of addressing the blind and the deaf.

Having learnt his language, I begin to feel something of the serio-comic embarrassment of the dedicated dramatist, who, in representing to you your condition of estrangement from the truth, is doomed to fail the more he succeeds, for the more truthfully he paints the condition, the less clearly can he indicate the truth from which it is estranged, the brighter his revelation of the truth in its order, its justice, its joy, the fainter shows his picture of your actual condition in all its drabness and sham, and, worse still, the more sharply he defines the estrangement itself – and, ultimately, what other aim and justification has he, what else exactly *is* the artistic gift which he is forbidden to hide, if not to make you unforgettably conscious of the ungarnished offended gap between what you so questionably are and what you are commanded without any question to become, of the unqualified No that opposes your every step in any direction?–the more he must strengthen your delusion that an awareness of the gap is in itself a bridge, your interest in your imprisonment a release, so that, far from your being led by him to contrition and surrender, the regarding of your defects in his mirror, your dialogue, using his words, with yourself about yourself, becomes the one activity which never, like devouring or collecting or spending, lets you down, the one game which can be guaranteed, whatever the company, to catch on, a madness of which you can only be cured by some shock quite outside his control, an unpredictable misting over of his glass or an absurd misprint in his text.

Our unfortunate dramatist, therefore, is placed in the unseemly predicament of having to give all his passion, all his skill, all his time to the task of 'doing' life–consciously to give anything less than all would be a gross betrayal of his gift and an unpardonable presumption–as if it lay in *his* power to solve this dilemma–yet of having at the same time to hope that some unforeseen mishap will intervene to ruin his effect, without, however, obliterating your disappointment, the expectation aroused by him that there was an effect to ruin, that, if the smiling interest never did arrive, it must, through no fault of its own, have got stuck somewhere; that, exhausted, ravenous, delayed by fog, mobbed and mauled by a thousand irrelevancies, it has, nevertheless, not forgotten its promise but is still trying desperately to get a connection.

Beating about for some large loose image to define the original drama which aroused his imitative passion, the first performance in which the players were their own audience, the worldly stage on which their behaving flesh was really sore and sorry–for the floods of tears were not caused by onions, the deformities and wounds did not come off after a good wash, the self-stabbed heroine could not pick herself up again to make a gracious bow nor her seducer go demurely home to his plain and middle-aged spouse–the fancy immediately flushed is of the greatest grandest opera rendered by a very provincial touring company indeed.

Our performance–for Ariel and I are, you know this now, just as deeply involved as any of you–which we were obliged, all of us, to go on with and sit through right to the final dissonant chord, has been so indescribably inexcusably awful. Sweating and shivering in our moth-eaten ill-fitting stock costumes which with only a change of hat and rearrangement of safety-pins, had to do for the *Landsknecht* and the Parisian art-student, bumping into, now a rippling palace, now a primeval forest full of holes, at cross purposes with the scraping bleating orchestra we could scarcely hear, for half the instruments were missing and the cottage piano which was filling-out must have stood for too many years in some damp parlour, we floundered on from fiasco to fiasco, the schmalz tenor never quite able at his big moments to get right up nor the ham bass right down, the stud contralto gargling through her maternal grief, the ravished coloratura trilling madly off-key and the re-united lovers half a bar apart, the knock-kneed armies shuffling limply through their bloody battles, the unearthly harvesters hysterically entangled in their honest fugato.

Now it is over. No, we have not dreamt it. Here we really stand, down stage with red faces and no applause; no effect, however simple, no piece of business, however unimportant, came off; there was not a single aspect of our production, not even the huge stuffed bird of happiness, for which a kind word could, however patronizingly, be said.

Yet, at this very moment when we do at last see ourselves as we are, neither cosy nor playful, but swaying out on the ultimate wind-whipped cornice that overhangs the unabiding void–we have never stood anywhere else,–when our reasons are silenced by the heavy huge derision,–There is nothing to say. There never has been,–and our wills chuck in their hands–There is no way out. There never was,–it is at this moment that for the first time in our lives we hear, not the sounds which, as born actors, we have hitherto condescended to use as an excellent vehicle for displaying our personalities and looks, but the real Word which is our only *raison d'être*. Not that we have improved; everything, the massacres, the whippings, the lies, the twaddle, and all their carbon copies are still present, more obviously than ever; nothing has been reconstructed; our shame, our fear, our incorrigible staginess, all wish and no resolve, are still, and more intensely than ever, all we have: only now it is not in spite of them but with them that we are blessed by that Wholly Other Life from which we are separated by an essential emphatic gulf of which our contrived fissures of mirror and proscenium arch—we understand them at last—are feebly figurative signs, so that all our meanings are reversed and it is precisely in its negative image of Judgment that we can positively envisage Mercy; it is just here, among the ruins and the bones, that we may rejoice in the perfected Work which is not ours. Its great coherences stand out through our secular blur in all their overwhelmingly righteous obligation; its voice speaks through our muffling banks of artificial flowers and unflinchingly delivers its authentic molar pardon; its spaces greet us with all their grand old prospect of wonder and width; the working charm is the full bloom of the unbothered state; the sounded note is the restored relation.

Postscript

(ARIEL *to Caliban. Echo by the* PROMPTER)

Weep no more but pity me,
Fleet persistent shadow cast
By your lameness, caught at last,
Helplessly in love with you,
Elegance, art, fascination,
   Fascinated by
   Drab mortality;
Spare me a humiliation,
   To your faults be true:
I can sing as you reply

                   . . . *I*

Wish for nothing lest you mar
The perfection in these eyes
Whose entire devotion lies
At the mercy of your will;
Tempt not your sworn comrade,–only
   As I am can I
   Love you as you are–
For my company be lonely
   For my health be ill:
I will sing if you will cry

                   . . . *I*

Never hope to say farewell,
For our lethargy is such
Heaven's kindness cannot touch
Nor earth's frankly brutal drum;
This was long ago decided,
   Both of us know why,
   Can, alas, foretell,
When our falsehoods are divided,
   What we shall become,
   One evaporating sigh

                    . . . I

The Age of Anxiety

A BAROQUE ECLOGUE

TO JOHN BETJEMAN

Lacrimosa dies illa
Qua resurget ex favilla
Iudicandus homo reus
Thomas a Celano (?)
Dies Irae

PART ONE

Prologue

Now the day is over,
Night is drawing nigh,
Shadows of the evening
Steal across the sky.
S. Baring-Gould

When the historical process breaks down and armies organize with their embossed debates the ensuing void which they can never consecrate, when necessity is associated with horror and freedom with boredom, then it looks good to the bar business.

In times of peace there are always a number of persons who wake up each morning excited by the prospect of another day of interesting and difficult work, or happily certain that the one with whom they shared their bed last night will be sharing it with them again the next, and who, in consequence, must be written off by the proprietor as a lost market. Not that he need worry. There will always be enough lonelies and enough failures who need desperately what he has to offer—namely, an unprejudiced space in which nothing particular ever happens, and a choice of physiological aids to the imagination whereby each may appropriate it for his or her private world of repentant felicitous forms, heavy expensive objects or avenging flames and floods—to guarantee him a handsome profit still.

But in wartime, when everybody is reduced to the anxious status of a shady character or a displaced person, when even the most prudent become worshippers of chance, and when, in comparison to the universal disorder of the world outside, his Bohemia seems as cosy and respectable as a suburban villa, he can count on making his fortune.

Looking up from his drink, QUANT caught the familiar eye of his reflection in the mirror behind the bar and wondered why he was still so interested in that tired old widower who would never be more now than a clerk in a shipping office near the Battery.

More, that is, as a public figure: for as so often happens in the modern world—and how much restlessness, envy and self-contempt it causes—there was no one-to-one correspondence between his social or economic position and his private mental life. He had come to America at the age of six when his father, implicated somehow in the shooting of a landlord, had had to leave Ireland in a hurry, and, from time to time, images, some highly-coloured, some violent, derived from a life he could not remember, would enter unexpectedly and incomprehensibly into his dreams. Then, again, in early manhood, when unemployed during a depression, he had spent many hours one winter in the Public Library reading for the most part—he could not have told you why—books on Mythology. The knowledge gained at that time had ever since lain oddly around in a corner of his mind like luggage left long ago in an emergency by some acquaintance and never reclaimed.

Watching the bubbles rise in his glass, MALIN was glad to forget for his few days of leave the uniform of the Canadian Air Force he was wearing and the life it represented, at once disjointed and mechanical, alternately exhausting and idle, of a Medical Intelligence officer; trying to recapture the old atmosphere of laboratory and lecture hall, he returned with pleasure to his real interests.

Lighting a cigarette, ROSETTA, too, ignored her surroundings but with less ease. Yes, she made lots of money—she was a buyer for a big department store and did it very well—and that was a great deal, for, like anyone who has ever been so, she had a sensible horror of being poor. Yes, America was the best place on earth to come to if you had to earn your living, but did it have to be so big and empty and noisy and messy? Why could she not have been rich? Yes, though she was not as young as she looked, there were plenty of men who either were deceived or preferred a girl who might be experienced—which indeed she was. But why were the men one liked not the sort who proposed marriage and the men who proposed marriage not the sort one liked? So she returned now to her favourite day-dream in which she indulged whenever she got a little high—which was rather too often—and conjured up, detail by detail, one of those landscapes familiar to all readers of English detective stories, those lovely innocent countrysides inhabited by charming eccentrics with independent means and amusing hobbies to whom, until the sudden intrusion of a horrid corpse onto the tennis court or into the greenhouse, work and law and guilt are just literary words.

EMBLE, on the other hand, put down his empty glass and looked about him as if he hoped to read in all those faces the answer to his own disquiet. Having enlisted in the Navy during his sophomore year at a Mid-Western university, he suffered from that anxiety about himself and his future which haunts, like a bad smell, the minds of most young men, though most of them are under the illusion that their lack of confidence is a unique and shameful fear which, if confessed, would make them an object of derision to their normal contemporaries. Accordingly, they watch others with a covert but passionate curiosity. What makes them tick? What would it feel like to be a success? Here is someone who is nobody in particular, there even an obvious failure, yet they do not seem to mind. How is that possible? What is their secret?

In certain cases—his was one—this general unease of youth is only aggravated by what would appear to alleviate it, a grace of person which grants them, without effort on their part, a succession of sexual triumphs. For then the longing for success, the doubt of ever being able to achieve the kinds of success which have to be earned, and the certainty of being able to have at this moment a kind which does not, play dangerously into each other's hands.

So, fully conscious of the attraction of his uniform to both sexes, he looked round him, slightly contemptuous when he caught an admiring glance, and slightly piqued when he did not.

It was the night of All Souls.

QUANT was thinking:

My deuce, my double, my dear image,
Is it lively there, that land of glass
Where song is a grimace, sound logic
A suite of gestures? You seem amused.
How well and witty when you wake up,
How glad and good when you go to bed,
Do you feel, my friend? What flavour has
That liquor you lift with your left hand;
Is it cold by contrast, cool as this
For a soiled soul; does your self like mine
Taste of untruth? Tell me, what are you
Hiding in your heart, some angel face,
Some shadowy she who shares in my absence,
Enjoys my jokes? I'm jealous, surely,
Nicer myself (though not as honest),
The marked man of romantic thrillers
Whose brow bears the brand of a winter
No priest can explain, the poet disguised,
Thinking over things in thieves' kitchens,
Wanted by the waste, whom women's love
Or his own silhouette might all too soon
Betray to its tortures. I'll track you down,
I'll make you confess how much you know who
View my vices with a valet's slight
But shameless shrug, the *Schadenfreude*
Of cooks at keyholes. Old comrade, tell me
The lie of my lifetime but look me up in
Your good graces; agree to be friends
Till our deaths differ; drink, strange future,
To your neighbour now.

258

MALIN was thinking:

> No chimpanzee
> Thinks it thinks. Things are divisible,
> Creatures are not. In chaos all bodies
> Would differ in weight. Dogs can learn to
> Fear the future. The faceless machine
> Lacks a surround. The laws of science have
> Never explained why novelty always
> Arrives to enrich (though the wrong question
> Initiates nothing). Nature rewards
> Perilous leaps. The prudent atom
> Simply insists upon its safety now,
> Security at all costs; the calm plant
> Masters matter then submits to itself,
> Busy but not brave; the beast assures
> A stabler status to stolen flesh,
> Assists though it enslaves: singular then
> Is the human way; for the ego is a dream
> Till a neighbour's need by name create it;
> Man has no mean; his mirrors distort;
> His greenest arcadias have ghosts too;
> His utopias tempt to eternal youth
> Or self-slaughter.

ROSETTA was thinking:

> From Seager's Folly
> We beheld what was ours. Undulant land
> Rose layer by layer till at last the sea
> Far away flashed; from fretted uplands
> That lay to the north, from limestone heights
> Incisive rains had dissected well,
> For down each dale industrious there ran
> A paternoster of ponds and mills,
> Came sweet waters, assembling quietly
> By a clear congress of accordant streams

A mild river that moseyed at will
Through parks and ploughland, purring southward
In a wide valley. Wolds on each side
Came dawdling downwards in double curves,
Mellow, mature, to meadowlands and
Sedentary orchards, settled places
Crowded with lives; fat cattle brooded
In the shade of great oaks, sheep grazed in
The ancient hollows of meander scars and
Long-legged ladies with little-legged dogs
Lolled with their lovers by lapsing brooks.
A couth region: consonant, lofty,
Volatile vault and vagrant buttress
Showed their shapeliness; with assured ease,
Proud on that plain, St. Peter Acorn,
St. Dill-in-the-Deep, St. Dust, St. Alb,
St. Bee-le-bone, St. Botolph-the-less,
High gothic growths in a grecian space,
Lorded over each leafy parish
Where country curates in cold bedrooms
Dreamed of deaneries till at day-break
The rector's rooks with relish described
Their stinted station.

EMBLE was thinking:

                                  Estranged, aloof,
They brood over being till the bars close,
The malcontented who might have been
The creative odd ones the average need
To suggest new goals. Self-judged they sit,
Sad haunters of Perhaps who after years
To grasp and gaze in get no further
Than their first beholding, phantoms who try
Through much drink by magic to restore
The primitive pact with pure feeling,

260

Their flesh as it felt before sex was,
(The archaic calm without cultural sin
Which her Adam is till his Eve does),
Eyeing the door, for ever expecting
Night after night the Nameless One, the
Smiling sea-god who shall safely land
Shy and broad-shouldered on the shore at last,
Enthusiastic, of their convenient
And dangerous dream; while days away, in
Prairie places where no person asks
What is suffered in ships, small tradesmen,
Wry relatives on rocking-chairs in
Moss-grown mansions, mothers whose causes
For right and wrong are unreal to them,
Grieve vaguely over theirs: their vision shrinks
As their dreams darken; with dulling voice
Each calls across a colder water,
Tense, optative, interrogating
Some sighing several who sadly fades.

But now the radio, suddenly breaking in with its banal noises upon
their separate senses of themselves, by compelling them to pay
attention to a common world of great slaughter and much sorrow,
began, without their knowledge, to draw these four strangers closer
to each other. For in response to its official doctored message:

Now the news. Night raids on
Five cities. Fires started.
Pressure applied by pincer movement
In threatening thrust. Third Division
Enlarges beachhead. Lucky charm
Saves sniper. Sabotage hinted
In steel-mill stoppage. Strong point held
By fanatical Nazis. Canal crossed
By heroic marines, Rochester barber

Fools foe. Finns ignore
Peace feeler. Pope condemns
Axis excesses. Underground
Blows up bridge. Thibetan prayer-wheels
Revolve for victory. Vital crossroads
Taken by tanks. Trend to the left
Forecast by Congressman. Cruiser sunk
In Valdivian Deep. Doomed sailors
Play poker. Reporter killed.

MALIN thought:

Untalkative and tense, we took off
Anxious into air; our instruments glowed,
Dials in darkness, for dawn was not yet;
Pulses pounded; we approached our target,
Conscious in common of our closed Here
And of Them out There thinking of Us
In a different dream, for we die in theirs
Who kill in ours and become fathers,
Not twisting tracks their trigger hands are
Given goals by; we began our run;
Death and damage darted at our will,
Bullets were about, blazing anger
Lunged from below, but we laid our eggs
Neatly in their nest, a nice deposit,
Hatched in an instant; houses flamed in
Shuddering sheets as we shed our big
Tears on their town: we turned to come back,
But at high altitudes, hostile brains
Waited in the west, a wily flock
Vowed to vengeance in the vast morning,
–A mild morning where no marriage was,
And gravity a god greater than love–
Fierce interferers. We fought them off
But paid a price; there was pain for some.

'Why have They killed me?' wondered our Bert, our
Greenhouse gunner, forgot our answer,
Then was not with us. We watched others
Drop into death; dully we mourned each
Flare as it fell with a friend's lifetime,
While we hurried on to our home bases
To the safe smells and a sacrament
Of tea with toast. At twenty to eight I
Stepped onto grass, still with the living,
While far and near a fioritura
Of brooks and blackbirds bravely struck the
International note with no sense
Of historic truth, of time meaning
Once and for all, and my watch stuttered:—
Many have perished; more will.

And QUANT thought:
All war's woes I can well imagine.
Gun barrels glint, gathered in ambush,
Mayhem among mountains; minerals break
In by order on intimate groups of
Tender tissues; at their tough visit
Flesh flusters that was so fluent till now,
Stammers some nonsense, stops and sits down,
Apathetic to all this. Thousands lie in
Ruins by roads, irrational in woods,
Insensitive upon snow-bound plains,
Or littered lifeless along low coasts
Where shingle shuffles as shambling waves
Feebly fiddle in the fading light
With bloated bodies, beached among groynes,
Male no longer, unmotivated,
Have-beens without hopes: Earth takes charge of,
Soil accepts for a serious purpose
The jettisoned blood of jokes and dreams,

Making buds from bone, from brains the good
Vague vegetable; survivors play
Cards in kitchens while candles flicker
And in blood-spattered barns bandaged men,
Their poor hands in a panic of need
Groping weakly for a gun-butt or
A friendly fist, are fetched off darkling.
Many have perished; more will.

And EMBLE thought:
High were those headlands; the eagles promised
Life without lawyers. Our long convoy
Turned away northward as tireless gulls
Wove over water webs of brightness
And sad sound. The insensible ocean,
Miles without mind, moaned all around our
Limited laughter, and below our songs
Were deaf deeps, denes of unaffection,
Their chill unchanging, chines where only
The whale is warm, their wildness haunted
By metal fauna moved by reason
To hunt not in hunger but for hate's sake,
Stalking our steamers. Strained with gazing
Our eyes ached, and our ears as we slept
Kept their care for the crash that would turn
Our fears into fact. In the fourth watch
A torpedo struck on the port bow:
The blast killed many; the burning oil
Suffocated some; some in lifebelts
Floated upright till they froze to death;
The younger swam but the yielding waves
Denied help; they were not supported,
They swallowed and sank, ceased thereafter
To appear in public; exposed to snap
Verdicts of sharks, to vague inquiries

Of amoeboid monsters, mobbed by slight
Unfriendly fry, refused persistence.
They are nothing but names assigned to
Anguish in others, areas of grief.
Many have perished; more will.

ROSETTA thought:
I see in my mind a besieged island,
That island in arms where my home once was.
Round green gardens, down grooves between white
Hawthorne-hedges, long hospital trains
Smoothly slide with their sensitized freight
Of mangled men, moving them homeward
In pain through pastures. In a packed hall
Two vicious rivals, two virtuosos
Appear on one platform and play duets
To war-orphans and widowed ladies,
Grieving in gloves; while to grosser ears
In clubs and cabarets crooners wail
Some *miserere* modern enough
In its thorough thinness. I think too of
The conquered condition, countries where
Arrogant officers, armed in cars,
Go roaring down roads on the wrong side,
Courts martial meet at midnight with drums,
And pudgy persons pace unsmiling
The quays and stations or cruise the nights
In vans for victims, to investigate
In sound-proof cells the Sense of Honour,
While in turkish baths with towels round them
Imperilled plotters plan in outline
Definitions and norms for new lives,
Half-truths for their times. As tense as these,
Four who are famous confer in a *schloss*
At night on nations. They are not equal:

Three stand thoughtful on a thick carpet
Awaiting the Fourth who wills they shall
Till, suddenly entering through a side-door,
Quick, quiet, unquestionable as death,
Grief or guilt, he greets them and sits down,
Lord of this life. He looks natural,
He smiles well, he smells of the future,
Odourless ages, an ordered world
Of planned pleasures and passport-control,
Sentry-go, sedatives, soft drinks and
Managed money, a moral planet
Tamed by terror: his telegram sets
Grey masses moving as the mud dries.
Many have perished; more will.

And when in conclusion the instrument said:

> *Buy a bond. Blood saves lives.*
> *Donate now. Name this station.*

they could no longer keep these thoughts to themselves, but turn-
ing towards each other on their high wooden stools, became
acquainted.

ROSETTA spoke first:
> Numbers and nightmares have news value.

Then MALIN:
> A crime has occurred, accusing all.

Then QUANT:
> The world needs a wash and a week's rest.

To which EMBLE said:
> Better this than barbarian misrule.
> History tells more often than not
> Of wickedness with will, wisdom but
> An interjection without a verb,

266

And the godless growing like green cedars
On righteous ruins. The reticent earth,
Exposed by the spade, speaks its warning
With successive layers of sacked temples
And dead civilians. They dwelt at ease
In their sown centres, sunny their minds,
Fine their features; their flesh was carried
On beautiful bones; they bore themselves
Lightly through life; they loved their children
And entertained with all their senses
A world of detail. Wave and pebble,
Boar and butterfly, birch and carp, they
Painted as persons, portraits that seem
Neighbours with names; one knows from them what
A leaf must feel. By lakes at twilight
They sang of swans and separations,
Mild, unmilitant, as the moon rose
And reeds rustled; ritual appointed
Tastes and textures; their touch preferred the
Spectrum of scents to Spartan morals,
Art to action. But, unexpected, as
Bells babbled in a blossoming month,
Near-sighted scholars on canal paths
Defined their terms, and fans made public
The hopes of young hearts, out of the north, from
Black tundras, from basalt and lichen,
Peripheral people, rancid ones
Stocky on horses, stomachs in need of
Game and grazing, by grass corridors
Coursed down on their concatenation
Of smiling cities. Swords and arrows
Accosted their calm; their climate knew
Fire and fear; they fell, they bled, not an
Eye was left open; all disappeared:
Utter oblivion they had after that.

MALIN said:

>But the new barbarian is no uncouth
>Desert-dweller; he does not emerge
>From fir forests; factories bred him;
>Corporate companies, college towns
>Mothered his mind, and many journals
>Backed his beliefs. He was born here. The
>Bravura of revolvers in vogue now
>And the cult of death are quite at home
>Inside the city.

QUANT said:

>   The soldiers' fear
>And the shots will cease in a short while,
>More ruined regions surrender to less,
>Prominent persons be put to death
>For mass-murder, and what moves us now,
>The defence of friends against foes' hate,
>Be over for ever. Then, after that,
>What shall we will? Why shall we practise
>Vice or virtue when victory comes?
>The celebrations are suddenly hushed,
>The coarse crowds uncomfortably still,
>For, arm-in-arm now, behind the festooned
>Conqueror's car there come his heirs, the
>Public hangman, the private wastrel.

ROSETTA said:

>Lies and lethargies police the world
>In its periods of peace. What pain taught
>Is soon forgotten; we celebrate
>What ought to happen as if it were done,
>Are blinded by our boasts. Then back they come,
>The fears that we fear. We fall asleep
>Only to meet the idiot children of
>Our revels and wrongs; farouche they appear,

Reluctant look-behinds, loitering through
The mooing gate, menacing or smiling,
Nocturnal trivia, torts and dramas,
Wrecks, arrivals, rose-bushes, armies,
Leopards and laughs, alarming growths of
Moulds and monsters on memories stuffed
With dead men's doodles, dossiers written
In lost lingos, too long an account
To take out in trade, no time either,
Since we wake up. We are warm, our active
Universe is young; yet we shiver:
For athwart our thinking the threat looms,
Huge and awful as the hump of Saturn
Over modest Mimas, of more deaths
And worse wars, a winter of distaste
To last a lifetime. Our lips are dry, our
Knees numb; the enormous disappointment
With a smiling sigh softly flings her
Indolent apron over our lives
And sits down on our day. Damning us,
On our present purpose the past weighs
Heavy as alps, for the absent are never
Mislaid or lost: as lawyers define
The grammar of our grief, their ghosts rise,
Hanged or headless, hosts who disputed
With good governors, their guilty flesh
Racked and raving but unreconciled,
The punished people to pass sentence
On the jolly and just; and, joining these
Come worse warlocks, the wailing infants
Who know now they will never be born,
Refused a future. Our failings give
Their resentment seizin; our Zion is
A doomed Sodom dancing its heart out
To treacly tunes, a tired Gomorrah

Infatuated with her former self
Whose dear dreams though they dominate still
Are formal facts which refresh no more.

  They fell silent and immediately became conscious again of the
radio, now blandly inexorably bringing to all John Doakes and
G.I. Joes tidings of great joy and saying

Definitely different. Has that democratic
Extra elegance. Easy to clean.
Will gladden grand-dad and your girl friend.
Lasts a lifetime. Leaves no odour.
American made. A modern product
Of nerve and know-how with a new thrill.
Patriotic to own. Is on its way
In a patent package. Pays to investigate.
Serves through science. Has something added
By skilled Scotchmen. Exclusively used
By upper classmen and Uncle Sam.
Tops in tests by teenagers.
Just ask for it always.

  Matter and manner set their teeth on edge, especially MALIN's
who felt like talking. So he ordered a round of drinks, then said:

Here we sit
Our bodies bound to these bar-room lights,
The night's odours, the noise of the El on
Third Avenue, but our thoughts are free . . .
Where shall they wander? To the wild past
When, beaten back, banished to their cirques
The horse-shoe glaciers curled up and died,
And cold-blooded through conifers slouched
Fumbling amphibians; forward into
Tidy utopias of eternal spring,

Vitamins, villas, visas for dogs
And art for all; and up and down through
Those hidden worlds of alien sizes
Which lenses elicit?

But EMBLE objected:
Muster no monsters, I'll meeken my own.

So did ROSETTA:
You may wish till you waste, I'll want here.

So did QUANT:
Too blank the blink of these blind heavens.

MALIN suggested:
Let us then
Consider rather the incessant Now of
The traveller through time, his tired mind
Biased towards bigness since his body must
Exaggerate to exist, possessed by hope,
Acquisitive, in quest of his own
Absconded self yet scared to find it
As he bumbles by from birth to death
Menaced by madness; whose mode of being,
Bashful or braggart, is to be at once
Outside and inside his own demand
For personal pattern. His pure I
Must give account of and greet his Me,
That field of force where he feels he thinks,
His past present, presupposing death,
Must ask what he is in order to be
And make meaning by omission and stress,
Avid of elseness. All that exists
Matters to man; he minds what happens

And feels he is at fault, a fallen soul
With power to place, to explain every
What in his world but why he is neither
God nor good, this guilt the insoluble
Final fact, infusing his private
Nexus of needs, his noted aims with
Incomprehensible comprehensive dread
At not being what he knows that before
This world was he was willed to become.

QUANT approved:
    Set him to song, the surly old dodger.

So did EMBLE:
    Relate his lies to his longing for truth.

So did ROSETTA:
    Question his crimes till his clues confess.

The radio attempted to interrupt by remarking

    And now Captain Kidd in his Quiz Programme
    HOW ALERT ARE YOU

But QUANT pointed a finger at it and it stopped immediately. He said:
    Listen, Box,
And keep quiet. Listen courteously to us
Four reformers who have founded—why not?—
The Gung-Ho Group, the Ganymede Club
The homesick young angels, the Arctic League
Of Tropical Fish, the Tomboy Fund
For Blushing Brides and the Bide-a-wees
Of Sans-Souci, assembled again
For a Think-Fest: Our theme tonight is

HOMO ABYSSUS OCCIDENTALIS
or
A CURIOUS CASE OF COLD FEET
or
SEVEN SELFISH SUPPERLESS AGES

And now, at ROSETTA's suggestion, they left their bar-stools and moved to the quieter intimacy of a booth. Drinks were ordered and the discussion began.

PART TWO

The Seven Ages

A sick toss'd vessel, dashing on each thing;
Nay, his own shelf:
My God, I mean myself.

George Herbert *Miserie*

MALIN began:
> Behold the infant, helpless in cradle and
> Righteous still, yet already there is
> Dread in his dreams at the deed of which
> He knows nothing but knows he can do,
> The gulf before him with guilt beyond,
> Whatever that is, whatever why
> Forbids his bound; till that ban tempts him;
> He jumps and is judged: he joins mankind,
> The fallen families, freedom lost,
> Love become Law. Now he looks at grown-ups
> With conscious care, and calculates on
> The effect of a frown or filial smile,
> Accuses with a cough, claims pity
> With scratched knees, skilfully avenges
> Pains and punishments on puny insects,
> Grows into a grin, and gladly shares his
> Small secret with the supplicating
> Instant present. His emptiness finds

Its joy in a gang and is joined to others
By crimes in common. Clumsy and alarmed,
As the blind bat obeys the warnings
Of its own echoes, his inner life
Is a zig-zag, a bizarre dance of
Feelings through facts, a foiled one learning
Shyness and shame, a shadowed flier.

QUANT said:

O

Secret meetings at the slaughter-house
With nickels and knives, initiations
Behind the billboards. Then the hammerpond looked
So green and grim, yet graciously its dank
Water made us welcome—once in, we
Swam without swearing. The smelting mill
We broke into had a big chimney
And huge engines; holding our breath, we
Lighted matches and looked at the gears,
The cruel cogwheels, the crank's absolute
Veto on pleasure. In a vacant lot
We built a bonfire and burned alive
Some stolen tyres. How strong and good one
Felt at first, how fagged coming home through
The urban evening. Heavy like us
Sank the gas-tanks—it was supper time.
In hot houses helpless babies and
Telephones gabbled untidy cries,
And on embankments black with burnt grass
Shambling freight-trains were shunted away
Past crimson clouds.

EMBLE said:

My cousins were both
Strong and stupid: they stole my candy,
They tied me to a tree, they twisted my arms,

275

Called me crybaby. 'Take care,' I sobbed,
'I could hold up my hand and hot water
Would come down on your drought and drown you all
In your big boots.' In our back garden
One dark afternoon I dug quite a hole
Planning to vanish.

ROSETTA said:

>   On picnic days
My dearest doll was deaf and spoke in
Grunts like grandfather. God understood
If we washed our necks he wasn't ever
To look in the loft where the Lamps were
And the Holy Hook. In the housekeeper's room there
Was currant cake and calves-foot jelly
As we did our sums while down below,
Tall in tweeds on the terrace gravel,
Father and his friends reformed régimes,
Monies and monarchs, and mother wrote
Swift and sure in the silk-hung saloon
Her large round letters. Along the esker,
Following a fox with our fingers crossed
Or after the ogre in Indian file,
We stole with our sticks through a still world of
Hilarious light, our lives united
Like fruit in a bowl, befriended by
The supple silence, incited by
Our shortened shadows.

MALIN went on to the Second Age:

>   With shaving comes
An hour when he halts, hearing the crescent
Roar of hazard, and realizes first
He has laid his life-bet with a lying self
Who wins or welches. Thus woken, he is
Amused no more by a merely given

Felt fact, the facile emergence of
Thought with thing, but, threatened from all sides,
Embarrassed by his body's bald statements,
His sacred soul obscenely tickled
And bellowed at by a blatant Without,
A dog by daylight, in dreams a lamb
Whom the nightmare ejects nude into
A ball of princes too big to feel
Disturbed by his distress, he starts off now,
Poor, unprepared, on his pilgrimage
To find his friends, the far-off *élite*,
And, knowing no one, a nameless young man,
Pictures as he plods his promised chair
In their small circle secret to those
With no analogies, unique persons,
The originals' ring, the round table
Of master minds. Mountains he loves now,
Piers and promontories, places where
Evening brings him all that grandeur
Of scope and scale which the sky is believed
To promise or recall, pacing by
In a sunset trance of self-pity,
While his toy tears with a touching grace
Like little balloons sail lonely away
To dusk and death.

QUANT said:

                     With diamonds to offer,
A cleaned tycoon in a cooled office,
I smiled at a siren with six breasts,
Leaning on leather, looking up at
Her righteous robber, her Robin Hood,
Her plump prince. All the public could see
Was a bus-boy brushing a table,
Sullen and slight.

ROSETTA said:

                    In my sixteenth year
          Before sleeping I fancied nightly
          The house on the headland I would own one day.
          Its long windows overlooked the sea
          And its turf terrace topped a sunny
          Sequestered cove. A corkscrew staircase
          From a green gate in the garden wall
          Descended the cliff, the sole entrance
          To my beach where bathers basked beside
          The watchet waves. Though One was special,
          All forms were friends who freely told their
          Secrets to me; but, safe in my purse
          I kept the key to the closet where
          A sliding panel concealed the lift,
          Known to none, which at night would take me
          Down through the dark to my dock below,
          A chamber chiselled in the chalk hill,
          Private and perfect; thence, putting forth
          Alone in my launch through a low tunnel
          Out to the ocean, while all others slept,
          Smiling and singing I sailed till dawn,
          Happy, hatless.

EMBLE said:

                    After a dreadful
          Row with father, I ran with burning
          Cheeks to the pasture and chopped wood, my
          Stomach like a stone. I strode that night
          Through wicked dreams: waking, I skipped to
          The shower and sang, ashamed to recall
          With whom or how; the hiss of the water
          Composed the tune, I supplied the words
          For a fine dirge which fifty years hence
          Massed choirs would sing as my coffin passed,

Grieved for and great on a gun-carriage.

MALIN went on, spoke of the Third Age:

Such pictures fade as his path is blocked
By Others from Elsewhere, alien bodies
Whose figures fasten on his free thoughts,
Ciphers and symbols secret to his flesh,
Uniquely near, needing his torments,
His lonely life, and he learns what real
Images are; that, however violent
Their wish to be one, that wild promise
Cannot be kept, their case is double;
For each now of need ignores the other as
By rival routes of recognition
Diminutive names that midnight hears
Intersect upon their instant way
To solid solitudes, and selves cross
Back to bodies, both insisting each
Proximate place a pertinent thing.
So, learning to love, at length he is taught
To know he does not.

QUANT said:

Since the neighbours did,
With a multitude I made the long
Visitors' voyage to Venus Island,
Elated as they, landed upon
The savage shore where old swains lay wrecked
Unfit for her fable, followed up
The basalt stairway bandying jokes with
The thoughtless throng, but then, avoiding
The great gate where she gives all pilgrims
Her local wine, I legged it over
A concrete wall, was cold sober as,
Pushing through brambles, I peeked out at
Her fascination. Frogs were shooting

Craps in a corner; cupids on stilts,
Their beautiful bottoms breaking wind,
Hunted hares with hurricane lanterns
Through woods on one side, while on the other,
Shining out through shivering poplars,
Stood a brick bath-house where burghers mixed
With light-fingered ladies and louche trade,
Dancing in serpents and daisy chains
To mad music. In the mid-distance
On deal chairs sat a dozen decayed
Gentlewomen with dejected backs
And raw fingers morosely stitching
Red flannel scivvies for heroic herms.
Primroses, peacocks and peachtrees made
A fair foreground but fairer there, with
An early Madonna's oval face
And lissom limbs, delighted that whole
Degraded glen, the Goddess herself
Presided smiling; a saucy wind,
Plucking from her thigh her pink wrapper
Of crêpe-de-chine, disclosed a very
Indolent ulcer.

ROSETTA said nothing but, placing a nickel in the Wallomatic,
selected a sad little tune *The Case is Closed* (*Tchaikovsky–Fink*) and
sang to it softly:

Deep in my dark the dream shines
Yes, of you, you dear always;
My cause to cry, cold but my
Story still, still my music.

Mild rose the moon, moving through our
Naked nights: tonight it rains;
Black umbrellas blossom out;
Gone the gold, my golden ball.

280

Heavy these hands. I believed
That pleased pause, your pause was me
To love alone till life's end:
I thought this; this was not true.

You touched, you took. Tears fall. O
Fair my far, when far ago
Like waterwheels wishes spun
Radiant robes: but the robes tore.

EMBLE did likewise but his choice was a hot number, *Bugs in the
Bed* by *Bog Myrtle & Her Two-Timers*. He sang gaily:

His Queen was forward, Her King was shy;
He hoped for Her Heart but He overbid;
When She ducked His Diamond down They went.

In Smuggler's Cove He smelt near Him
Her musical mermaids; She met His angels
In Locksmith's Lane, the little dears.

He said to Her: 'You're a hazy truth;'
She said to Him: 'You're a shining lie;'
Each went to a washroom and wept much.

The public applauded and the poets drew
A moral for marriage: 'The moths will get you
If the wolves won't, so why not now?'

The consequence was Both claimed the insurance
And the furniture gave what-for to Their elbows.
A reason for One, a risk on the Pair.

MALIN went on, spoke of the Fourth Age:

> Now unreckoned with, rough, his road descends
> From the haughty and high, the humourless places
> His dreams would prefer, and drops him till,
> As his forefathers did, he finds out
> Where his world lies. By the water's edge,
> The unthinking flood, down there, yes, is his
> Proper place, the polychrome Oval
> With its kleig lights and crowd engineers,
> The mutable circus where mobs rule
> The arena with roars, the real world of
> Theology and horses, our home because
> In that doubt-condemning dual kingdom
> Signs and insignia decide our cause,
> Fanatics of the Egg or Knights sworn to
> Die for the Dolphin, and our deeds wear
> Heretic green or orthodox blue,
> Safe and certain.

ROSETTA said:

>   Too soon we embrace that
> Impermanent appetitive flux,
> Humorous and hard, which adults fear
> Is real and right, the irreverent place,
> The clown's cosmos.

EMBLE said:

>   Who is comforted by it?
> Pent in the packed compulsory ring
> Round father's frown each *famus* waits his
> Day to dominate. Here a dean sits
> Making bedroom eyes at a beef steak,
> As wholly oral as the avid creatures
> Of the celibate sea; there, sly and wise

Commuters mimic the Middle Way,
Trudging on time to a tidy fortune.
(A senator said: 'From swimming-hole
To board-meeting is a big distance.')
Financiers on knolls, noses pointing
East towards oil fields, inhale the surplus
Their bowels boast of, while boys and girls, their
Hot hearts covered over with marriage
To tyrant functions, turn by degrees
To cold fish, though, precarious on the
Fringes of their feeling, a fuzzy hope
Persists somehow that sometime all this
Will walk away, and a wish gestates
For explosive pain, a punishing
Demanded moment of mortal change,
The Night of the Knock when none shall sleep,
The Absolute Instant.

QUANT said:

                    It is here, now.
For the huge wild beast of the Unexpected
Leaps on the lax recollecting back;
Unknown to him, binoculars follow
The leaping lad; lightning at noonday
Swiftly stooping to the summer-house
Engraves its disgust on engrossed flesh,
And at tea-times through tall french windows
Hurtle anonymous hostile stones.
No soul is safe. Let slight infection
Disturb a trifle some tiny gland,
And Caustic Keith grows kind and silly
Or Dainty Daisy dirties herself.
We are mocked by unmeaning; among us fall
Aimless arrows, hurting at random
As we plan to pain.

MALIN went on, spoke of the Fifth Age:

> In peace or war,
> Married or single, he muddles on,
> Offending, fumbling, falling over,
> And then, rather suddenly, there he is
> Standing up, an astonished victor
> Gliding over the good glib waters
> Of the social harbour to set foot
> On its welcoming shore where at last
> Recognition surrounds his days with
> Her felicitous light. He likes that;
> He fairly blooms; his fever almost
> Relaxes its hold. He learns to speak
> Softer and slower, not to seem so eager;
> His body acquires the blander motions
> Of the approved state. His positive glow
> Of fiscal health affects that unseen
> Just judge, that Generalized Other
> To whom he thinks and is understood by,
> Who grows less gruff as if gravely impressed
> By his evident air of having now
> Really arrived, bereaved of every
> Low relation.

EMBLE said:

> Why leave out the worst
> Pang of youth? The princes of fiction,
> Who ride through risks to rescue their loves,
> Know their business, are not really
> As young as they look. To be young means
> To be all on edge, to be held waiting in
> A packed lounge for a Personal Call
> From Long Distance, for the low voice that
> Defines one's future. The fears we know

Are of not knowing. Will nightfall bring us
Some awful order–Keep a hardware store
In a small town. . . . Teach science for life to
Progressive girls–? It is getting late.
Shall we ever be asked for? Are we simply
Not wanted at all?

QUANT said:

                                    Well, you will soon
Not bother but acknowledge yourself
As market-made, a commodity
Whose value varies, a vendor who has
To obey his buyer, will embrace moreover
The problems put you by opposing time,
The fight with work, the feud of marriage,
Whose detonating details day and night
Invest your breathing and veto sleep,
As their own answers, like others find
The train-ride between your two natures,
The morning-evening moment when
You are free to reflect on your faults still,
Is an awkward hiatus, is indeed
The real risk to be read away with
Print and pictures, reports of what should
Never have happened, will no longer
Expect more pattern, more purpose than
Your finite fate.

ROSETTA said:

                          I refuse to accept
Your plain place, your unprivileged time.
No. No. I shall not apologize
Nor retire contempt for this tawdry age.
The juke-box jives rejoicing madly
As life after life lapses out of

Its essential self and sinks into
One press-applauded public untruth
And, massed to its music, all march in step
Led by that liar, the lukewarm Spirit
Of the Escalator, ever timely,
His whims their will, away from freedom
To a locker-room life at low tension,
Abnormal none, anonymous hosts
Driven like Danaids by drill sergeants
To ply well-paid repetitive tasks
(Dowdy they'll die who have so dimly lived)
In cosy crowds. Till the caring poet,
Child of his chamber, chooses rightly
His pleased picture of pure solitudes
Where gusts gamble over gaunt areas
Frozen and futile but far enough
From vile civilities vouched for by
Statisticians, this stupid world where
Gadgets are gods and we go on talking,
Many about much, but remain alone,
Alive but alone, belonging–where?–
Unattached as tumbleweed. Time flies.

QUANT said:
No, Time returns, a continuous Now
As the clock counts. The captain sober
Gulps his beer as the galley-boy drunk
Gives away his water; William East is
Entering Olive as Alfred West
Is leaving Elaine; Lucky McGuire
Divides the spoil as Vacuous Molly
Joins in the joke; Justice van Diemen
Foresees the day when the slaves rise and
Ragamuffins roll around the block
His cone-shaped skull, while Convict 90

286

Remembers his mother. We move on
As the wheel wills; one revolution
Registers all things, the rise and fall
In pay and prices, peregrinations
Of lies and loves, colossal bangs and
Their sequential quiets in quick order.
And who runs may read written on walls
Eternal truths: 'Teddy Peterson
Never washes.' 'I'm not your father
You slobbering Swede.' 'Sulky Moses
Has bees in his bush.' 'Betty is thinner
But Connie lays.'—Who closes his eyes
Sees the blonde vistas bathed in sunlight,
The temples, tombs, and terminal god,
Tall by a torrent, the etruscan landscape
Of Man's Memory. His myths of Being
Are there always. In that unchanging
Lucid lake where he looks for ever
Narcissus sees the sensitive face
He's too intelligent to trust or like,
Pleading his pardon. Polyphemus
Curses his cave or, catching a nymph,
Begs for brotherhood with a big stick,
Hobbledehoy and helpless. Kind Orpheus lies
Violently slain on the virid bank,
That smooth sward where he sinned against kind,
And, wild by the water, women stone
The broken torso but the bloody head,
In the far distance, floating away
Down the steady stream, still opening
Its charming mouth, goes chanting on in
Fortissimo tones, a tenor lyre
Dinning the doom into a deaf Nature
Of her loose chaos. For Long-Ago has been
Ever-After since Ur-Papa gave

The Primal Yawn that expressed all things
(In His Boredom their beings) and brought forth
The wit of this world. One-Eye's mistake
Is sorry He spoke.

MALIN went on, spoke of the Sixth Age:

                    Our subject has changed.
He looks far from well; he has fattened on
His public perch; takes pills for vigour
And sound sleep, and sees in his mirror
The jawing genius of a jackass age,
A rich bore. When he recollects his
Designed life, the presented pomp is
A case of chaos, a constituted
Famine of effect. Feverish in
Their bony building his brain cells keep
Their hectic still, but his heart transfixed
By the ice-splinter of an ingrown tear,
Comatose in her cave, cares little
What the senses say; at the same time,
Dedicated, clandestine under
The guilt and grime of a great career,
The bruise of his boyhood is as blue still,
Horrid and hurting, hostile to his life
As a praised person. He pines for some
Nameless Eden where he never was
But where in his wishes once again
On hallowed acres, without a stitch
Of achievement on, the children play
Nor care how comely they couldn't be
Since they needn't know they're not happy.

QUANT said:
So do the ignored. In the soft-footed

288

Hours of darkness when elevators
Raise blondes aloft to bachelor suites
And the night-nurse notices a change
In the patient's breathing, and Pride lies
Awake in himself too weak to stir
As Shame and Regret shove into his their
Inflamed faces, we failures inquire
For the treasure also. I too have shed
The tears of parting at Traitor's Halt
Where comforts finished and kind but dull,
In low landaus and electric broughams,
Through wrought-iron gates, down rhododendron
Avenues they came, Sir Ambrose Touch,
Fat Lady Feel, Professor Howling,
Doctor Dort, dear Mrs. Pollybore,
And the Scarsdale boy with a school friend
To see us off. (But someone important,
Alas, was not there.) Some laughed of course.
Ha-ha, ha-ha, cried Hairy Mary
The lighthouse lady, little Miss Odd,
And Will Walton the watercress man,
And pointed northward. Repellent there
A storm was brewing, but we started out
In carpet-slippers by candlelight
Through Wastewood in the wane of the year,
Past Torture Tower and Twisting Ovens,
Their ruins ruled by the arrested insect
And abortive bird. In the bleak dawn
We reached Red River; on Wrynose Weir
Lay a dead salmon; when the dogs got wind
They turned tail. We talked very little;
Thunder thudded; on the thirteenth day
Our diseased guide deserted with all
The milk chocolate. Emerging from
Forests to foothills, our fears increased,

For roads grew rougher and ridges were
Congested with gibbets. We had just reached
The monastery bridge; the mist cleared;
I got one glimpse of the granite walls
And the glaciers guarding the Good Place.
(A giant jawbone jutted from that ice;
Condors on those crags coldly observed our
Helpless anguish.) My hands in my pockets,
Whistling ruefully I wandered back
By Maiden Moor and Mockbeggar Lane
To Nettlenaze where nightingales sang
Of my own evil.

ROSETTA said:

     Yet holy are the dolls
Who, junior for ever, just begin
Their open lives in absolute space,
Are simply themselves, deceiving none,
Their clothes creatures, so clearly expressing,
Tearless, timeless, the paternal world
Of pillars and parks. O Primal Age
When we danced deisal, our dream-wishes
Vert and volant, unvetoed our song.
For crows brought cups of cold water to
Ewes that were with young; unicorn herds
Galumphed through lilies; little mice played
With great cock-a-hoop cats; courteous griffins
Waltzed with wyverns, and the wild horses
Drew nigh their neighbours and neighed with joy,
All feasting with friends. What faded you
To this drab dusk? O the drains are clogged,
Rain-rusted, the roofs of the privies
Have fallen in, the flag is covered
With stale stains and the stable-clock face
Mottled with moss. Mocking blows the wind

Into my mouth. O but they've left me.
I wronged. Then they ran. I'm running down.
Wafna. Wafna. Who's to wind me now
In this lost land?

EMBLE said:

                                 I've lost the key to
The garden gate. How green it was there,
How large long ago when I looked out,
Excited by sand, the sad glitter
Of desert dreck, not dreaming I saw
My future home. It foils my magic:
Right is the ritual but wrong the time,
The place improper.

QUANT said:

                                     Reproaches come,
Emanating from some hidden centre,
Cold radiations directed at us
In waves unawares, and we are shaken
By a sceptical sigh from a Scotch Fir,
The Accuser crying in a cocktail glass.

Someone had put on the juke box a silly number *With That Thing*
as played by *The Three Snorts*, and to this he sang:

Let me sell you a song, the most side-splitting tale
Since old Chaos caught young Cosmos bending
With his back bare and his braces down,
Homo Vulgaris, the Asterisk Man.

He burned all his boats and both pink ends
Of his crowing candle, cooked his goose-flesh.
Jumped his bailiwick, jilted his heirs
And pickled his piper, the Approximate Man.

With his knees to the north and the night in his stride
He advanced on the parlours, then vanished upstairs
As a bath-tub admiral to bark commands
At his ten hammer toes, the Transient Man.

Once in his while his wit erupted
One pure little puff, one pretty idea;
A fumerole since, he has fizzled a cloud
Of gossip and gas, the Guttering Man.

Soon his soul will be sent up to Secret Inks,
His body be bought by the Breakdown Gang;
It's time for the Ticklers to take him away
In a closed cab, the Camouflage Man.

So look for a laundress to lay him out cold,
A fanciful fairy to fashion his tomb
In Rest-room Roman; get ready to pray
In a wheel-chair voice for the Watery Man.

MALIN went on once more, spoke of the Seventh Age:

His last chapter has litttle to say.
He grows backward with gradual loss of
Muscular tone and mental quickness:
He lies down; he looks through the window
Ailing at autumn, asks a sign but
The afternoons are inert, none come to
Quit his quarrel or quicken the long
Years of yawning and he yearns only
For total extinction. He is tired out;
His last illusions have lost patience
With the human enterprise. The end comes: he
Joins the majority, the jaw-dropped
Mildewed mob and is modest at last.
There his case rests: let who can disprove.

So their discussion concluded. MALIN excused himself and went to the men's room. QUANT went to the bar to fetch more drinks. ROSETTA and EMBLE sat silent, occupied with memories of a distant or recent, a real or imaginary past.

ROSETTA was thinking:

> There was Lord Lugar at Lighthazels,
> Violent-tempered; he voted against
> The Banking Bill. At Brothers Intake
> Sir William Wand; his Water Treaty
> Enriched Arabia. At Rotherhope
> General Locke, a genial man who
> Kept cormorants. At Craven Ladies
> Old Tillingham-Trench; he had two passions,
> Women and walking-sticks. At Wheels Rake,
> In his low library loving Greek
> Bishop Bottrel; he came back from the East
> With a fat notebook full of antique
> Liturgies and laws, long-forgotten
> Christian creeds occluded within a
> Feldspar fortress. Fay was his daughter;
> A truant mutation, she took up art,
> Carved in crystal, became the friend of
> Green-eyed Gelert the great dressmaker,
> And died in Rome. There was Dr Sykes
> At Mugglers Mound; his monograph on
> The chronic cough is a classic still;
> He was loved by all. At Lantern Byepew
> Susan O'Rourke, a sensitive who
> Prayed for the plants. They have perished now; their
> Level lawns and logical vistas
> Are obliterated; their big stone
> Houses are shut. Ease is rejected,
> Poor and penalized the private state.

EMBLE was thinking:

> I have friends already, faces I know
> In that calm crowd, wearing clothes like mine,
> Who have settled down, accepted at once,
> Contemporary with Trojan Knights
> And Bronze-Age bagmen; Bud and Whitey
> And Clifford Monahan and Clem Lifschutz,
> Dicky Lamb, Dominic Moreno,
> Svensson, Seidel: they seem already
> Like anyone else. Must I end like that?

Waiting to be served, QUANT caught sight of himself again in the bar mirror and thought:

> Ingenious George reached his journey's end
> Killed by a cop in a comfort station,
> Dan dropped dead at his dinner table,
> Mrs O'Malley with Miss De Young
> Wandered away into wild places
> Where desert dogs reduced their status
> To squandered bones, and it's scared you look,
> Dear friend of a friend, to face me now.
> How limply you've aged, how loose you stand
> A frog in your fork, my far-away
> Primrose prince, but a passenger here
> Retreating to his tent. Whose trump hails your
> Shenanigans now? Kneel to your bones
> And cuddle your cough. Your castle's down.
> It rains as you run, rusts where you lie.
> Beware my weakness. Worse will follow.
> The Blue Little Boys should blow their horns
> Louder and longer, for the lost sheep
> Are nibbling nightshade. But never mind . . .

MALIN returned and QUANT brought back drinks to the table. Then raising his glass to ROSETTA, QUANT said:

> Come, peregrine nymph, display your warm
> Euphoric flanks in their full glory
> Of liberal life; with luscious note
> Smoothly sing the softer data of an
> Unyielding universe, youth, money,
> Liquor and love; delight your shepherds
> For crazed we come and coarsened we go
> Our wobbling way: there's a white silence
> Of antiseptics and instruments
> At both ends, but a babble between
> And a shame surely. O show us the route
> Into hope and health; give each the required
> Pass to appease the superior archons;
> Be our good guide.

To which ROSETTA answered:

>   What gift of direction
> Is entrusted to me to take charge
> Of an expedition any may
> Suggest or join? For the journey homeward
> Arriving by roads already known
> At sites and sounds one has sensed before,
> The knowledge needed is not special,
> The sole essential a sad unrest
> Which no life can lack. Long is the way
> Of the Seven Stages, slow the going,
> And few, maybe, are faithful to the end,
> But all start out with the hope of success,
> Arm in arm with their opposite type
> Like dashing Adonis dressed to kill
> And worn Wat with his walrus moustache,
> Or one by one like Wandering Jews,

Bullet-headed bandit, broad churchman,
Lobbyist, legatee, loud virago,
Uncle and aunt and alien cousin,
Mute or maddening through the Maze of Time,
Seek its centre, desiring like us
The Quiet Kingdom. Comfort your wills then
With hungry hopes; to this indagation
Allay your longings: may our luck find the
Regressive road to Grandmother's House.

As everyone knows, many people reveal in a state of semi-intoxication capacities which are quite beyond them when they are sober: the shy talk easily and brilliantly to total strangers, the stammerers get through complicated sentences without a hitch, the unathletic is translated into a weight-lifter or a sprinter, the prosaic show an intuitive grasp of myth and symbol. A less noted and a more significant phenomenon, however, is the way in which our faith in the existence of other selves, normally rather wobbly, is greatly strengthened and receives, perhaps precisely because, for once, doubt is so completely overcome, the most startling justifications. For it can happen, if circumstances are otherwise propitious, that members of a group in this condition establish a rapport in which communication of thoughts and feelings is so accurate and instantaneous, that they appear to function as a single organism.

So it was now as they sought that state of prehistoric happiness which, by human beings, can only be imagined in terms of a landscape bearing a symbolic resemblance to the human body. The more completely these four forgot their surroundings and lost their sense of time, the more sensitively aware of each other they became, until they achieved in their dream that rare community which is otherwise only attained in states of extreme wakefulness. But this did not happen all at once.

PART THREE

The Seven Stages

O Patria, patria! Quanto mi costi!
A. Ghislanzoni *Aida*

At first all is dark and each walks alone. What they share is only
the feeling of remoteness and desertion, of having marched for miles
and miles, of having lost their bearings, of a restless urge to find
water. Gradually for each in turn the darkness begins to dissolve and
their vision to take shape.

QUANT is the first to see anything. He says:

> Groping through fog, I begin to hear
>   A salt lake lapping:
> Dotterels and dunlins on its dark shores
>   Scurry this way and that.

Now ROSETTA perceives clearly and says:

> In the centre of a sad plain
> Without forests or footpaths,
> Rimmed with rushes and moss
> I see a tacit tarn.

> Some oddling angler in summer
> May visit the spot, or a spy
> Come here to cache a stolen
> Map or meet a rival.

297

But who remarks the beehive mounds,
Graves of creatures who cooked
And wanted to be worshipped and perhaps
Were the first to feel our sorrow?

And now MALIN:

How still it is; the horses
Have moved into the shade, our mothers
Have followed their migrating gardens.

Curlews on kettle moraines
Foretell the end of time,
The doom of paradox

But lovelorn sighs ascend
From wretched greedy regions
Which cannot include themselves;

And the freckled orphan flinging
Ducks and drakes at the pond
Stops looking for stones,

And wishes he were a steamboat,
Or Lugalzaggisi, the loud
Tyrant of Erech and Umma.

And last EMBLE:

The earth looks woeful and wet;
On the raw horizon regiments pass
Tense against twilight, tired beneath
Their corresponsive spears.

Slogging on through slush
By broken bridges and burnt hamlets
Where the starving stand, staring past them
At remote inedible hills.

And now, though separate still, they begin to advance from their several starting-points into the same mountainous district. ROSETTA says:

> Now peaks oppose to the ploughman's march
>   Their twin confederate forms,
> In a warm weather, white with lilies,
>   Evergreen for grazing.
>
> Smooth the surfaces, sweeping the curves
>   Of these comely frolic clouds,
> Where the great go to forget themselves.
>   The beautiful and boon to die.

QUANT says:

> Lights are moving
> On domed hills
> Where little monks
> Get up in the dark.
>
> Though wild volcanoes
> Growl in their sleep
> At a green world,
> Inside their cloisters
>
> They sit translating
> A vision into
> The vulgar lingo
> Of armed cities,
>
> Where brides arrive
> Through great doors
> And robbers' bones
> Dangle from gallows.

EMBLE says:

> Bending forward
> With stern faces,
> Pilgrims puff
> Up the steep bank
> In huge hats.
>
> Shouting, I run
> In the other direction,
> Cheerful, unchaste,
> With open shirt
> And tinkling guitar.

MALIN says:

> Looming over my head
> Mountains menace my life,
> But on either hand, let down
> From U-valleys like yarn,
> Waterfalls all the way
> Quietly encourage me on.

And now one by one they enter the same valley and begin to ascend the same steep pass. ROSETTA is in front, then EMBLE, then MALIN and QUANT last.

ROSETTA says:

> These hills may be hollow; I've a horror of dwarfs
> And a streaming cold.

EMBLE says:

> This stony pass
> Is bad for my back. My boots are too small
> My haversack too heavy. I hate my knees
> But like my legs.

MALIN says:
>   The less I feel
>   The more I mind. I should meet death
>   With great regret.

QUANT says:
>   Thank God I was warned
>   To bring an umbrella and had bribes enough
>   For the red-haired rascals, for the reservoir guard
>   A celluloid sandwich, and silk eggs
>   For the lead smelters; for Lizzie O'Flynn,
>   The capering cowgirl with clay on her hands,
>   Tasty truffles in utopian jars,
>   And dungarees with Danish buttons
>   For Shilly and Shally the shepherd kings.

Now ROSETTA says:
>   The ground's aggression is growing less.
>   The clouds are clearing.

EMBLE says:
>   My cape is dry.
>   I can reckon correctly.

MALIN says:
>   My real intentions
>   Are nicer now.

And QUANT says:
>   I'm nearing the top.
>   When I hear what I'm up to, how I shall laugh.

And so, on a treeless watershed, at the tumbledown Mariners Tavern (which is miles inland) the four assemble, having completed the first stage of their journey. They look about them, and everything seems somehow familiar. EMBLE says:

> The railroads like the rivers run for the most part
> > East and west, and from here
> On a clear day both coasts are visible
> > And the long piers of their ports.
> To the south one sees the sawtooth range
> > Our nickel and copper come from,
> And beyond it the Barrens used for Army
> > Manœuvres; while to the north
> A brown blur of buildings marks
> > Some sacred or secular town.

MALIN says:
> Every evening the oddest collection
> > Of characters crowd this inn:
> Here a face from a farm, its frankness yearning
> > For corruption and riches; there
> A gaunt gospel whom grinning miners
> > Will stone to death by a dolmen;
> Heroes confess to whores, detectives
> > Chat or play chess with thieves.

QUANT says:
> And one finds it hard to fall asleep here.
> > Lying awake and listening
> To the creak of new creeds on the kitchen stairs
> > Or the sob of a dream next door,
> (By pass and port they percolated,
> > By friendships and official channels)
> Gentler grows the heart, gentler and much
> > Less certain it will succeed.

But ROSETTA says impatiently:
>Questioned by these crossroads our common hope
>Replies we must part; in pairs proceed
>By bicycle, barge, or bumbling local,
>As vagabonds or in wagon-lits,
>On weedy waters, up winding lanes,
>Down rational roads the Romans built,
>Over or into, under or round
>Mosses dismal or mountains sudden,
>Farmlands or fenlands or factory towns,
>Left and right till the loop be complete
>And we meet once more.

EMBLE whispers to himself:
>Do I mind with whom?
>Yes, a great deal.

And MALIN:
>In youth I would have cared,
>But not now.

And QUANT:
>I know what will happen,
>Am sincerely sorry.

They divide thus, youth with youth and age with age. To the left go ROSETTA and EMBLE, to the right QUANT and MALIN, these on foot, those by car, moving outwards in opposite directions from the high heartland to the maritime plains.

EMBLE says:
>As I pull on my gloves and prepare
>For another day-long drive,
>The landscape is full of life:
>Nieces of millionaires
>Twitter on terraces,

Peasant wives are pounding
Linen on stones by a stream,
And a doctor's silk hat dances
On top of a hedge as he hurries
Along a sunken lane.

All these and theirs are at home,
May love or hate their age
And the beds they are built to fit;
Only I have no work
But my endless journey, its joy
The whirr of wheels, the hiss
As moonlit miles flash by,
Its grief the glimpse of a face
Whose unique beauty cannot
Be asked to alter with me.

Or must everyone see himself
As I, as the pilgrim prince
Whose life belongs to his quest
For the Truth, the tall princess,
The buried gold or the Grail,
The important thought-of Thing
Which is never here and now
Like this world through which he goes
That all the others appear
To possess the secret of?

QUANT says:
> Between pollarded poplars
> This rural road
> Ambles downhill
> In search of the sea.

Nothing, neither
The farms nor the flowers,
The cows nor the clouds,
Look restive or wrong.

Then why without warning,
In my old age,
My duty done,
Do I change to a child,

And shake with shame,
Afraid of Father,
Demanding Mother's
Forgiveness again?

ROSETTA says:
The light collaborates with a land of ease,
    And rivers meander at random
Through meadowsweet massed on moist pastures,
    Past decrepit palaces
Where, brim from belvederes, bred for riding
    And graceful dancing, gaze
Fine old families who fear dishonour.

But modern on the margin of marshy ground
    Glitter the glassier homes
Of more practical people with plainer minds,
    And along the vacationer's coast,
Distributed between its hotels and casinos,
    Ex-monarchs remember a past
Of wars and waltzes as they wait for death.

MALIN says:
Though dunes still hide from the eye
    The shining shore,

Already by a certain exciting
    Kind of discomfort
I know the ocean near.

For wind and whining gull
    Are saying something,
Or trying to say, about time
    And the anxious heart
Which a matter-snob would dismiss.

So, arriving two and two at the rival ports, they complete the
second stage of their journey.

ROSETTA says:
            These ancient harbours are hailed by the morning
                        Light that untidies
            Warehouses and wharves and wilder rocks
                        Where intolerant lives
            Fight and feed in the fucoid thickets
                        Of popular pools.

EMBLE says:
            Reflected fleets, feeling in awe
                Of their sheltered lagoons,
            Stand still, a steady congregation
                Of gigantic shadows;
            Derricks on these docks adore in silence
                The noon they denote.

MALIN says:
            Quiet falls the dusk at this queasy juncture
                Of water and earth,
            And lamps are lit on the long esplanade;
                Urgent whispers
            Promise peace, and impatience shakes
                Ephemeral flesh.

And QUANT says:

> As, far from furniture and formal gardens
>> The desperate spirit
> Thinks of its end in the third person,
>> As a speck drowning
> In those wanton mansions where the whales take
>> Their huge fruitions.

But here they may not linger long. EMBLE says to ROSETTA:

> A private plane, its propeller tied
> With red ribbons is ready waiting
> To take us to town.

MALIN says to QUANT:

>> A train whistles
> For the last time. We must leave at once.

And so by air, by rail, they turn inland again towards a common goal.

QUANT says:

> Autumn has come early; evening falls;
> Our train is traversing at top speed
> A pallid province of puddles and stumps
> Where helpless objects, an orphaned quarry,
> A waif of a works, a widowed engine,
> For a sorry second sigh and are gone
> As we race through the rain with rattling windows
> Bound for a borough all bankers revere.

ROSETTA says:

> Lulled by an engine's hum,
> Our insulated lives
> Go floating freely through
> Space in a metal spore.

White hangs the waning moon,
A scruple on the sky,
And constellations crowd
Our neighbourhood the night.

QUANT says:
    In the smoking cars all seats are taken
    By melancholics mewed in their dumps,
    Elegant old-school ex-lieutenants
    Cashiered for shuddering, short blowhards,
    Thwarted geniuses in threadbare coats,
    Once well-to-do's at their wits' end,
    And underpaid agents of underground powers
    The faded and failing in flight towards town.

ROSETTA says:
    Just visible but vague,
    Way down below us lies
    The world of hares and hounds,
    Open to our contempt.

    Escaping by our skill
    Its public prison, we
    Could love ourselves and live
    In just anarchic joy.

QUANT says:
    The parlour cars and Pullmans are packed also
    With scented assassins, salad-eaters
    Who murder on milk, merry expressives,
    Pert pyknics with pumpkin heads,
    Clever cardinals with clammy hands,
    Jolly logicians with juvenile books,
    Farmers, philistines, *filles-de-joie*,
    The successful smilers the city can use.

ROSETTA says:
>What fear of freedom then
>Causes our clasping hands
>To make in miniature
>That earth anew, and now
>By choice instead of chance
>To suffer from the same
>Attraction and untruth,
>Suspicion and respect?

QUANT says:
>What mad oracle could have made us believe
>The capital will be kind when the country is not,
>And value our vanities, provide our souls
>With play and pasture and permanent water?

They lose altitude, they slow down, they arrive at the city, having completed the third stage of the journey, and are united once more, greet each other.

EMBLE says:
>Here we are.

MALIN says:
>As we hoped we have come
>Together again.

ROSETTA says:
>I am glad, I think.
>It is fun to be four.

QUANT says:
>The flushed animations
>Of crowds and couples look comic to friends.

They look about them with great curiosity. Then MALIN says:

The scene has all the signs of a facetious culture,
Publishing houses, pawnshops and pay-toilets;
August and Graeco-Roman are the granite temples
Of the medicine men whose magic keeps this body
          Politic free from fevers,
          Cancer and constipation.

The rooms near the railroad-station are rented mainly
By the criminally inclined; the Castle is open on Sundays;
There are parks for plump and playgrounds for pasty
                                                children;
The police must be large, but little men are hired to
          Service the subterranean
          Miles of dendritic drainage.

A married tribe commutes, mild from suburbia,
Whom ritual rules protect against raids by the nomad
Misfortunes they fear; for they flinch in their dreams at
                                                the scratch
Of coarse pecuniary claws, at crying images,
          Petulant, thin, reproachful,
          Destitute shades of dear ones.

Well, here I am but how, how, asks the visitor,
Strolling through the strange streets, can I start to discover
The fashionable feminine fret, or the form of insult
Minded most by the men? In what myth do their sages
          Locate the cause of evil?
          How are these people punished?

How, above all, will they end? By any natural
Fascination of frost or flood, or from the artful
Obliterating bang whereby God's rebellious image
After thousands of thankless years spent in thinking about it,

> Finally finds a solid
> Proof of its independence?

Now a trolley car comes, going northward. They take it. EMBLE
says:

> This tortuous route through town
> Was planned, it seems, to serve
> Its institutions; for we halt
> With a jerk at the Gothic gates
> Of the Women's Prison, the whitewashed
> Hexagonal Orphanage for
> Doomed children, the driveway,
> Bordered with trees in tubs
> Of the Orthopædic Hospital,
> And are crowded by the close relatives
> Of suffering, who sit upright
> With little offerings on their laps
> Of candy, magazines, comics,
> Avoiding each other's eyes,
> Shy of a rival shame.
>
> Slums are replaced by suburbs,
> Suburbs by tennis-courts, tennis-courts
> By greenhouses and vegetable gardens.
> The penultimate is the State
> Aslyum, a large Palladian
> Edifice in acres of grounds
> Surrounded by iron railings;
> And now there is no one left
> For the final run through fields
> But ourselves whose diseases as yet
> Are undiagnosed, and the driver
> Who is anxious to get home to his tea.
>
> The buttercups glitter; our bell
> Clangs loudly; and the lark's

Song is swallowed up in
The blazing blue: we are set
Down and do not care
Very much but wonder why.

Now they see before them, standing, half hidden by trees, on a little insurrection of red sandstone above a coiling river, the big house which marks the end of their journey's fourth stage. ROSETTA is enthusiastic and runs forward saying:

In I shall go, out I shall look.

But the others are tired and MALIN says:

Very well, we will wait, watch from outside.

QUANT says:
A scholarly old scoundrel,
Whose fortune was founded on the follies of others,
    Built it for his young bride.
She died in childbed; he died on the gallows;
    The property passed to the Crown.

The façade has a lifeless look,
For no one uses the enormous ballroom;
    But in book-lined rooms at the back
Committees meet, and many strange
    Decisions are secretly taken.

High up in the East Tower,
A pale-faced widow looks pensively down
    At the terrace outside where the snow
Flutters and flurries round the formal heads
    Of statues that stare at the park.

And the guards at the front gate
Change with the seasons; in cheerful Spring
    How engaging their glances; but how

312

Morose in Fall: ruined kitchen-maids
　　Blubber behind the bushes.

ROSETTA returns, more slowly than she left. EMBLE asks:

Well, how was it? What did you see?

ROSETTA answers:
　　Opera glasses on the ormolu table,
　　Frock-coated father framed on the wall
　　In a bath-chair facing a big bow-window,
　　With valley and village invitingly spread,
　　　　　I got what is going on.

At the bend of the Bourne where the brambles grow
　　　　　　　　　　　　　　　thickest
　　Major Mott joins Millicent Rusk;
　　Discreetly the kingfisher keeps his distance
　　But an old cob swan looks on as they
　　　　　Commit the sanguine sin.

Heavy the orchards; there's Alison pinching
　　Her baby brother, Bobby and Dick
　　Frying a frog with their father's reading-glass,
　　Conrad and Kay in the carpentry shed
　　　　　Where they've no business to be.

Cold are the clays of Kibroth-Hattaavah,
　　Babel's urbanities buried in sand,
　　Red the geraniums in the rectory garden
　　Where the present incumbent reads Plato in French
　　　　　And has lost his belief in Hell.

From the gravel-pits in Groaning Hollow
　　To the monkey-puzzle on Murderer's Hill,
　　From the Wellington Arms to the white steam laundry,

313

The significant note is nature's cry
        Of long-divided love.

I have watched through a window a World that is fallen,
The mating and malice of men and beasts,
The corporate greed of quiet vegetation,
And the homesick little obstinate sobs
        Of things thrown into being.

I would gladly forget; let us go quickly.

EMBLE said:
        Yonder, look, is a yew avenue,
        A mossy mile. For amusement's sake
        Let us run a race till we reach the end.

   This, willing or unwilling, they start to do and, as they run, their
rival natures, by art comparing and compared, reveal themselves.
Thus MALIN mutters:

        'Alas,' say my legs, 'if we lose it will be
        A sign you have sinned.'

And QUANT:
                        The safest place
        Is more or less middling: the mean average
        Is not noticed.

And EMBLE:
                        How nice it feels
        To be out ahead: I'm always lucky
        But must remember how modest to look.

And ROSETTA:
        Let them call; I don't care. I shall keep them waiting.
        They ought to have helped me. I can't hope to be first
        So let me be last.

314

In this manner, sooner or later they come to the crumbling lichen-covered wall of the forgotten graveyard which marks the end of the fifth stage of their journey. At their feet lies a fallen wooden sign, bearing in faded letters the warning:

No Entrance Here Without a Subject

and underneath this, in smaller, barely decipherable script, some verses which EMBLE starts to read aloud:

> Stranger, this still
> Museum exhibits
> The results of life:
> Thoughtfully, therefore,
> Peer as you pass
> These cases clouded
> By vetch and eyebright
> And viper's bugloss
> At each little collection
> Loosely arranged
> Of dated dust.
>
> Here it is holy,
> Here at last
> In mute marble
> The Master closed
> His splendid period;
> A spot haunted
> By goat-faced grasshoppers
> And gangling boys
> Taunted by talents
> Which tell them more
> Than their flesh can feel.
>
> Here impulse loses
> Its impetus: thus
> Far and no farther
> Their legs, resolutions

And longings carried
The big, the ambitious,
The beautiful; all
Stopped in mid-stride
At this straggling border
Where wildflowers begin
And wealth ends.

Yet around their rest
Flittermice, finches
And flies restore
Their lost milieu;
An inconsequential
Host of pert
Occasional creatures,
Blindly, playfully,
Bridging death's
Eternal gap
With quotidian joy.

MALIN sighs and says what they are all thinking but wish they were
not.

> Again we must digress, go by different
> Paths in pairs to explore the land.

Knowing they will never be able to agree as to who shall accom-
pany whom, they cast lots and so it falls out that ROSETTA is to go
with QUANT and EMBLE with MALIN. Two are disappointed, two
are disturbed.

QUANT mutters:
> This bodes badly.

And MALIN:
>   So be it. Who knows
> If we wish what we will?

And ROSETTA:

> Will you forget
> If you know that I won't?

And EMBLE:

> Will your need be me?

They depart now, MALIN and EMBLE westward on bicycles, QUANT and ROSETTA eastward by boat, sad through fair scenes, thinking of another and talking to themselves.

MALIN says:

> As we cycle silent through a serious land
> For hens and horses, my hunger for a live
> Person to father impassions my sense
> Of this boy's beauty in battle with time.
>
> These old-world hamlets and haphazard lanes
> Are perilous places; how plausible here
> All arcadian cults of carnal perfection,
> How intoxicating the platonic myth.

EMBLE says:

> Pleasant my companion but I pine for another.

QUANT says:

> Our canoe makes no noise; monotonous
> Ramparts of reeds surround our navigation;
> The waterway winds as it wants through the hush:
> O fortunate fluid her fingers caress.
>
> Welcome her, world; sedge-warblers, betray your
> Hiding places with song; and eddy, butterflies,
> In frivolous flights about that fair head:
> How apt your homage to her innocent disdain.

317

ROSETTA says:

> The figure I prefer is far away.

MALIN says:

> To know nature is not enough for the ego;
> The aim of its eros is to create a soul,
> The start of its magic is stolen flesh.

QUANT says:

> Let nature unite us whose needs belong to
> Separate systems that make no sense to each other:
> She is not my sister and I am not her friend.

EMBLE says:

> Unequal our happiness: his is greater.

ROSETTA says:

> Lovelier would this look if my love were with me.

MALIN says:

> Girlishly glad that my glance is not chaste,
> He wants me to want what he would refuse:
> For sons have this desire for a slave also.

QUANT says:

> Both graves of the stream are agog as here
> Comes a bride for a bridegroom in a boat ferried
> By a dying man dreaming of a daughter-wife.

Now they arrive, two and two, east and west, at the hermetic gardens and the sixth stage of their journey is completed. They gaze about them entranced at the massive mildness of these survivals from an age of cypresses and cisterns.

318

ROSETTA says:

>How tempting to trespass in these Italian gardens
>With their smirk ouches and sweet-smelling borders,
>>To lean on the low
>Parapet of some pursive fountain
>>And drowse through the unctuous day.

EMBLE says:

>There are special perspectives for speculation,
>Random rose-walks, and rustic bridges
>>Over neat canals;
>A miniature railroad with mossy halts
>>Wambles through wanton groves.

QUANT says:

>Yet this is a theatre where thought becomes act
>And beside a sundial, in the silent umbrage
>>Of some dark daedal,
>The ruined rebel is recreated
>>And chooses a chosen self.

>From lawns and relievos the leisure makes
>Its uncomfortable claim and, caught off its guard,
>>His hardened heart
>Consents to suffer, and the sudden instant
>>Touches his time at last.

MALIN says:

>Tense on the parterre, he takes the hero's
>Leap into love; then, unlatching the wicket
>>Gate he goes:
>The plains of his triumph appear empty,
>>But now among their motionless

Avenues and urns with extra élan
Faster revolves the invisible corps
   Of pirouetting angels,
And a chronic chorus of cascades and birds
   Cuts loose in a wild cabaletta.

  Presently the extraordinary charm of these gardens begins to work upon them also. It seems an accusation. They become uneasy and unwell.

EMBLE says:
   I would stay to be saved but the stillness here
   Reminds me too much of my mother's grief;
   It scorns and scares me.

QUANT says:
          My excuses throb
   Louder and lamer.

ROSETTA says:
        The long shadows
   Disapprove of my person.

MALIN says:
          Reproached by the doves,
   My groin groans.

ROSETTA:
        I've got a headache,
   And my nose is inflamed.

QUANT:
          My knees are stiff.

EMBLE:
   My teeth need attention.

Then QUANT says:

> Who will trust me now,
> Who with broad jokes have bored my children
> And, warm by my wife, have wished her dead
> Yet turned her over, who have told strangers
> Of the cars and castles that accrued with the fortune
> I might have made?

And EMBLE says:

> My mortal body
> Has sinned on sofas; assigning to each
> Points for pleasure, I have pencilled on envelopes
> Lists of my loves.

And ROSETTA says:

> Alas for my sneers
> At the poor and plain: I must pay for thinking
> Failure funny.

And MALIN says:

> I have felt too good
> At being better than the best of my colleagues:
> Walking by water, have worked out smiling
> Deadly reviews. My deeds forbid me
> To linger longer. I'll leave my friend,
> Be sorry by myself.

Then EMBLE again:

> I must slip off
> To the woods to worry.

Then ROSETTA:

> I want to retire
> To some private place and pray to be made
> A good girl.

And then QUANT:

> I must go away
> With my terrors until I have taught them to sing.

So one by one they plunge into the labyrinthine forest and vanish down solitary paths, with no guide but their sorrows, no companion but their own voices. Their ways cross and recross yet never once do they meet though now and then one catches somewhere not far off a brief snatch of another's song. Thus QUANT's voice is heard singing:

> A vagrant veteran I,
> Discharged with grizzled chin,
> Sans youth or use, sans uniform,
> A tiger turned an ass.

Then MALIN's.

> These branches deaf and dumb
> Were woeful suitors once;
> Mourning unmanned, and moping turned
> Their sullen souls to wood.

Then ROSETTA's:

> My dress is torn, my tears
> Are running as I run
> Through forests far from father's eye
> To look for a true love.

Then EMBLE's:

> My mother weeps for me
> Who disappeared at play
> From home and hope like all who chase
> The blue elusive bird.

Now QUANT's again:

> Through gloomy woods I go
> Ex-demigod; the damp
> Awakes my wound; I want my tea
> But needed am of none.

Now EMBLE'S:

>   More faint, more far away
>   The huntsman's social horn
> Calls through the cold uncanny woods
>   And nearer draws the night.

Now ROSETTA'S:

>   Dear God, regard thy child;
>   Repugn or pacify
> All furry forms and fangs that lurk
>   Within this horrid shade.

Now MALIN'S:

>   Their given names forget,
>   Mere species of despair,
> On whims of win their wills depend,
>   On temperatures their mood.

And yet once more QUANT'S:

>   So, whistling as I walk
>   Through brake and copse, I keep
> A lookout for the Limping One
>   Who buys abandoned souls.

Obedient to their own mysterious laws of direction, their twisting paths converge, approach their several voices, and collect the four for a startled reunion at the forest's edge. They stare at what they see.

QUANT says:

>   The climate of enclosure, the cool forest
>   Break off abruptly:
>   Giddy with the glare and ungoverned heat,
>   We stop astonished,
>   Interdicted by desert, its dryness edged
>   By a scanty scrub

Of Joshua trees and giant cacti;
    Then, vacant of value,
Incoherent and infamous sands,
    Rainless regions
Swarming with serpents, ancestral wastes,
    Lands beyond love.

Now, with only the last half of the seventh stage to go to finish their journey, for the first time fear and doubt dismay them. Is triumph possible? If so, are they chosen? Is triumph worth it? If so, are they worthy?

MALIN says:
    Boring and bare of shade,
    Devoid of souvenirs and voices,
    It takes will to cross this waste

    Which is really empty: the mirage
    Need not be tasty to tempt;
    For the senses arouse themselves,

    And an image of humpbacked girls
    Or plates of roasted rats
    Can make the mouth water.

    With nothing to know about,
    The mind reflects on its movements
    And so doubles any distance.

    Even if we had time
    To read through all the wrinkled
    Reports of explorers who claim

    That hidden arrant streams
    Chuckle through this chapped land
    In profound and meagre fissures,

Or that this desert is dotted with
Oases where acrobats dwell
Who make unbelievable leaps,

We should never have proof they were not
Deceiving us. For the only certain
Truth is that they returned,

And that we cannot be deaf to the question:
'Do I love this world so well
That I have to know how it ends?'

EMBLE says:

    As yet the young hero's
    Brow is unkissed by battle,
    But he knows how necessary
    Is his defiance of fate
    And, serene already, he sails
    Down the gorge between the august
    Faces carved in the cliffs
    Towards the lordship of the world.

    And the gentle majority are not
    Afraid either, but, owl-like
    And sedate in their glass globes
    The wedded couples wave
    At the bandits racing by
    With affection, and the learned relax
    On pinguid plains among
    A swarm of flying flowers.

    But otherwise is it with the play
    Of the child whom chance decrees
    To say what all men suffer:
    For he wishes against his will
    To be lost, and his fear leads him

To dales of driving rain
Where peasants with penthouse eyebrows
Sullenly guard the sluices.

And his steps follow the stream
Past rusting apparatus
To its gloomy beginning, the original
Chasm where brambles block
The entrance to the underworld;
There the silence blesses his sorrow,
And holy to his dread is that dark
Which will neither promise nor explain.

ROSETTA says:
Are our dreams indicative? Does it exist,
   That last landscape
Of gloom and glaciers and great storms
Where, cold into chasms, cataracts
   Topple, and torrents
Through rocky ruptures rage for ever
In a winter twilight watched by ravens,
      Birds on basalt,
And shadows of ships long-shattered lie,
Preserved disasters, in the solid ice
   Of frowning fjords?
Does the Moon's message mean what it says:
'In that oldest and most hidden of all places
   Number is unknown?'
Can lying lovers believe their bones'
   Unshaken assurance
That all the elegance, all the promise
Of the world they wish is waiting there?

Even while she is still speaking, their fears are confirmed, their
hopes denied. For the world from which their journey has been one

long flight rises up before them now as if the whole time it had been hiding in ambush, only waiting for the worst moment to reappear to its fugitives in all the majesty of its perpetual fury.

QUANT says:
>My shoulders shiver. A shadow chills me
>As thunderheads threaten the sun.

MALIN says:
>Righteous wrath is raising its hands
>To strike and destroy.

EMBLE says:
>   Storm invades
>The Euclidean calm. The clouds explode.
>The scene dissolves, is succeeded by
>A grinning gap, a growth of nothing
>Pervaded by vagueness.

ROSETTA says:
>   Violent winds
>Tear us apart. Terror scatters us
>To the four coigns. Faintly our sounds
>Echo each other, unrelated
>Groans of grief at a great distance.

QUANT says:
>In the wild West they are whipping each other.

EMBLE says:
>In the hungry East they are eating their books.

ROSETTA says:
>In the numb North there are no more cradles.

MALIN says:
>The sullen South has been set on fire.

EMBLE says:

> Dull through the darkness, indifferent tongues
> From bombed buildings, from blacked-out towns,
> Camps and cockpits, from cold trenches,
> Submarines and cells, recite in unison
> A common creed, declaring their weak
> Faith in confusion. The floods are rising;
> Rain ruins on the routed fragments
> Of all the armies; indistinct
> Are friend and foe, one flux of bodies
> Miles from mother, marriage, or any
> Workable world.

QUANT says:

>   The wall is fallen
> That Balbus built, and back they come
> The Dark Ones to dwell in the statues,
> Manias in marble, messengers from
> The Nothing who nothings. Night descends;
> Through thickening darkness thin uneases,
> Ravenous unreals, perambulate
> Our paths and pickles.

MALIN says:

>   The primary colours
> Are all mixed up; the whole numbers
> Have broken down, the big situations
> Ceased to excite.

ROSETTA says

>   Sick of time,
> Long Ada and her Eleven Daughters,
> The standing stones, stagger, disrupt
> Their petrified polka on Pillicock Mound;
> The chefs and shepherds have shot themselves,

The dowagers dropped in their Dutch gardens,
The battle-axe and the bosomed war-horse
Swept grand to their graves. Graven on all things,
Inscribed on skies, escarpments, trees,
Notepaper, neckties, napkin rings,
Brickwalls and barns, or branded into
The livid limbs of lambs and men,
Is the same symbol, the signature
Of reluctant allegiance to a lost cause.

MALIN says:

    Our ideas have got drunk and drop their H's.

EMBLE:

    We err what we are as if we were not.

ROSETTA:

    The honest and holy are hissed at the races.

QUANT:

    God's in his greenhouse, his geese in the world.

    Saying this, they woke up and recognized where they sat and who
they were. The darkness which had invaded their dream was ex-
plained, for it was closing time and the bartender was turning off the
lights. What they had just dreamed they could no longer recall
exactly, but when EMBLE and ROSETTA looked at each other, they
were conscious of some sweet shared secret which it might be
dangerous to remember too well. Perhaps it was this which prompted
ROSETTA to suggest that they all come back to her apartment for a
snack and a nightcap for, when they accepted, she realized that she
had been expecting QUANT and MALIN to decline. But it was too
late now. They were out in the street already and EMBLE had hailed
a cab.

PART FOUR

The Dirge

His mighty work for the nation,
Strengthening peace and securing union,
Always at it since on the throne,
Has saved the country more than one billion.
Broadsheet *on the death of King Edward VII*

As they drove through the half-lit almost empty streets, the effect of their dream had not yet worn off but persisted as a mutual mood of discouragement. Whether they thought of Nature, of her unending stream of irrelevant events without composition or centre, her reckless waste of value, her alternate looks of idiotic inertia and insane ferocity, or whether they thought of Man, of the torpor of his spirit, the indigent dryness of his soul, his bottomless credulity, his perverse preference for the meretricious or the insipid–it seemed impossible to them that either could have survived so long had not some semi-divine stranger with superhuman powers, some Gilgamesh or Napoleon, some Solon or Sherlock Holmes, appeared from time to time to rescue both, for a brief bright instant, from their egregious destructive blunders. And for such a great one who, long or lately, has always died or disappeared, they now lamented thus.

Sob, heavy world,
Sob as you spin
Mantled in mist, remote from the happy:
The washerwomen have wailed all night,

330

The disconsolate clocks are crying together,
    And the bells toll and toll
For tall Agrippa who touched the sky:
    Shut is that shining eye
Which enlightened the lampless and lifted up
The flat and foundering, reformed the weeds
Into civil cereals and sobered the bulls;
    Away the cylinder seal,
The didactic digit and dreaded voice
Which imposed peace on the pullulating
Primordial mess. Mourn for him now,
    Our lost dad,
    Our colossal father.

    For seven cycles
    For seven years
Past vice and virtue, surviving both,
Through pluvial periods, paroxysms
Of wind and wet, through whirlpools of heat,
    And comas of deadly cold,
On an old white horse, an ugly nag,
    In his faithful youth he followed
The black ball as it bowled downhill
On the spotted spirit's spiral journey,
Its purgative path to that point of rest
    Where longing leaves it, and saw
Shimmering in the shade the shrine of gold,
The magical marvel no man dare touch,
Between the towers the tree of life
    And the well of wishes
    The waters of joy.

    Then he harrowed hell,
    Healed the abyss
Of torpid instinct and trifling flux,
Laundered it, lighted it, made it lovable with

Cathedrals and theories; thanks to him
      Brisker smells abet us,
Cleaner clouds accost our vision
      And honest sounds our ears.
For he ignored the Nightmares and annexed their ranges,
Put the clawing Chimaeras in cold storage,
Berated the Riddle till it roared and fled,
      Won the Battle of Whispers,
Stopped the Stupids, stormed into
The Fumblers' Forts, confined the Sulky
To their drab ditches and drove the Crashing
      Bores to their bogs,
      Their beastly moor.

      In the high heavens,
      The ageless places,
The gods are wringing their great worn hands
For their watchman is away, their world-engine
Creaking and cracking. Conjured no more
      By his master music to wed
Their truths to times, the Eternal Objects
      Drift about in a daze:
O the lepers are loose in Lombard Street,
The rents are rising in the river basins,
The insects are angry. Who will dust
      The cobwebbed kingdoms now?
For our lawgiver lies below his people,
Bigger bones of a better kind,
Unwarped by their weight, as white limestone
      Under green grass,
      The grass that fades.

But now the cab stopped at ROSETTA's apartment house. As they
went up in the elevator, they were silent but each was making a
secret resolve to banish such gloomy reflections and become, or at
least appear, carefree and cheerful.

PART FIVE

The Masque

'Oh, Heaven help me,' she prayed, 'to be decorative and to do right.'
Ronald Firbank *The Flower beneath the Foot*

Rosetta had shown the men where everything was and, as they trotted between the kitchen and the living room cutting sandwiches and fixing drinks, all felt that it was time something exciting happened and decided to do their best to see that it did. Had they been perfectly honest with themselves, they would have had to admit that they were tired and wanted to go home alone to bed. That they were not was in part due, of course, to vanity, the fear of getting too old to want fun or too ugly to get it, but also to unselfishness, the fear of spoiling the fun for others. Besides, only animals who are below civilization and the angels who are beyond it can be sincere. Human beings are, necessarily, actors who cannot become something before they have first pretended to be it; and they can be divided, not into the hypocritical and the sincere, but into the sane who know they are acting and the mad who do not. So it was now as ROSETTA switched on the radio which said:

> *Music past midnight. For men in the armed*
> *Forces on furlough and their feminine consorts,*
> *For war-workers and women in labour,*
> *For Bohemian artists and owls of the night,*
> *We present a series of savage selections*

333

By brutal bands from bestial tribes,
The Quaraquorams and the Quaromanlics,
The Arsocids and the Alonites,
The Ghuzz, the Guptas, the gloomy Krimchaks,
The Timurids and Torguts, with terrible cries
Will drag you off to their dream retreats
To dance with your deaths till the dykes collapse.

EMBLE asked ROSETTA to dance. The others sat watching. QUANT waved his cigar in time to the music and sang a verse from an old prospector's ballad.

When Laura lay on her ledger side
And nicely threw her north cheek up,
How pleasing the plight of her promising grove
And how rich the random I reached with a rise.

Whereupon MALIN sang a verse of a folksong from a Fen District.

When in wan hope I wandered away and alone,
How brag were the birds, how buxom the sky,
But sad were the sallows and slow were the brooks
And how dismal that day when I danced with my dear.

Moving well together to the music, ROSETTA and EMBLE were becoming obviously attracted to each other. In times of war even the crudest kind of positive affection between persons seems extraordinarily beautiful, a noble symbol of the peace and forgiveness of which the whole world stands so desperately in need. So to dancers and spectators alike, this quite casual attraction seemed and was of immense importance.

ROSETTA and EMBLE sang together:

Hushed is the lake of hawks
Bright with our excitement,

334

And all the sky of skulls
Glows with scarlet roses;
The melter of men and salt
Admires the drinker of iron:
Bold banners of meaning
Blaze o'er the host of days.

MALIN has been building a little altar of sandwiches. Now he placed an olive upon it and invoked the Queen of love.

Hasten earthward, Heavenly Venus,
Mistress of motion, Mother of loves,
A signal from whom excites time to
Confused outbursts, filling spaces with
Lights and leaves. In pelagic meadows
The plankton open their parachutes;
The mountains are amused; mobs of birds
Shout at fat shopkeepers. 'Shucks! We are free.
Imitate us—' and out of the blue
Come bright boys with bells on their ankles
To tease with roses Cartesian monks
Till their heads ache, geometers vexed by
Irrelevant reds. May your right hand,
Lightly alighting on their longing flesh,
Promise this pair what their prayers demand,
Bliss in both, born of each other, a
Double dearness; let their dreams descend
Into concrete conduct. Claim your own.

ROSETTA and EMBLE had stopped dancing and sat down on the couch. Now he put his arm around her and said:

Enter my aim from all directions, O
Special spirit whose expressions are
My carnal care, my consolation:
Be many or one. Meet me by chance on

335

Credulous coasts where cults intersect
Or join as arranged by the Giants' Graves,
Titanic tombs which at twilight bring
Greetings from the great misguided dead;
Hide from, haunt me, on hills to be seen
Far away through the forelegs of mares;
Stay till I come in the startling light
When the tunnel turns to teach surprise,
Or face me and fight for a final stand
With a brave blade in your buffer states,
My visible verb, my very dear,
Till I die, darling.

ROSETTA laid her head on his shoulder and said:

O the deep roots
Of the cross-roads yew, calm for so long,
Have felt you afar and faintly begin
To tingle now. What twitters there'll be in
The brook bushes at the bright sound of
Your bicycle bell. What barking then
As you stride the stiles to startle one
Great cry in the kitchen when you come home,
My doom, my darling.

They kissed. Then EMBLE said:

Till death divide
May the Four Faces Feeling can make
Assent to our sighs.

She said:

The snap of the Three
Grim Spinning Sisters' Spectacle Case
Uphold our honours.

336

He said:

> The Heavenly Twins
> Guard our togetherness from ghostly ills.

She said:

> The Outer Owner, that Oldest One whom
> This world is with, be witness to our vows.

Which vows they now alternately swore.

> If you blush, I'll build breakwaters.
> When you're tired, I'll tidy your table.
> If you cry, I'll climb crags.
> When you're sick, I'll sit at your side.
> If you frown, I'll fence fields.
> When you're ashamed, I'll shine your shoes.
> If you laugh, I'll liberate lands.
> When you're depressed, I'll play you the piano.
> If you sigh, I'll sack cities.
> When you're unlucky, I'll launder your linen.
> If you sing, I'll save souls.
> When you're hurt, I'll hold your hand.
> If you smile, I'll smelt silver.
> When you're afraid, I'll fetch you food.
> If you talk, I'll track down trolls.
> When you're on edge, I'll empty your ash-tray.
> If you whisper, I'll wage wars.
> When you're cross, I'll clean your coat.
> If you whistle, I'll water wastes.
> When you're bored, I'll bathe your brows.

Again they embraced. QUANT poured out the dregs of the glass on the carpet as a libation and invoked the local spirits.

Ye little larvae, lords of the household,
Potty, P-P, Peppermill, Lampshade,
Funnybone, Faucet, Face-in-the-wall,
Head-over-heels and Upsy-daisy
And Collywobbles and Cupboard-Love,
Be good, little gods, and guard these lives,
Innocent be all your indiscretions,
That no paranoic notion obsess
Nor dazing dump bedevil their minds
With faceless fears; no filter-passing
Virus invade; no invisible germ,
Transgressing rash or gadding tumour
Attach their tissues; nor, taking by
Spiteful surprise, conspiring objects
With slip or sharpness or sly fracture
Menace or mangle the morbid flesh
Of our king and queen.

Now, turning to ROSETTA, MALIN said:

> O clear Princess,
Learn from your hero his love of play,
Cherish his childishness, choose in him
Your task and toy, your betrayer also
Who gives gladly but forgets as soon
What and why, for the world he is true to
Is his own creation; to act like father,
And beget like God a gayer echo,
And unserious self, is the sole thought
Of this bragging boy. Be to him always
The mother-moment which makes him dream
He is lord of time. Belong to his journey:
O rest on his rock in your red dress,
His youth and future.

338

Then, turning to EMBLE, he said:

> And you, bright Prince,
> Invent your steps, go variously about
> Her pleasant places, disposed to joy;
> O stiffly stand, a staid monadnock,
> On her peneplain; placidly graze
> On her outwash apron, her own steed;
> Dance, a wild deer, in her dark thickets;
> Run, a river, all relish through her vales.

Alcohol, lust, fatigue, and the longing to be good, had by now induced in them all a euphoric state in which it seemed as if it were only some trifling and easily rectifiable error, improper diet, inadequate schooling, or an outmoded moral code which was keeping mankind from the millennial Earthly Paradise. Just a little more effort, perhaps merely the discovery of the right terms in which to describe it, and surely absolute pleasure must immediately descend upon the astonished armies of this world and abolish for ever all their hate and suffering. So, such effort as at that moment they could, they made. ROSETTA cried:

> Let brazen bands abrupt their din and
> Song grow civil, for the siege is raised.
> The mad gym-mistress, made to resign,
> Can pinch no more.

EMBLE cried:

> Deprived of their files,
> The vice-squads cavort in the mountains,
> The Visa-Division vouch for all.

Then ROSETTA:

> The shops which displayed shining weapons
> And crime-stories carry delicate
> Pastoral poems and porcelain groups.

Then EMBLE:
>Nor money, magic, nor martial law,
>Hardness of heart nor hocus-pocus
>Are needed now on the novel earth.

ROSETTA:
>Nor terrors, tides, contagion longer
>Lustrate her stables: their strictures yield
>To play and peace.

EMBLE:
>   Where pampered opulent
>Grudges governed, the Graces shall dance
>In excellent order with hands linked.

ROSETTA:
>Where, cold and cruel, critical faces
>Watched from windows, shall wanton putti
>Loose floods of flowers.

EMBLE:
>   Where frontier sentries
>Stood so glumly on guard, young girls shall pass
>Trespassing in extravagant clothes.

ROSETTA:
>Where plains winced as punishing engines
>Raised woeful welts, tall windmills shall pat
>The flexible air and fan good cows.

EMBLE:
>Where hunted hundreds helplessly drowned,
>Rose-cheeked riders shall rein their horses
>To smile at swans.

The others joined in chorus. MALIN cried:

> It is safe to endure:
> Each flat defect has found its solid
> Gift to shadow, each goal its unique
> Longing to lure, relatedness its
> Invariant base, since Venus has now
> Agreed so gladly to guarantee
> Plenty of water to the plants this year,
> Aid to the beasts, to all human demands
> Full satisfaction with fresh structures
> For crucial regions.

QUANT cried:

> A kind word and
> A fatherly peak not far away
> For city orphans.

Then ROSETTA again:

> Synchronized watches
> And a long lane with a lot of twists
> For both sexes.

And EMBLE:

> Barns and shrubberies
> For game-playing gangs.

QUANT:

> Grates full of logs and
> Hinterland homes for old proconsuls
> And pensioned pairs.

EMBLE:

> Places of silence
> For real readers.

ROSETTA:
>   A room with a view
> For a shut-in soul.

MALIN:
>   A shady walk
> There and back for a thinker or two.

EMBLE:
> A gentle jaunt for dejected nerves
> Over warm waters.

ROSETTA:
>   A wild party
> Every night for the outgoing classes.

MALIN:
> A long soliloquy to learn by heart
> For the verbal type.

QUANT:
>   Vast museums
> For the acquisitive kind to keep tidy.

MALIN:
> Spigots to open for the spendthrift lot,
> And choke-pear choices for champion wills.

MALIN caught QUANT's eye and they rose to take their leave. As they were getting their hats and coats, QUANT sang:

> O gifted ghosts, be gone now to affirm
> Your dedication; dwell in your choice:
>   Venus with grace preventing
>   Requires what she may quicken.

342

Royal with roses be your resting place,
Balmy the airways, blue the welkin that
    Attend your time of passage,
    And easy seas assist you.

MALIN sang:
    Redeem with a clear
    Configuration
    Of routes and goals
    The ages of anguish,
    All griefs endured
    At the feet of appalling
    Fortresses; may
    Your present motions
    Satisfy all
    Their antecedents.

ROSETTA went with them to the elevator. As they waited in the
corridor for it to come up, QUANT went on singing:

    Wonder warm you with its wisdom now,
    Genial joy rejuvenate your days,
      A light of self-translation,
      A blessed interior brightness,

    Animate also your object world
    Till its pure profiles appear again,
      Losing their latter vagueness,
      In the sharp shapes of childhood.

So did MALIN as they entered the elevator:

    Plumed and potent
    Go forth, fulfil
    A happy future
    And occupy that

Permanent kingdom
Parameters rule,
Loved by infinite
Populations
Of possible cases:
Away. Farewell.

Then they sank from her sight. When she got back to her apartment, she found that EMBLE had gone into her bedroom and passed out. She looked down at him, half sadly, half relieved, and thought thus:

Blind on the bride-bed, the bridegroom snores,
Too aloof to love. Did you lose your nerve
And cloud your conscience because I wasn't
Your dish really? You danced so bravely
Till I wished I were. Will you remain
Such a pleasant prince? Probably not.
But you're handsome, aren't you? even now
A kindly corpse. I'll coffin you up till
You rule again. Rest for us both and
Dream, dear one. I'll be dressed when you wake
To get coffee. You'll be glad you didn't
While your headache lasts, and I won't shine
In the sobering sun. We're so apart
When our ways have crossed and our words touched
On Babylon's banks. You'll build here, be
Satisfied soon, while I sit waiting
On my light luggage to leave if called
For some new exile, with enough clothes
But no merry maypole. Make your home
With some glowing girl; forget with her what
Happens also. If ever you see
A fuss forming in the far distance,
Lots of police, and a little group
In terrible trouble, don't try to help;

They'd make you mock and you might be ashamed.
As long as you live may your lying be
Poetic only. I'd hate you to think
How gentile you feel when you join in
The rowdy cries at Rimmon's party;
'—Fasten your figleaf, the Fleet is in.
Caesar is sitting in solemn thought,
Do not disturb. I'm dying to-night with
The tragic poets—' for you'll trust them all,
Be at home in there where a host of creatures,
Shot or squashed, have insured good-luck to
Their bandit bodies, blond mausoleums
Of the inner life. How could I share their
Light elations who belong after
Such hopes end? So be off to the game, dear,
And meet your mischief. I'll mind the shop.
You'll never notice what's not for sale
To charming children. Don't choose to ask me.
You're too late to believe. Your lie is showing,
Your creed is creased. But have Christian luck.
Your Jesus has wept; you may joke now,
Be spick and span, spell out the bumptious
Morals on monuments, mind your poise
And take up your cues, attract Who's-Who,
Ignore What's-Not. Niceness is all and
The rest bores. I'm too rude a question.
You'd learn to loathe, your legs forget their
Store of proverbs, the staircase wit of
The sleep-walker. You'd slip and blame me
When you came to, and couldn't accept
Our anxious hope with no household god or
Harpist's Haven for hearty climbers.
So fluke through unflustered with full marks in
House-geography: let history be.
Time is our trade, to be tense our gift

Whose woe is our weight; for we are His Chosen,
His ragged remnant with our ripe flesh
And our hats on, sent out of the room
By their dying grandees and doleful slaves,
Kicked in corridors and cold-shouldered
At toll-bridges, teased upon the stage,
Snubbed at sea, to seep through boundaries,
Diffuse like firearms through frightened lands,
Transpose our plight like a poignant theme
Into twenty tongues, time-tormented
But His People still. We'll point for Him,
Be as obvious always if He won't show
To threaten their thinking in their way,
Nor His strong arm that stood no nonsense,
Fly, let's face it, to defend us now
When bruised or broiled our bodies are chucked
Like cracked crocks onto kitchen middens
In the time He takes. We'll trust. He'll slay
If His Wisdom will. He won't alter
Nor fake one fact. Though I fly to Wall Street
Or Publisher's Row, or pass out, or
Submerge in music, or marry well,
Marooned on riches, He'll be right there
With His Eye upon me. Should I hide away
My secret sins in consulting rooms,
My fears are before Him; He'll find all,
Ignore nothing. He'll never let me
Conceal from Him the semi-detached
Brick villa in Laburnum Crescent,
The poky parlour, the pink bows on
The landing-curtains, or the lawn-mower
That wouldn't work, for He won't pretend to
Forget how I began, nor grant belief
In the mythical scenes I make up
Of a home like theirs, the Innocent Place where

His Law can't look, the leaves are so thick.
I've made their magic but their Momma Earth
Is His stone still, and their stately groves,
Though I wished to worship, His wood to me.
More boys like this one may embrace me yet
I shan't find shelter, I shan't be at peace
Till I really take your restless hands,
My poor fat father. How appalling was
Your taste in ties. How you tried to have fun,
You so longed to be liked. You lied so,
Didn't you, dad? When the doll never came,
When mother was sick and the maid laughed.
—Yes, I heard you in the attic. At her grave you
Wept and wilted. Was that why you chose
So blatant a voice, such button eyes
To play house with you then? Did you ever love
Stepmother Stupid? You'd a strange look,
Sad as the sea, when she searched your clothes.
Don't be cruel and cry. I couldn't stay to
Be your baby. We both were asking
For a warmth there wasn't, and then wouldn't write.
We mustn't, must we? Moses will scold if
We're not all there for the next meeting
At some brackish well or broken arch,
Tired as we are. We must try to get on
Though mobs run amok and markets fall,
Though lights burn late at police stations,
Though passsports expire and ports are watched,
Though thousands tumble. Must their blue glare
Outlast the lions? Who'll be left to see it
Disconcerted? I'll be dumb before
The barracks burn and boisterous Pharaoh
Grow ashamed and shy. *Sh'ma' Yisra'el.*
*'*donai '*e*lohenu, '*a*donai 'echad.*

PART SIX

Epilogue

Some natural tears they drop'd, but wip'd them soon;
The world was all before them, where to choose . . .
John Milton *Paradise Lost*

Meanwhile in the street outside, QUANT and MALIN, after expressing their mutual pleasure at having met, after exchanging addresses and promising to look each other up some time, had parted and immediately forgotten each other's existence. Now MALIN was travelling southward by subway while QUANT was walking eastward, each to his own place. Dawn had begun to break.

Walking through the streets, QUANT sang to himself an impromptu ballad:

> When the Victory Powers convened at Byzantium,
> The shiners declined to show their faces,
> And the ambiences of heaven uttered a plethora
> Of admonitory monsters which dismayed the illiterate.

Sitting in the train, MALIN thought:

> Age softens the sense of defeat
> As well as the will to success,
> Till the unchangeable losses of childhood,
> The forbidden affections rebel
> No more; so now in the mornings
> I wake, neither warned nor refreshed,

From dreams without daring, a series
Of vaguely disquieting adventures
Which never end in horror,
Grief or forgiving embraces.

QUANT sang:

But peace was promised by the public hepatoscopists
As the Ministers met to remodel the Commonwealth
In what was formerly the Museum of Fashion and
                                        Handicrafts,
While husky spectres haunted the corridors.

MALIN thought:

Do we learn from the past? The police,
The dress-designers, etc.
Who manage the mirrors, say–No.
A hundred centuries hence
The gross and aggressive will still
Be putting their trust in a patron
Saint or a family fortress,
The seedy be taking the same
Old treatments for tedium vitae,
Religion, Politics, Love.

QUANT sang:

The Laurentian Landshield was ruthlessly gerrymandered,
And there was a terrible tussle over the Tethys Ocean;
Commentators broadcast by the courtesy of a
                                        shaving-cream
Blow by blow the whole debate on the Peninsulas.

MALIN thought:

Both professor and prophet depress,
For vision and longer view
Agree in predicting a day

349

Of convulsion and vast evil,
When the Cold Societies clash
Or the mosses are set in motion
To overrun the earth,
And the great brain which began
With lucid dialectics
Ends in a horrid madness.

QUANT sang:

But there were some sensible settlements in the
                                    sub-committees:
The Duodecimal System was adopted unanimously,
The price of obsidian pegged for a decade,
Technicians sent north to get nitrogen from the ice-cap.

MALIN thought:

Yet the noble despair of the poets
Is nothing of the sort; it is silly
To refuse the tasks of time
And, overlooking our lives,
Cry – 'Miserable wicked me,
How interesting I am.'
We would rather be ruined than changed,
We would rather die in our dread
Than climb the cross of the moment
And let our illusions die.

QUANT sang:

Outside these decisions the cycle of Nature
Revolved as usual, and voluble sages
Preached from park-benches to passing fornicators
A Confucian faith in the Functional Society.

MALIN thought:

We're quite in the dark: we do not
Know the connection between

The clock we are bound to obey
And the miracle we must not despair of;
We simply cannot conceive
With any feelings we have
How the raging lion is to lime
With the yearning unicorn;
Nor shall we, till total shipwreck
Deprive us of our persons.

QUANT had now reached the house where he lived and, as he started to climb the steps of his stoop, he tripped and almost fell. At which he said:

Why, Miss *ME*, what's the matter? *Must* you go
                                                    woolgathering?
Once I was your wonder. How short-winded you've
                                                    gotten.
Come, Tinklebell, trot. Let's pretend you're a
                                                    thoroughbred
Over the hill now into Abraham's Bosom.

So saying, he opened his front door and disappeared. But MALIN's journey was still not done. He was thinking:

For the new locus is never
Hidden inside the old one
Where Reason could rout it out,
Nor guarded by dragons in distant
Mountains where Imagination
Could explore it; the place of birth
Is too obvious and near to notice,
Some dull dogpatch a stone's throw
Outside the walls, reserved
For the eyes of faith to find.

Now the train came out onto the Manhattan Bridge. The sun had risen. The East River glittered. It would be a bright clear day for work and for war.

MALIN thought:

> For the others, like me, there is only the flash
> Of negative knowledge, the night when, drunk, one
> Staggers to the bathroom and stares in the glass
> To meet one's madness, when what mother said seems
> Such darling rubbish and the decent advice
> Of the liberal weeklies as lost an art
> As peasant pottery, for plainly it is not
> To the Cross or to *Clarté* or to Common Sense
> Our passions pray but to primitive totems
> As absurd as they are savage; science or no science,
> It is Bacchus or the Great Boyg or Baal-Peor,
> Fortune's Ferris-wheel or the physical sound
> Of our own names which they actually adore as their
> Ground and goal. Yet the grossest of our dreams is
> No worse than our worship which for the most part
> Is so much galimatias to get out of
> Knowing our neighbour, all the needs and conceits of
> The poor muddled maddened mundane animal
> Who is hostess to us all, for each contributes his
> Personal panic, his predatory note
> To her gregarious grunt as she gropes in the dark
> For her lost lollypop. We belong to our kind,
> Are judged as we judge, for all gestures of time
> And all species of space respond in our own
> Contradictory dialect, the double talk
> Of ambiguous bodies, born like us to that
> Natural neighbourhood which denial itself
> Like a friend confirms; they reflect our status,
> Temporals pleading for eternal life with
> The infinite impetus of anxious spirits,

352

Finite in fact yet refusing to be real,
Wanting our own way, unwilling to say Yes
To the Self-So which is the same at all times,
That Always-Opposite which is the whole subject
Of our not-knowing, yet from no necessity
Condescended to exist and to suffer death
And, scorned on a scaffold, ensconced in His life
The human household. In our anguish we struggle
To elude Him, to lie to Him, yet His love observes
His appalling promise; His predilection
As we wander and weep is with us to the end,
Minding our meanings, our least matter dear to Him,
His Good ingressant on our gross occasions
Envisages our advance, valuing for us
Though our bodies too blind or too bored to examine
What sorts excite them are slain interjecting
Their childish Ows and, in choosing how many
And how much they will love, our minds insist on
Their own disorder as their own punishment,
His Question disqualifies our quick senses,
His Truth makes our theories historical sins,
It is where we are wounded that is when He speaks
Our creaturely cry, concluding His children   .
In their mad unbelief to have mercy on them all
As they wait unawares for His World to come.

.So thinking, he returned to duty, reclaimed by the actual world
where time is real and in which, therefore, poetry can take no interest.
   Facing another long day of servitude to wilful authority and blind
accident, creation lay in pain and earnest, once more reprieved from
self-destruction, its adoption, as usual, postponed.

WYSTAN HUGH AUDEN was born in York, England, in 1907. He came to the United States in 1939, and became an American citizen in 1946. Educated at Gresham's School, Holt, and at Christ Church, Oxford, he was associated with a small group of young writers in London—among them Stephen Spender and Christopher Isherwood—who became recognized as the most promising of the new generation in English letters. He collaborated with Isherwood on the plays *The Dog Beneath the Skin, The Ascent of F-6,* and *On the Frontier,* as well as on *Journey to a War,* a prose record of experiences in China. He edited many anthologies, including *The Oxford Book of Light Verse* and, with Norman Holmes Pearson, *Poets of the English Language.* In collaboration with Chester Kallman, he also wrote the libretto for Igor Stravinsky's opera *The Rake's Progress* and for Hans Henze's opera *Elegy for Young Lovers.* His selected essays, *The Dyer's Hand,* appeared in 1962. *Academic Graffiti,* with illustrations by Filippo Sanjust, appeared in 1972. *Forewords and Afterwords,* a collection of essays—his last book—was published in 1973.

Among his volumes of poetry are *The Double Man, For the Time Being, The Age of Anxiety, Nones,* and *The Shield of Achilles,* which received the National Book Award in 1956. Much of his poetry can be found in the volumes *Collected Shorter Poems, Collected Longer Poems* and *Selected Poetry.* His most recent collections of poetry are *City Without Walls* (1969) and *Epistle to a Godson* (1972).

In 1972 Mr. Auden returned to Oxford, where he resided at Christ Church as an honorary student. He died in 1973.